RELIGION IN LATE ROMAN BRITAIN

Forces of change

Dorothy Watts

London and New York

First published 1998
by Routledge
2 Park Square, Milton Park, Abingdon, Oxon, OX14 4RN

Simultaneously published in the USA and Canada
by Routledge
270 Madison Ave, New York NY 10016

First issued in paperback 2011

Typeset in Garamond by Routledge

British Library Cataloguing in Publication Data
A catalogue record for this book is available from the British Library

Library of Congress Cataloguing in Publication Data
Watts, Dorothy.
Religion in late Roman Britain: forces of change/Dorothy Watts.
p.   cm.
Includes bibliographical references and index.
1.Great Britain–Religion–To 449. I. Title.
BL980.G7W37   1998
200'.9361'09015–dc21   97–19773
CIP

ISBN10: 0–415–11855–7 (hbk)
ISBN10: 0–415–62002–3 (pbk)

ISBN13: 978–0–415–11855–2 (hbk)
ISBN13: 978–0–415–62002–4 (pbk)

Publisher's Note

The publisher has gone to great lengths to ensure the quality of this reprint
but points out that some imperfections in the original may be apparent.

ὦ Φοῖβ᾽ Ἄπολλον, ἔμβαλέ μοι τὴν
δεξιάν ·

CONTENTS

LIST OF FIGURES

PREFACE

Since writing *Christians and Pagans in Roman Britain* (published in 1991), I have been concerned that Christianity in Late Roman Britain not be viewed as something which sprang Athena-like and fully armed from the head of Zeus; rather, it was a religion which developed, reached its apogee and subsequently faltered as it reacted to the forces which operated around and even against it in the late fourth century. In *Christians and Pagans* I sought to map out the extent of Christianity from the literary and archaeological evidence, and to show that it was far more widespread and had more pagan content than had previously been thought. What I did not explore then was the chronology of Christianity in Roman Britain, nor did I look at what was happening in the non-Christian cults or what had been the causes of the changes in religion in the last century of Roman occupation there.

Religion in Late Roman Britain seeks to address those questions. It makes use of the identification of cemeteries and churches already made in the earlier work. It also casts the net wider to include what I hope will be a useful study of some pagan practices, including the much-debated rite of decapitated burial, and the fate of the pagan cults as well. The whole has been set against the political and economic background of the fourth and early fifth centuries, and particularly the events in the Western Empire.

The investigation has traced the rise of Christianity in the fourth century, the effects of the revival of paganism by Julian the Apostate and of policies of religious toleration by his successors, and has sought to explain why Christianity failed to become the dominant religion in Britain as it had elsewhere in the Roman Empire. At the same time an analysis has been made of the types of pagan cults which survived up to and beyond the withdrawal of the Romans.

The question of syncretism as a feature of Romano-British religion is also discussed.

This work will, it is hoped, provoke further comment and debate; only by re-examining the evidence, both historical and archaeological, and combining that with new finds can we hope to advance knowledge in this important aspect of Romano-British studies.

My research has been made immeasurably easier with the recent publication of some key archaeological reports, many of the details of which were not accessible previously. Other reports have yet to be published, and it is my pleasure to thank the following for permission to use unpublished material: Mr D. G. Benson (Rushton Mount), Mr R. A. Chambers (Oxfordshire decapitations), Mr B. Dix (Ashton), Emeritus Prof. P. A. Rahtz (Cannington), Mr B. R. G. Turner (Witham) and Mr D. Wilson (Ancaster). For permission to reprint an article in *Britannia* on the lead tank fragment from Brough, I thank the Society for the Promotion of Roman Studies. I should also like to record my gratitude to the following academics and archaeologists for information, advice and for long and some-times passionate discussions about various aspects of a project which has been carried on over the past six years, generally in the depths of the northern winter: Mr D. G. Benson, Prof. K. Branigan, Mr I. Caruana, Mr R. A. Chambers, Mr J. Casey, Prof. J. Collis, Ms N. Crummy, Mr P. Crummy, Bro. E. deBhaldraithe, Dr A. Detsicas, Mr B. Dix, Mr R. Feachem, Rev. Emeritus Prof. W. H. C. Frend, Ms C. Johns, Mr M. Jones, Mr D. Knight, Mr P. Leach, Mr J. Magilton, Dr A. McWhirr, Mr I. Meadows, Mr D. Miles, Prof. M. Millett, Mr C. Newman, Ms R. Niblett, Dr E. O'Brien, Emeritus Prof. P. A. Rahtz, Dr R. Reece, Dr A. Ross, Prof. E. Rynne, Ms L. Watts and Dr A. Woodward.

For funding of this research I am most grateful to the Australian Academy of Humanities, the Australian Research Council and the University of Queensland. The project was completed during extended study leave from the Department of Classics and Ancient History, University of Queensland. I thank Prof. Robert Milns and Mr Don Barrett for reading the typescript and for their helpful suggestions for improvement of the text, other colleagues for their forbearance, my postgraduate students for their stimulating and critical discussions of ideas and theories, my husband, Dr Keith Watts, for help with the tables, and Mrs Penny Peel for research assistance and for once again preparing the index. To them and the other scholars noted above I acknowledge my debt; for any errors of fact and for opinions expressed here (except as acknowledged) I alone am responsible.

Long-suffering family members and friends have probably by now grown accustomed to being deserted at Christmas as I travel to the other end of the world in response to the call of my Muse. To them and to my 'adopted family' in Sheffield I express my appreciation for their love and support. Klio and Apollo have much to answer for.

Dorothy Watts
University of Queensland
Brisbane, Australia
March 1997

1

HISTORICAL
BACKGROUND AD 294–360

By the mid-fourth century of the Christian era, Britain had been part of the Roman Empire for over 300 years. Once divided up by tribes which did not always peacefully co-exist, it was progressively conquered by the Roman army and became one, two and ultimately five[1] Roman provinces. These were administered from Rome through provincial governors, if necessary with the help of the large army which was stationed there. The Romans brought not only peace and the material trappings of *romanitas* but also their language, culture and religion. The historian Tacitus (*Agric.* 21) describes how the native aristocracy, at least, readily adopted Roman ways:

> [Agricola] . . . provided a liberal education for the sons of the chiefs, and showed such a preference for the natural powers of the Britons over the industry of the Gauls that they who lately disdained the tongue of Rome now coveted its eloquence. Hence, too, a liking sprang up for our style of dress, and the toga became fashionable. Step by step they were led to . . . the lounge, the bath, the elegant banquet.

As a general policy, Rome had always practised tolerance towards the religions of a conquered people, provided there was no threat to the state. The influence of the Druids had been regarded by Caesar with a certain amount of macabre fascination (e.g. *B.G.* 6.13–16). Augustus also tolerated their activities, banning their cults only to citizens, but Tiberius took steps to abolish the Druids in Gaul, and Claudius their practices (Pliny *N.H.* 30.13; Suetonius *Claud.* 25.5). After the conquest of Britain, the Druids on Anglesey were seen to be subversive and were eliminated[2] by Suetonius Paulinus (Tacitus *Ann.* 14.30; Dio *Epit.* 52.7).[3] Some of the activities associated with their religion which were abhorrent to the Romans, such as human sacrifice, headhunting and even cannibalism, were rigorously suppressed (Strabo 4.4.5; Pliny *N.H.* 30.13).

The cults of Iron Age Britain were many and varied, frequently animistic, and usually associated with war, nature or fertility: the earth itself, the sun, trees or groves, streams, marshes, animals and birds were invested with religious significance. There were few cult buildings or anthropomorphic representations of deity. On the other hand, the religious practices of the conqueror were well developed, and gradually the native people came to build temples (mostly of a distinctively 'Romano-Celtic' type, rather than the classical style), to represent their gods as humans, and to bury their dead more in the Roman way. It may be that they also adopted Roman gods, or conflated them with their own.[4] There was at least a veneer of Romanisation. Certainly cults which were followed by Romans themselves were found where acculturation was at its greatest: in the towns, the 'villa belts' and areas of occupation by the Roman army.

As in other parts of the empire, the Imperial Cult was introduced and formed part of the official religious life of the province after initial opposition and revolt (Tacitus *Ann.* 14.31). To Britain also came Jupiter, Juno, Minerva and a host of lesser gods, along with more exotic imports such as Cybele, Isis, Mithras and Bacchus.

Some time in the late second or early third century, Christianity reached Britain. The peak of expansion was probably *c.*340–60. After this, the impetus seemed to have slowed, and in some parts halted altogether. In line with events at Rome, paganism revived to some extent in the years 360–90, but in Britain it seems to have been mainly in Celtic form. Despite Theodosius' closure of the temples and banning of pagan cults in 391, Christianity failed to become established by the end of the fourth century, as it had in the Eastern Empire and in Gaul, as the dominant religion.

The reasons for the failure of Christianity and for the resurgence of paganism in Britain are manifold. The present work is intended to determine what changes occurred in religion in Britain in the late fourth century, to examine the forces that contributed to them and to assess the state of religion at the time of the withdrawal of the official Roman presence by AD 410. It is helpful to begin by looking at the empire as a whole.

The empire: Diocletian, Constantine and his house[5]

The third century was, for the Roman Empire, one of turmoil and uncertainty. Serious problems included spiralling inflation, an out-of-control army, and barbarian incursions. Frequent political assassinations and usurpations, resulting in the rapid turnover of emperors, also contributed to the degeneration of the empire. This was temporarily arrested by the actions of the emperor Diocletian, who, having seized power nine years earlier, proceeded to introduce administrative and constitutional reforms. In 293 he divided the state into East and West,[6] each with its own head or Augustus and a junior Caesar to provide practical (military) support and a peaceful succession.

Diocletian's reforms, dependent as they were on mutual cooperation and trust between members of the tetrarchy, proved to be unworkable, and during the fourth century various ambitious and capable generals were able to achieve sole power, or to be the senior Augustus dominating a weaker partner.

It was against this background that Christianity came to be, first, the religion of the imperial family, a religion tolerated by the state and, finally, by the end of the century, the official religion of the empire. Yet this progress was not without setbacks, as a brief survey of the years 294–361 (below) and 361–91 (Chapter 2) will show.

By the end of the third century, Christianity had expanded greatly (Eusebius *H.E.* 8.1.1). Whole towns in the eastern part of the empire had become Christian[7] and North Africa was rapidly doing the same. While it was generally the ordinary folk who were attracted to the faith, there were converts even in high positions in the imperial administration. These were to be especial targets for persecution.

It is not known precisely why Diocletian instituted one of the most severe persecutions against Christians in 303. It may have been the result of his inherently conservative nature that he saw the Christians as a threat to the religion of the state, and thus to the state itself. His Caesar in the east, Galerius, was a fierce pagan. At first, martyrdoms, a feature of earlier persecutions,[8] were avoided. Instead Diocletian concentrated on the fabric of the Church – buildings and copies of Scripture. Christians lost their positions in public office. But successive imperial edicts increased the intensity of the purge, and Christian lives were lost when, with the fourth edict, all citizens of the empire were required to sacrifice on pain of death.

3

In the Western Empire, the Augustus, Maximian, and his Caesar, Constantius (father of Constantine), carried out the persecution with far less zeal. Lactantius (*De Mort. Pers.* 15.7) and Eusebius (*H.E.* 8.13.13) tell us that Constantius, who was responsible for Britain, Spain, Gaul and the Rhineland, took little action against Christians. Church buildings seem to have been the main casualties. Indeed, there is no certainty that the edict concerning sacrifice was ever proclaimed in the Western Empire (A. H. M. Jones 1964: 72).

Although the abdication of Diocletian and Maximian in 305 did not bring Christians any immediate respite from their sufferings, the next quarter of a century was to prove the most significant period in the growth of Christianity since the apostolic era. Constantine had been passed over in the formation of the Second Tetrarchy of 305 (Galerius and Constantius as Augusti, Maximin and Severus as Caesars) and was named Caesar only in 306, despite his having been acclaimed Augustus by the army on his father's death at York. Yet in a series of manoeuvres, he came to be in a strong position to achieve sole power. He married the daughter of the old Emperor Maximian, who had come out of retirement to support the campaign of his son, Maxentius, for the throne, and also bestowed on his son-in-law the title of Augustus. In 308, at a conference at Carnuntum, Constantine refused to resign as Augustus and take instead the title *filius Augusti*. In his way were (by now) three other Augusti,[9] Galerius, Licinius and Maximin[10] and, by 310, the renegade Maxentius.

Up to this point there had been no indication of Constantine's turning to Christianity, but that was to change. Galerius died in 311, after a deathbed edict putting an end to the persecution of Christians. Maximin moved quickly east to take over Galerius' eastern dominions and once more institute a harsh persecution.[11] He may have formed some kind of an alliance with Maxentius, who had been declared a public enemy in 308 but was still head of an army and gaining ground. Constantine and Licinius were each marshalling armies. It was the former who met Maxentius in battle near the Milvian Bridge outside Rome in 312. His victory, with the help of the God of the Christians (Eusebius *V. Const.* 1.28; Lactantius *De Mort. Pers.* 44), sealed his commitment to Christianity, and changed the western world for the next sixteen centuries. Maximin died a fugitive in 313, and in the same year an Edict of Toleration (the so-called Edict of Milan) was issued by Constantine and Licinius. Licinius, however, later reneged on this agreement and was ousted by his fellow Augustus. In 324

Constantine became sole emperor, and the House of Constantine the powerful patrons of Christianity throughout the empire.

Constantine's conversion, while not necessarily a smooth progression spiritually, had an immediate and far-reaching effect materially. Impressive churches sprang up, those in Italy and at Rome and Jerusalem in particular being heavily endowed from the royal purse. The influence of men such as Lactantius and Eusebius of Caesarea (Frend 1984: 482–7, 502–5) ensured that the clergy had privilege and immunities, and eventually the status of magistrates. Funds flowed into the imperial coffers with the confiscation of temple treasure, and were disbursed to family, friends and the Church.

This positive advancement for Christianity was, however, marred by schisms and reprisal. The first, arising in 311, was a movement led by Donatus against the supposed 'traitors' to the faith during the persecutions in North Africa; Constantine's personal intervention failed to suppress the Donatists or to produce Church unity. In the east, a doctrinal dispute led to the rise of Arianism. Arius, a presbyter at Alexandria, had questioned the nature of the Trinity and for his pains was exiled in 318–19. He reappeared in Nicomedia, Licinius' eastern capital, whence his teachings took root and spread. The Council of Nicaea of 325, convened and chaired by Constantine, reinforced orthodoxy by producing the Nicaean Creed. Conciliation later brought the two sides together, yet Arius and his doctrine remained to simmer in the east.

Constantine died in 337, but his hopes that political and religious peace would be maintained were in vain. Although he had planned the restoration of the tetrarchy, the army had other ideas, and in September of 337 they acclaimed his three remaining sons,[12] Constantine II, Constantius II and Constans, as Augusti. Their territories were the western provinces, the eastern provinces, and Italy and North Africa, respectively. Other male family members, with the exception of the young Julian and his half-brother Gallus, were murdered. The triumvirate had a short life, however. Constantine died in an attempt on the domains of Constans in 340, after which Constans came to control the greater part of the empire (including Britain). Constans himself was murdered by the rebellious Magnentius in 350; and Constantius, after finally defeating Magnentius in 353, became sole ruler until his death in 361.

The sons of Constantine had been brought up as Christians, and were all, in their own way, totally committed to the Christian cause, although Constantius leaned towards Arianism and his brothers to orthodoxy. During the years 337–60 Christianity continued to make great advances, despite the recalcitrance of some bishops (especially Athanasius of Alexandria, a passionate opponent of Arianism), the resurgence of Donatism in Africa and the continued existence of Arius' doctrines in the East. Bans increased against paganism, temples were closed (*C.Th.* 16.10.3–4) and altars removed. Among these was the Altar of Victory from the Senate House in Rome, when Constantius visited the city in 357 (Ambrose *Ep.* 18.32; Ammianus 16.10.1). This was to be a bone of contention with pagan senators until almost the end of the century (see below, Chapter 2). The clergy and the Church gained a privileged position,[13] financial immunities to clergy were extended and even allowed to their children, and the wealthy admitted to orders without having to surrender their property. Part of state funds was directed to the Church in some provinces. Throughout the empire the religion expanded and flourished. The growth of the Church in distant Britain was also probably the result of these stimuli during the reign of the sons of Constantine.

Britain: paganism and the rise of Christianity

As noted earlier, by the fourth century Britain had long been part of the empire, although Romanisation does not seem to have been as thoroughgoing as it had been elsewhere.[14] Resistance to the Occupation from AD 43 had generally been firm and prolonged; the attempted conquest of Scotland had had to be abandoned along with the wall built in the time of the Antonines. Clearly the people of Britannia were less amenable than many others conquered by Rome. But conquered they were and, by the end of the second century or early into the third, peace prevailed in the lowlands, and was restored[15] in the territory north, up to the wall built by Hadrian. Yet even then Romanisation was not adopted with great enthusiasm in many parts.

It is likely that this resistance to *romanitas* was reflected in religion in much of the province. That Britons initially opposed the Imperial Cult and what it stood for cannot be doubted. Tacitus (*Ann.* 14.31–2) tells us that the temple of Claudius in Colchester, built in the 50s,[16] was a prime target in the revolt begun by Boudicca in 60/1.[17] The failure to build temples in the classical style also suggests a reluctance to adopt Roman ways. Very few were built during more than 300 years of occupation.[18] Of those that Lewis (1966) categorises as classical, only two, the one at Colchester and another at Bath, have origins in the first or early second century.

The Bath temple had Celtic connections, perhaps making it more acceptable to a suspicious native population. The building probably dates to the late first century (Blagg 1979) and is dedicated to Sulis-Minerva. Sulis was a Celtic deity, one of whose aspects was healing. She could thus be equated by the Romans with Minerva Medica (Henig 1984: 43). While the temple itself exhibits many of the characteristics of Roman architecture, it has at the centre of its pediment a representation of a fierce male head usually interpreted as a male Medusa or Neptune (Henig 1984: 43) or a Gorgon (Richmond and Toynbee 1955; Lewis 1966: 60), the usual decoration on the aegis of Minerva.[19] The Celtic aspects of the visage have been noted.[20] Lead curse tablets (*defixiones*) from the sacred pool are mostly addressed or refer to Sulis or Sulis Minerva. Tomlin (1988: 80, 96–8) points out that the names of the petitioners are those of 'humbler people', not of legionaries such as were recorded on stone altars and tombstones at Bath.

To the casual observer, the temple of Sulis-Minerva at Bath could be interpreted as a demonstration of the early Romanisation of the native population, and the syncretic nature of Romano-British religion. Such perceptions will be discussed more fully later (Chapter 6), but it might be pointed out here that the lack of evidence for any continuation of the 'tradition of sanctity' (Lewis 1966: 50) in the siting of classical temples in Britain suggests that, initially, they had very little to do with the native population. Although it is unlikely that the hot springs at Bath escaped the religious devotion of Iron Age Britons, it is not certain that the actual site of the temple of Sulis-Minerva was previously the location of a native shrine or sacred place. There is little pre-Roman evidence for religious or even domestic activity. There is no known evidence for any pre-Roman cults at the sites of the other classical temples, all of which were built in the later second or early third century.[21]

This is far from the case with the more common type of temple found in Britain, the Romano-Celtic, a style normally with a square cella-and-ambulatory plan found also on the Continent. Lewis (1966: 9) is probably correct in suggesting that this type of temple first emerged in Gaul, the result of Roman architectural influences on the simpler Celtic religious structures,[22] and was carried to Britain after the Occupation. A number from rural Britain have certain or almost certain Iron Age predecessors (see below), but none from urban centres.

It seems that Romano-Celtic temples appeared in Britain first in the towns, and later in the country (Lewis 1966: 51–5; Horne 1981:

Figure 3.1), surviving longer in the rural areas. Only one Romano-Celtic temple in Britain can so far be dated to before the Boudiccan revolt and that, significantly, comes from close by the earliest Roman settlement, at Colchester.[23] It may well be that, where Roman influence was strongest, a move to erect religious structures new in design but in reality very little removed from those of the Iron Age was fairly well received by wealthy Britons. In the country, however, the old sacred places or simple shrines would usually suffice sometimes for one, two or even three centuries before a cella-and-ambulatory structure appeared (for example, Maiden Castle and Harlow). One exception to this is the Romano-Celtic temple at Hayling Island, built on the site of an earlier Iron Age shrine c. AD 60–70; but the excavator points out that this temple was built in a tribal area which saw very early Roman building activity, in particular the 'palace' at Fishbourne (King 1990: 231). A further exception is the first Romano-Celtic temple at Uley. It will be considered later in this study (Chapter 6). Few new urban Romano-Celtic temples appear in Britain after about 200[24], but in the country a number of temples were being built or refurbished until almost the end of the fourth century.[25]

Other temples of simpler plan (single-celled and round, rectangular or polygonal) were also erected in the Roman period, and several of these had pre-Roman antecedents. In his study of Iron Age religion and ritual, Wait (1986: 173, 183) was able to find considerable evidence of continuity of religious tradition into the Roman period: 60 per cent of all the Celtic religious sites he examined went on into the Roman period, and a number of temples (including several of Romano-Celtic plan) he believed had Iron Age predecessors.[26] To his examples a few others might be added, with temples built on the site of earlier sacred foci such as trees or groves, an artificial mound, or even a standing stone.[27]

Since water also played an important part in Celtic religion, it is likely that the temples at Carrawburgh and Springhead 2[28] were built over sacred springs. The building at Carrawburgh (Allason-Jones and McKay 1985) is unusual in that it began life as a Roman stone-lined cistern containing a natural spring. As the spring had had a religious significance the cistern came to be a place of veneration, and votives continued to be offered into the fifth century, long after the end of the Occupation. A similar situation may have arisen at Witham, where, during the early Roman period, an artificial pond was created in an area with a natural spring. This in turn became a sacred focus, with a Romano-Celtic temple built beside it in the late third/early fourth century (Turner 1982).

Few dedications for temples other than classical are known: examples include Apollo Cunomaglus from Nettleton (Wedlake 1982), Mercury/Mars/Silvanus from Uley (Woodward and Leach 1993) – where there may have been some doubt in the minds of the native British supplicants as to the identity of the god (see below, Chapter 6), Nodens at Lydney (Wheeler and Wheeler 1932; Casey 1981), and Coventina at Carrawburgh (Allason-Jones and McKay 1985). Further evidence from inscriptions on altars and metal plaques indicates the presence of many of the gods of the Roman pantheon, regularly paired with a Celtic deity by the votary.[29]

From the above, it can be seen that temples in Britain from the time of the Occupation reflected far more the continuity of native traditions than a wholesale conversion to the religions of the Romans; and even if a dedication was to a Roman deity, the chances are that this deity was viewed as such only by Romans or Romanised Britons. For the bulk of the population living in the country, the spirit of the place, whether named or unnamed, was still accorded veneration, and little had changed from the Iron Age.

This does not mean, of course, that the influence of the Romans did not penetrate British culture and customs at all. Such influence is reflected in changed burial rites and in approaches to religious art. If we can generalise, a late Iron Age burial involved interment into a rough grave in foetal or crouched position with head to the north, and with little grave furniture. With the coming of Rome this changed rapidly to supine and extended burial in properly cut graves, sometimes in a coffin, and part of a recognisable burial ground. More commonly, and certainly by the end of the first century, Romano-Britons, in line with Rome, adopted cremation as the main method of disposal of the dead. It was only by the third century that inhumation came once more to predominate.[30] Because of this, most of our cemetery evidence is from the late third and fourth century. It is clear, however, that while the methods of Roman burial were followed in Britain, the native practices were not totally abandoned. Indeed, in the fourth century, even with the advent of Christianity, burials in Roman Britain reflected a strong Celtic influence (Watts 1991: 209–14). This point will be taken up later, in discussions on decapitated burial and syncretism (Chapters 4 and 6).

As with burials, Roman influence on religious art in Britain was apparent from an early period, with native sculptors taking the lead from the Romans and representing their deities in anthropomorphic

9

form to an increasing extent. The early indigenous attempts are clumsy and naive in comparison with their Roman models, but by the fourth century Romano-British art had reached a much higher (classical) standard, while retaining some of its Celtic heritage. The Mercury sculpture from Uley is one of the most significant works to illustrate this (Henig 1995: 99, 111). That such a level of artistic achievement was lost as soon as the Roman influence disappeared from Britain suggests that it was not a natural Celtic preference to represent gods anthropomorphically.

Other pagan religions in Britain had representations of their deities, but these were cults brought in mainly by the soldiers of the Roman army, and such art would not be native British. Of the imported cults,[31] the most significant was Mithraism, but its significance was probably out of proportion to the number of its adherents because it was seen as a direct threat to Christianity. The threat must have been more perceived than real, since it was an exclusive cult, its membership comprising mainly soldiers and men engaged in trade. In Britain, dedications to the god are all by soldiers,[32] and mainly by officers. There is nothing to suggest that the cult held any attraction for native Britons, especially those living away from the cities and the forts.

Mithraea were found in London and several centres along the frontiers. They were built in the late second to early third century and most were desecrated or destroyed by the mid-fourth. The destruction of the Mithraea in Roman Britain is generally held by scholars to be the work of Christians.[33]

Further exotic religious imports to Britain included the cults of Jupiter Dolichenus, Isis, Cybele (Magna Mater) and Bacchus. The first two had associations with the army, but the appeal of Cybele and Bacchus seems to have been more widespread. Jupiter Dolichenus had a Hittite-Syrian origin and is known only from inscriptions from military areas.[34] Evidence for the cult of Isis, originating in Egypt, is equally rare and as yet found only in London.[35] The cult of the Great Mother, Cybele, on the other hand, is attested in Britain not only by inscriptions from Cavoran (*RIB* 1791 and 1792) but also by archaeological evidence from London, Dunstable and Verulamium. Bacchus, too, had a wider following and he may have been a relatively early import to Britain: Dionysius 'Periegetes', writing around the time of the Emperor Hadrian (AD 117–38), tells of islands near Jersey and Guernsey where the rites of Bacchus were performed.[36] While inscriptions to the god are not known from Britain, there are many representations of him and of the maenads and satyrs that accompany him. From a comprehensive study of his cult in Britain by Hutchinson (1986), it seems that although the evidence is widespread it occurs mainly in towns and on villa sites.

As well as being the god of wine, equating to the Greek Dionysus, Bacchus was also a saviour god. Resurrection or regeneration was a concept which his cult had in common with those of Mithras, Isis and Cybele. The appeal of these salvation cults seemed to grow, along with that of Christianity, with the uncertainties of the later empire. By the end of the fourth century, however, Christianity had by far the strongest position among them.

Christianity is likely to have come to Britain from Gaul: there was already a significant number of converts in that province by 177, when forty-eight were martyred at Lyon (Eusebius *H.E.* 5.1). There were 'many . . . of both sexes' – who were British martyrs, too, although Bede (*H.E.* 1.7) gives the names of only three: Alban, Aaron and Julius. He goes on to tell us (*H.E.* 1.8) that following the persecution of Diocletian 'faithful Christians . . . rebuilt the ruined churches'; but these 'churches' were more than likely house-churches, indistinguishable from other domestic buildings until the emergence of a distinctive church architecture. So Christianity remained archaeologically invisible in Britain until the Peace of the Church in 313. From that time on, buildings recognisable as churches were established, as well as cemeteries set aside for Christian use.

It is difficult to trace chronologically the growth of Christianity in Roman Britain, since dating evidence is very sparse, particularly for cemeteries. Nevertheless, a number of major sites have been published in the past few years since the present author's earlier research on the subject (Watts 1991). An attempt will thus be made here to put all available evidence together for the years up to the accession of Julian in 360; the further development of Christianity and the effects of his revival of paganism in Britain will be discussed later in this work. The evidence to be considered cannot include that which is not datable or provenanced. Many individual items, such as those appearing in Thomas (1981) and Mawer (1995), must therefore be excluded from this discussion. There will be heavy reliance on the identification of sites in the author's 1991 work.

Our earliest knowledge of the arrival of Christianity in Britain comes from Tertullian (*c.*160–*c.*240), who, writing around the beginning of the third century (*Adv. Iudaeos* 7), mentions

Christianity in parts of Britain beyond Roman settlement. A few decades later, Origen (c.185–c.255) described Christianity as a unifying force there (*Homily 4 on Ezekiel*). While the value of these sources has been questioned,[37] there is little reason to doubt such evidence, even if there is some element of exaggeration.[38] With a considerable number of Christians already in Gaul by 177, it was only a matter of time before their faith was carried to Britain. Bishop Irenaeus of Lyon, successor to the martyred Pothinus, did much to spread the influence of the Church in the west by carrying the Gospel to the Gauls in their own language. Undoubtedly such influence spread, as did so many other features of *romanitas*, to Britain.

Although the dates are not known, the martyrdoms of Alban, Aaron and Julius certainly took place in Britain before the Peace of the Church in 313,[39] and in 314 three bishops attended the Council of Arles, attended by two lesser clergy. This Council, coming so soon after the Edict of Toleration, must have provided a stimulus for Christian communities in the provinces to adopt a more public profile and perhaps now to build recognisable churches.

We know that these bishops came from London, York and *Londinensium* (variously claimed to be Lincoln, Colchester and Cirencester),[40] which indicates Christian communities in those centres by 314; and Thomas (1981: 198) suggests that by the last decades of the fourth century there could have been 'twenty or more' bishops in Britain. That the orthodox faith was followed in Britain is confirmed by Athanasius of Alexandria (*Ad Iovian. Imp.* 2; *Apol. cont. Arianos* 1). The relative poverty of the church c.360 has been postulated on the evidence of Sulpicius Severus (*Hist. Sacr.* 2.41),[41] and the growing body of archaeological evidence has done little to dispel that impression.

The earliest archaeological evidence we have for Christianity in Britain (Figures 1 and 2) may have been less than two decades after Constantine's decree. It is no surprise that it comes from Colchester, the oldest *colonia* in Britain and, perhaps, the See of the Primate. The church at Butt Road, Colchester (Crummy *et al.* 1993: 60, 159), was first built and burials in the cemetery laid west–east around 320–30 (over earlier north–south graves dating from c.270). As a cemetery church, the building is unlikely to have been the main Christian church in Colchester. Perhaps within a decade, a Christian community was established at Roman *Durobrivae*, better known as Water Newton,[42] and continued until some threat resulted in the deposition of silver communion plate and a hoard of

Site	Type of Evidence	320	330	340	350	360	370	380	390	400	410
Ancaster	Cem		? ··	··· —	—					··?	
Ashton	Cem			—	—			··			
Bradley Hill	Cem				·:—	—					→
Brean Down	Cem/Ch				·:—	—					→
Cannington	Cem			?	:—	—					→
Canterbury St Pancras	Ch			···	:·	—					→
Colchester Butt Road	Cem/Ch	··	—								··→
Dorchester Crown Bldgs	Cem		·	—		· ·					
Dorchester Poundbury	Cem		·	—						····	··→
Frampton	M	·	····					····	···	····	?
Hinton St Mary	M	·	·····					····	···		?
Icklingham	Cem/Ch/B			··	—				···		····
Lamyatt Beacon	Cem/Ch				·	—	—				→
Lincoln Paul-in-the-Bail	Ch							?	····	—	→
Lullingstone	House Ch				·	—	—			·	
Nettleton Bldg 23	Ch/Cem		··	—		·					
Nettleton Octagonal	Ch		··	—		·					
Richborough	Ch							··	—	· ···	
Shepton Mallett	Cem			?	:—	—				?	
Silchester	Ch/B		····							···	
Stone by Faversham	Ch				·	—	—				··→
Uley	Ch										→
Verulamium 7	Cem/Ch			···	:·		····				
Water Newton	H			·	—	·					
Winchester Lankhills F6	Cem			··	—		·				
Witham	Ch/B			··	—						

Figure 1. Archaeological evidence for Romano-British Christianity
B = Baptistery; Cem = Cemetery; Ch = Church; H = Hoard; M = Mosaic.

coins around 350 or a few years later (Painter 1977; Thomas 1981: 119). Still in East Anglia, a cemetery at Ancaster was begun some time in the earlier part of the century (D. R. Wilson 1968), and by *c.*330–40 Christians had built a small chapel and associated baptistery on a previously pagan site at Witham. These buildings were in existence until *c.*360 (Turner 1982 and personal communication).

Around 340–50,[43] an extra-mural church was established at Verulamium, perhaps after the destruction of a pagan shrine (Watts 1991: 106), and a small Christian cemetery was begun (Anthony 1968). In view of the size of the cemetery, the church probably did not remain in use until the last quarter of the century. It is extremely unlikely that this was the only church at Verulamium, however: the elaborate shrine to the martyred St Alban (Bede *H.E.* 1.7) must certainly have existed by the fourth century.

Other churches and cemeteries appeared around 340–50, and we may here already be beginning to see the effects of the promotion of Christianity by the sons of Constantine. The church at Silchester

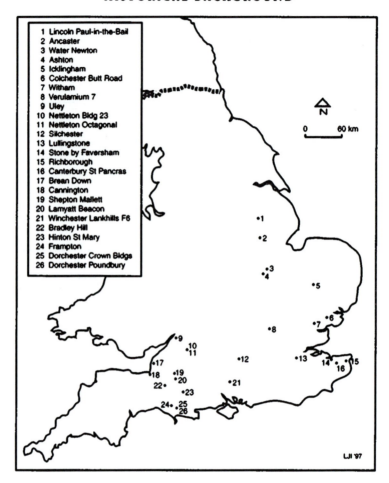

1 Lincoln Paul-in-the-Bail
2 Ancaster
3 Water Newton
4 Ashton
5 Icklingham
6 Colchester Butt Road
7 Witham
8 Verulamium 7
9 Uley
10 Nettleton Bldg 23
11 Nettleton Octagonal
12 Silchester
13 Lullingstone
14 Stone by Faversham
15 Richborough
16 Canterbury St Pancras
17 Brean Down
18 Cannington
19 Shepton Mallett
20 Lamyatt Beacon
21 Winchester Lankhills F6
22 Bradley Hill
23 Hinton St Mary
24 Frampton
25 Dorchester Crown Bldgs
26 Dorchester Poundbury

Figure 2. Map of datable Christian sites of the fourth century

(Frere 1975) and perhaps that on the site of St Pancras, Canterbury, were built *c.*340–50, although the latter could have been a decade or so later (Jenkins 1976).[44] The small rural church/baptistery/cemetery complex at Icklingham (West 1976), the house-church at Lullingstone (Meates 1979) and perhaps the mausoleum/church at Stone-by-Faversham (Fletcher and Meates 1969, 1977) appeared soon after (*c.*345–50). The formal cemetery at the small Roman town at Ashton, Northants, was begun around 340, and was in use until at least 380 (Dix 1984 and personal communication; Frere 1983: 305–6; 1984: 300–1).

In the central south and the south west, Christianity followed the distribution pattern of Romanisation in Britain, and first appeared at about the same time as elsewhere in Britain. Relatively dense evidence comes particularly from the towns and the villa belts of Hampshire and Gloucestershire. Feature 6 of Lankhills cemetery, Winchester, was probably used by Christians as early as c.330 (G. Clarke 1979), continuing until around 360–5. Two cemeteries in Dorchester, the Crown Buildings site (Green et al. 1982) and Poundbury Camp (Farwell and Molleson 1993), saw their earliest Christian burials c.335. The Crown Buildings cemetery was out of use by 360–5, but the large burial ground at Poundbury lasted until at least the end of the century.

By c.325–40, too, wealthy Christians may have already built villas with Christian motifs incorporated into their mosaics: the Hinton St Mary and Frampton mosaics are dated by D. J. Smith (1963) to around this period.[45] Further west, the first- to fourth-century pagan temple site at Nettleton (Wedlake 1982) saw Christian intrusion. A Christian cemetery and associated chapel were established c.330, and a temple converted to a church, in use until c.360. At two further sites, in Somerset, the west–east cemeteries at Cannington (Rahtz 1977, 1991) and Shepton Mallet (Leach 1990, 1991)[46] probably began mid-century; however, detail is sparse as these sites still await full publication.

The evidence, it must be admitted, is still limited and imprecise. While the picture is not altogether clear, it seems that in the eastern part of the country the growth of Christianity was steady over the whole period 320–60, with an intensification from c.340 onward. The evidence from the south and west suggests that Christianity also came early to this part of Britain. In some cases, at least, it was not long-lived. As we shall see, a further burst of Christian activity and conversion took place in both areas towards the end of the century.[47]

With the growth and spread of Christianity in Britain in the fourth century, there was a corresponding decline in the pagan cults. Christianity had grown and co-existed with pagan religions in the atmosphere of religious toleration which Constantine had proclaimed early in his reign. His sons took a progressively harder line in the period 341–61: the year 341 saw the first ban on sacrifice, and official endorsement for the destruction of urban temples implied, if not actually stated (C.Th. 16.10.2–3).[48] In 356 Constantius closed temples everywhere and banned sacrifice (C.Th. 16.10.4, 6). Even so, there is little evidence for the wholesale destruction of pagan sites in distant Britain at this time.

15

This may have been the result of official appointments for these years, and the religion of the office holders. As we are reminded (Croke and Harries 1982: 26), the effectiveness of the anti-pagan laws was dependent on the local officials who were to implement them. The praetorian prefect of Gaul was responsible for seeing that imperial policy was implemented in Britain. For the period of the sole rule of Constantius (353–61), the prefects he appointed to Gaul were Rufinus (354), Volusianus (355), Honoratius (355–7), Florentius (357–60) and Nebridius (360–1). The *vicarius* in Britain for 353–4 was Martinus, and for 358 and probably until 360, Alypius.

Vulcacius Rufinus was a pagan, Martinus very likely so. But during his term Martinus seems to have been too busy attempting to ward off the excesses of the *notarius* Paulus (Catena, 'the Chain': Ammianus 14.5.6–8) in the aftermath of the usurpation of Magnentius to have carried out zealously any anti-pagan orders of the emperor, had they been transmitted to him with any degree of enthusiasm by Rufinus, his superior in Gaul. Although Martinus' religion is not known, from Ammianus' description of him[49] he seems unlikely to have been the kind of man who would have stirred up opposition among the people. Volusianus, the prefect in 355, was also a pagan. His *vicarius* in Britain is not known.

The religion of the next two prefects, Honoratius and Florentius, is not recorded, but the latter may have been a Christian.[50] Alypius, his *vicarius*, was a pagan and an associate of Julian. It was during Florentius' term of office that the more severe anti-pagan legislation of Constantius was introduced. Yet Alypius evidently was rather tardy in carrying out his orders, in much the same way that Constantius, father of Constantine, had avoided destroying Christian churches in the Great Persecution at the beginning of the century. There is little archaeological evidence to suggest that the situation resembled that in Greece, where, according to Libanius (see below), no altar remained.

As Florentius was now dealing with barbarian hordes and a young and ambitious Caesar, Alypius' position in Britain was very likely even more comfortable. Julian was at that time Caesar in Gaul and, to all appearances, a Christian, since it would have been politically suicidal for him to have professed openly his commitment to the pagan gods. We are told by Ammianus (21.2.4) that only a few shared his secret (*arcanorum participibus paucis*) as he wanted to win popularity, presumably to get support for his planned coup. Alypius may well have been one of those in Julian's confidence, since Julian's letter to him (*To Alypius* 402D–403C) speaks openly of 'the gods'. In another (*To Alypius* 403C–404B) Julian refers to 'the god' and calls Alypius 'dearest and most loved brother'. This was a veiled reference, it is thought, to their being initiates in the cult of Mithras (W. C. Wright 1990: xxxiii).[51] There is another likely clue in this second letter: Julian says, 'With regard to your administration of affairs, inasmuch as you study to act in all cases both energetically and humanely, I am well pleased with it.' This is a curious statement from a man who had had nothing to do with Alypius' appointment, and who was not responsible for the actions of the *vicarius*. That Julian wrote in cryptic terms[52] to Alypius is confirmed by the postscript in his first letter: he suggests that there is good hunting where he is, and urges Alypius to join him (402B–C). This is taken to be an allusion to Julian's plot to overthrow Constantius (W. C. Wright 1990: 18, n. 1). In the passage quoted above, Julian may be congratulating Alypius on activities which did not harm the pagan cause. The animosity between Julian and Florentius is well documented by Ammianus (e.g. 17.3, 18.2.7)[53] and Libanius (*Or.* 18.48); and there is no doubt that, as the Caesar, Julian could go over the head of the prefect if he had a mind to. It is possible that the absence of evidence for large-scale destruction of pagan sites in Britain in the late 350s, as compared with other parts of the empire, was due to Julian's presence in Gaul and his influence, or even secret counter-instructions. Alypius was still in favour when Julian became emperor: it was he who was entrusted to superintend the rebuilding of the Temple at Jerusalem (Ammianus 23.1.3), a project which was abandoned by 363.

The results elsewhere of the edicts of the sons of Constantine are recorded by Libanius. He describes in highly coloured terms[54] the situation in the east prior to 354: temples deserted, altars overturned and sacrifices suppressed, temple lands and revenue confiscated, and priests expelled (*Or.* 18.23). Following the edict of 356, in some cases destruction was complete, but in others the law was defied. He tells us, now more realistically (*Or.* 18.114, 116, 126), that there were no longer any altars in Greece, that sacrifices had not been offered for a long time and that temples had been pulled down and the stone reused for houses. Yet he also says that Julian gave great favours to cities which had kept their temples standing and unpolluted (*Or.* 18.129). In other words, even in the eastern part of the empire there had not been universal destruction of pagan sites.

The situation in Britain from 341 to 361 may be compared with that described above. While there is no archaeological evidence for large-scale attacks on paganism, there are signs of the gradual but not necessarily general conversion to Christianity. This is reflected in the treatment of cultic buildings and also in burial practices. For temples, there is some evidence of destruction or abandonment in the first half of the fourth century. A few may have been casualties of the decrees of 341 and 356, or even prompted by the visit of Constans to Britain in midwinter 342–3 (Ammianus 20.1.1; Firmicus Maternus *Err. prof. rel.* 28.6). A couple of temples were probably converted to churches, even if temporarily; and changed burial practices in discrete cemeteries indicate adoption of Christianity. On the other hand, there is evidence for the continuation of pagan religious activity, despite the edict of Constantius.

In many cases deliberate attacks on pagan sites may as readily be attributed to the spread of Christianity and the reaction of zealous Christians to pagan cults as to any official policy. There is, after all, no literary evidence for any 'official' destruction of temples until the time of Constans and Constantius.[55] The fate of the Mithraea in London and along the frontiers suggests such a situation. In London, the temple was under attack sometime in the first half of the fourth century, when pieces of religious statuary were destroyed, but a beautiful imported marble head of Serapis was hidden away along with other art and ritual objects. The fate of this Mithraeum is not known: it may have had further use as a temple, but, clearly, in a town which boasted a bishop Christians would be unlikely to tolerate the overt practice of paganism, except in the short period when paganism was officially revived by Julian from 360 to 363. Along the northern border, Mithraea at Housesteads, Carrawburgh and Rudchester suffered damage at the end of the third century, probably at the hands of invaders from the north. Only the last two were rebuilt. The shrine at Carrawburgh was destroyed in the Constantinian period, perhaps around 324 (Richmond and Gillam 1951: 39–43), and the Rudchester building also relatively early in the fourth century (Gillam and MacIvor 1954: 218). The attacks on both these buildings may have been the result of Christians taking the law into their own hands (Harris and Harris 1965: 28–36). The end of the Mithraeum at Caernarvon probably does reflect a reaction to the anti-pagan laws, however. It was abandoned at the end of the third century, at the time of the withdrawal of the garrison from the town, and appears to have been burnt down and its remaining altars smashed about 350 (Boon 1961: 153–6).

Other shrines or small temples near military sites along Hadrian's Wall had been attacked or abandoned before mid-fourth century. Two shrines, located beside a stream some 3.2 km south of the Roman fort at Bowes, and with altars dedicated by soldiers to a local god, Vinotonus Silvanus (*RIB* 732, 733), were used only until early in the fourth century. Fragmentary remains of other altars (Lewis 1966: 79; R. P. Wright 1947) point to a violent end. A small apsidal shrine at Housesteads, probably for a cult of a spring, was abandoned about 320 (Birley 1961).

In the towns of Roman Britain there is similar evidence. The second-century classical temple at Wroxeter was probably derelict, its sculptures smashed, early in the fourth century (Bushe-Fox 1914). Of the many temples at Colchester, the one dedicated to Jupiter in the Sheepen complex was maintained until at least 333 before it fell into disuse. It seems to have been deliberately dismantled in the late fourth century. At Gosbeck's Farm, also on the outskirts of Colchester, a temple associated with a theatre and perhaps dedicated to Mercury was out of use by about 350 (Hull 1958: 229–30; Lewis 1966: 141; Crummy 1980).[56] Similarly, the temple in Insula XIV at Verulamium was unlikely to have been still in use by mid-century, since the theatre which adjoined it was at least by about 360 used as a rubbish dump (Niblett 1990; Reece 1984: 17).[57] There was always a close connection between the theatre and religion.[58] Thus it is reasonable to assume that if the theatre was no longer in use, so too had the focus of the cult lost its importance. At York, a temple located on the main road from the fortress and perhaps built in classical style was in use from the second to the fourth century, but was derelict by about 350.[59] This same date may have seen the violent end of a pagan cult and temple at Southwark, where the sculpture of a hunter-god was found in a well, along with burnt building debris (Merrifield 1986).[60] There is no evidence that the fate of these temples was directly linked to the legislation of 341 and 356, although the abandonment of urban temples could represent a response to these laws. Since the pagan Alypius was *vicarius* from 358, it is more likely to be the result of the growth of Christianity and of Christians' individual efforts to stamp out paganism. As a Roman religion (Watts 1991: 7–9), and one adopted by the imperial family, Christianity would have had an impact on the pagan cults in such centres. These towns were among the most important and most thoroughly Romanised in Britain, and literary sources and various archaeological finds indicate that they had a Christian presence.[61]

From the countryside, however, there is considerable evidence for Romano-Celtic temples which continued into or were built in the fourth century. An analysis of such rural sites [62] shows that, of those that were abandoned by about 350–60, a number had merely ceased to be used, and some of those had evidence of Christian activity if not reuse; at least two may have been converted to Christian use; and still others met a violent end. Examples may be considered briefly.

Those rural temples which fell into disuse by mid-fourth century include three at Springhead, and the temples at Harlow and Chedworth. Springhead had a number of shrines and was probably a healing cult centre. The archaeological record has been reappraised (Detsicas 1983: 60–76), with the result that four structures, renumbered 1, 2, 3 and 10, have now been identified as cult buildings.[63] Of these, at least two were in use in the fourth century, and one (no. 2) lasted until the middle of the century.[64] The temple at Chedworth, dedicated perhaps to Silvanus or a similar hunting–healing-type deity (Baddeley 1930; Goodburn 1983: 34; Lewis 1966: 48), appears to have survived until at least the early part of the fourth. The Harlow temple, possibly to a martial deity and first built in the Flavian period, was in a state of decay by the middle of the fourth century (France and Gobel 1985). These last two sites have evidence for a Christian presence.[65]

Mention has already been made of two pagan sites which are believed to have been converted to Christian use in the period to 360: Nettleton Scrub, Wiltshire and Witham in Essex. The octagonal shrine of Apollo Cunomaglus at Nettleton was probably converted to a cruciform church around 330, and at the same time another building, no. 23, was erected in association with an adjacent west–east cemetery (Wedlake 1982: 75–7; Watts 1991: 110, 138–9). In the east, also around 330, the Romano-Celtic site at Witham saw its sacred pool drained, its sacred trees uprooted and a small oratory-style building and baptistery built in their place (Turner 1982 and personal communication).[66] Such reuse of pagan sites is well attested in literary sources of the fourth century and later: Socrates (4.24), when describing the conversion of a pagan island to Christianity c.380, says that the new Christians changed the form of their temple into that of a church. Similarly, Sozomen (7.15) relates the reuse of the temple of Dionysus at Alexandria. But, as will be seen, the conversion of the churches at Nettleton and Witham to Christian use was to be short-lived.

Christians were not always ready to reuse pagan sites, but often merely desecrated them. The circular temple at Frilford (Bradford and Goodchild 1939) seems to have been burnt down before 350–60. The mosaics of another at Great Chesterford may also have been the target of Christian zealots (Lewis 1966: 144; Powell 1963: 83). On the other hand, while the octagonal temple at Pagans Hill was damaged at some time after 333–5 (perhaps mid-century), its cultic purpose was resumed for a period after 367 (Rahtz and Watts 1989; Rahtz 1991: 12).

In line with the situation in the east of the empire,[67] there were some temples which survived the anti-pagan laws at least to around 360. Others lasted even until the end of the century and beyond. They included urban, military and rural temples. These sites are marked on the map as pagan survivors for the years 341–60 (Figure 3), but their fate will be considered later.

Although pagan burial practices also continued into the late fourth century, the period to 361 saw an increase in the numbers of Christians being buried in cemeteries set aside for their use. But there is little evidence that the advent of these cemeteries meant an end to or even a tapering off of what were typical pagan burial rituals in clearly pagan cemeteries.[68]

The cemetery at Butt Road, Colchester, had changed from north–south to west–east around 320, and by 340 it had all the characteristics of a Christian cemetery.[69] Icklingham cemetery probably began at the same time as the church there, following the sealing of an earlier pagan level some time around 345–50. At Nettleton, despite the limited published evidence, it is likely that Cemetery A dated to the same period as building 22, identified as a small chapel, and built as early as 330. At other sites, pagan and Christian funerary rites were contemporaneous in separate cemeteries or burial areas: for example, at Poundbury Camp, Dorchester (Farwell and Molleson 1993; C. J. S. Green 1982), Lankhills, Winchester (G. Clarke 1979) and Ashton (Watts 1991: 64–5). In yet other cemeteries, such as Dunstable (C. L. Matthews 1981), Bath Gate at Cirencester (McWhirr *et al.* 1982) and Frilford (Buxton 1921), pagan burials continued much as before, seemingly unaffected by the growth of Christianity.[70] At Radley, however, one burial ground contained fourth-century burials oriented north–south (Atkinson 1952–3), while another, still to be reported fully, contained at least nine cremations, thirty-eight north–south inhumations and, in a cluster at the southern end, nine west–east burials (Frere 1984; D. Miles, personal communication). This last-mentioned group included decapitated bodies and hobnails. Thus,

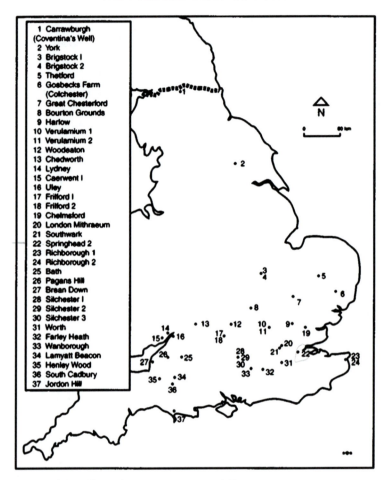

Figure 3. Map of temples surviving to AD 360

while there was possibly an influence from Christian funerary practice on the orientation of the bodies here (and this is a contentious issue),[71] in all other respects Radley II was a typical fourth-century pagan cemetery. There were to be other subtle changes in burial practices in Roman Britain from the accession of Julian onwards.

Such, then, was the state of religion in Britain to the mid-fourth century, and the position of Christianity within that framework. In keeping with trends in the rest of the empire, Christianity had gone from being a proscribed religion to one which had the patronage and favour of the imperial family, and it had become a visible religion.

With the elevation of Julian as Augustus in February 360, changes would occur which, had he survived for any length of time, would have shaken the security of the Church. That 'little cloud' (Sozomen 5.15.3) would soon pass, however, but Julian's legacy was to be a revival of paganism which was to slow down the spread of Christianity in Britain and weaken the Church to the extent that it barely survived in the following two centuries.

2

THE PAGAN REVIVAL OF
THE LATE FOURTH
CENTURY AD 360–90

For the central part of the Roman Empire in the second half of the fourth century, paganism[1] had two major parallel and at times seemingly coalescing strands: a revived interest in and devotion to the ancient cults, as promoted by the Emperor Julian, and a continuing resistance to Christianity by certain elements of the old aristocratic society at Rome. Yet the two never really melded; and with the death of Julian and the effective end of his 'outreach' programme, and because of political events from 363 to 394, paganism in the central Mediterranean area did not survive in any major form to the close of the fourth century. It was weakened by increasingly severe legislation, and brought to its knees by the sword.[2] Any significant revival of Graeco-Roman paganism in distant parts of the empire originating from Julian's religious policies was precluded by the very nature of paganism at Rome, although local cults continued to attract allegiance. Generally, successive emperors followed a policy of appointing Christians to positions whereby such paganism might be contained (see Appendix 1). In Britain there was also a revival, but in character it was mostly far removed from the paganism of Julian and the Roman aristocracy.

It is easy, in hindsight, to conclude that with the conversion of Constantine and the adoption of the religion by subsequent emperors the victory of Christianity over paganism was assured. But this was not necessarily so. Had Julian lived to implement his proposed religious reforms, the victory of Christianity might not have been so soon won. In fact, it may not have been won at all, when the barbarian invasions were beginning to have such an effect on the stability of the empire; and Julian's immediate successors, though Christian, usually followed a policy of religious toleration. On the other hand, the pagan element in the Senate at Rome was conservative, exclusive, inward-looking and clung to traditions from Rome's mythical past, its members steeping themselves in the study of Vergil and Cicero and ignoring Julian's reforms and the realities of a changed world. It did not reach out to the people as Julian's revived paganism was planned to do, and could not survive political events of the late fourth century.

Although this senatorial pagan resistance appears to have been a Roman phenomenon, there were numerous links with the religious practices and cults promoted by Julian. But Julian's reign itself must be seen against a background of expanding Christianity since the battle of Milvian Bridge and the conversion of Constantine in 312. Constantine's tolerance of pagan cults had been replaced by the progressively harsher line of his sons. From 356 on, all temples had been closed in all cities and in all places (*C.Th.* 16.10.4), and sacrifice banned. There were severe penalties: law-breakers, as well as governors of provinces who failed to see the law was carried out, were to be executed and their property confiscated. These measures were all cancelled by Julian when he became sole Augustus in November 361. In the previous year, in a letter to the Senate and People of Athens, he had openly professed his paganism. With the death of Constantius, he ordered the temples to be opened, sacrifice resumed and the worship of the pagan gods reinstituted (Ammianus 22.5.2).

The paganism of Julian

Julian's paganism[3] was as complex as the emperor himself. It was a mix of Greek and oriental religions, with the gods he promotes in his *Oration* 4 (*To Helios*), the major gods of Greece, Egypt, Asia and Persia, seen as manifestations of a supreme sun god.[4] He was immersed in hellenistic culture and philosophy ('I myself . . . am a Greek in my habits' (*Misop.* 367C), seeing himself as a philosopher-emperor in the mould of Marcus Aurelius. He perceived it as his mission to restore the ancient religions.[5] It was an austere religion that he promoted, one which in itself would have had little appeal to the masses, or to the sophisticated Greeks of great cities such as Antioch. Yet Julian was astute enough to recognise the appeal of Christianity to the lower classes, and he began to reorganise pagan religion, borrowing much from Christianity itself. He built on the earlier reforming work of the pagan Augustus Maximin in *c.*310, as well as introducing measures to curtail Christian activity. He was also able to turn his knowledge of Scripture, a legacy of his Christian upbringing, to the promotion of the pagan cause. His pamphlet highly critical of Christian doctrine, *Against the Galilaeans*,[6] which was undoubtedly circulated throughout the empire, was, some forty years later, still considered sufficiently dangerous for Cyril of Alexandria to publish a rebuttal (*Against Julian*).

The measures taken against Christianity cannot be said to amount to persecution in a physical sense.[7] However, such was the tenor of Julian's writing on the subject, and particularly the venom of the *Misopogon*, it is very likely that had he survived the Persian campaign he would have dealt with the 'Galilaeans' in earnest.

There is no doubt that, even at this time, Christians were disadvantaged. Their property, sacred vessels and relics were threatened and their privileges lost. On 4 February 362 Julian proclaimed religious freedom in the empire. Christian heretical leaders were recalled from exile (Julian *To the Alexandrians, an Edict* 398C–9), a measure calculated, according to Ammianus (22.5.4), to increase acrimony among Christians.[8] Jews were singled out as preferable to Christians (Julian *To the Alexandrians* 433C), instructions were given for the rebuilding of the temple at Jerusalem (Ammianus 23.1.2)[9] and it was said (Gregory of Nazianzus *Second Invective* 3) that the emperor deliberately stirred up trouble between Jews and Christians. The visible symbols of Christianity now came under attack. Zealous pagans (to whom Julian referred as 'Hellenes') turned the tables on the Christians and burnt churches, or converted them into temples,[10] and temples which had been destroyed by Christians were to be restored, or new ones built (Libanius *Or.* 18.126).[11] Church plate was confiscated[12] and the destruction of church property and buildings ignored, if not actually encouraged (Gregory of Nazianzus *First Invective* 86–90).

Old cults were revived. Ammianus (22.14.6) relates that a new Apis bull was found in Egypt, after a long search. The oracle of Apollo at Daphne, near Antioch, was restored: the remains of the Christian martyr Babylas were removed from the vicinity of the temple (Sozomen 5.19) and other bodies from around the Castalian spring nearby.[13] Julian sought to reopen the spring, closed since the days of Trajan, and, in an effort to purify the site, ordered the same ritual as had been used by the Athenians in the days of Peisistratus when they purified (and removed bodies from) Delos (Ammianus 22.12.8; Herodotus 1.64). There was thus an attempt to revert to old religious formulae, although Julian seems frustrated that in some long-Christianised places like Antioch the pagan rites had been forgotten (*To Theodorus* 453D; *To Aristoxenus* 375A–C).

See p.38

Christians ceased to have a privileged position, and traditions were attacked. Pagans were to be preferred for public office (Julian *To Artarbius* 376–D), Christian priests lost their immunity from public service (e.g. *To the Citizens of Byzacium* 380D–381A) and bishops their free use of the *cursus publicus* (*C.Th.* 8.5.12–13). Henceforth, funerals were no longer to take place in the daytime, as had been the Christian custom (Julian *Edict on Funerals* (Hertlein 77); *C.Th.* 9.17.5); and – the measure with perhaps the most serious ramifications – Christians were forbidden to teach the 'classics' (Julian *Rescript on Christian Teachers* 422A–424A; Ammianus 22.10.7).

Julian went still further. He attempted to put his revived pagan religion on an organised, hierarchical footing, as Christianity was. He was concerned that the 'hellenic' religion was not prospering as he wished, so set about laying down standards of conduct expected from priests and, to a lesser extent, the people. Moreover, he realised that his religion must reach out to the people, and planned agencies to do this.

Considerable detail can be drawn from Julian's correspondence. It is clear that high priests were set up over local ones, in the manner of bishops over lower Christian clergy, and Julian himself was the Supreme Pontiff (*To an Official* 451B). In his letter *To Arsacius* (429C–432A) he instructs the high priest of Galatia to live a virtuous life, and to see that all the priests under his control do the same, on pain of dismissal.[14] They were forbidden to enter theatres or drink in taverns, or to control any trade that lacked respectability. In the same letter, Julian exhorts priests to ensure that their whole households, including wives, children and slaves,[15] convert to paganism; to teach the people to contribute to the needy, as the Christians do; and to encourage villages to give first fruits to the gods. Hostels were to be set up for the care of strangers and the poor. To encourage public donations to such schemes in Galatia at least, Julian ordered that wine and corn be given from state supplies each year. Priests were to be given precedence over military men once they entered a temple, and so their moral authority was bolstered.

Much the same ground, but in rather more detail, is covered in Julian's (fragmentary) letter *To a Priest* (288A–310D). Priests must exhort men not to transgress religious law; they should encourage them to adopt the life of a priest, since it is more holy than a political life; and they themselves must be philanthropic, but not only to the helpless and the poor of good character: it is a pious act to give aid even to the wicked, such as those in prison, and to strangers. In fact, he comes close in his exhortations (291C–D) to the first and second Commandments: 'Thou shalt love the Lord thy God . . . and thy neighbour . . . ' (Matthew 22.37–9). Guidelines for priests' personal conduct are again set down: to avoid licentiousness, shameful acts and speech, and certain reading material such as Old Comedy, the works of Archilochus or Hipponax, and the philosophies of Epicurus and Pyrrho.[16] They are not to attend the theatre, to have actors or chariot drivers as friends, nor to attend games where women attend or compete, or shows with hunting dogs. This last is so depraved that even the sons of priests are forbidden to attend. A priest is to learn by heart the hymns sung in the temples, and to pray in private and in public, if possible three times a day. He is also to avoid contamination with others when engaged in temple service, and not even to enter a house or a marketplace at this time. For his priestly duties he is expected to robe himself in gorgeous array,[17] but on resuming his ordinary life, to adopt a moderate way of life and dress. Julian finishes by emphasising that priests should demonstrate their love for God (*philotheon*) by caring for others, and points out that it is the poor who, neglected by the pagan priests, are the recipients of Christian charity, and 'very many' (*pleistous*) have in this way been won over to Christianity.[18]

Thus Julian drew heavily on his knowledge and experience of Christianity. Gregory of Nazianzus relates (*First Invective* 111, 113) that the emperor also intended to set up some kind of religious school in each town for the spread of heathen doctrines. Forms of prayer with congregational response were to be introduced, penance pronounced for sinners, and a form of initiation brought in. Other features of Christianity were to be copied, such as monasteries and convents, inns and hospices, places for meditation, the provision of charity to prisoners, and the use of letters of recommendation to fellow Christians. All of these, Gregory says, Julian especially admired in the Christian religion. But it was, in his view, not so much *copying* as *parodying* the Christians.

There seemed to be plenty of time to carry out religious reform, but Julian died during the campaign against the Persians in June 363. The immediate results of his pagan revival are hard to assess, given the generally strong Christian or pagan bias of the sources. The army was probably the first to be affected by Julian's apostasy, as some, at least, were devoted to him.[19] Julian writes (*To Maximus* 414A–415D) that even before he had become sole Augustus his whole army worshipped the gods with him. This is confirmed by

Gregory of Nazianzus, a contemporary but hostile (Christian) source, who says (*First Invective* 82–4) that the soldiery was won over by the emperor's own efforts and by the efforts of his officers. The officers themselves were an easy target because they saw in apostasy the hope of promotion, because they knew no law but the will of the emperor, and because of their own simplicity. (Here he tells the story of soldiers who, after having burnt incense on the pay parade, received the emperor's donative of a gold piece, unaware that they had, in so doing, renounced Christ). Indeed, it is likely that the majority of the rank and file had never converted to Christianity, even in the Constantinian era,[20], and it has been pointed out (A. H. M. Jones 1964: 137) that by this time the army was mostly barbarian or peasant, from areas where Christianity would as yet have made little headway. Ammianus (22.12.6) describes the enthusiasm with which the auxiliary units of Celtae and Petulantes, in particular, took part in the excesses of sacrifice ordered by the emperor.

There is also evidence (Julian *To a Priest* (Hertlein 78)) that some Christian priests apostasised even before pressure was applied by Julian to do so; and Libanius (*Or.* 18.115–16) relates that the Athenians had reverted to paganism prior to Constantius' death.

Despite the eulogistic nature of his oration, Libanius does not go so far as to claim the revival as a great triumph for Julian. It seems likely that at the time of the emperor's death not 'everybody' yet came to the pagan altars, or that former Christians now willingly sacrificed to the gods (*Or.* 18.281–2). Nor does Ammianus, another pagan historian whose testimony was first hand, make extravagant claims of success. He records (22.14.2) the hostility of the Antiochenes to Julian, and their singular lack of enthusiasm for his revived paganism. He also tells of the brutal murder of Bishop George at the hands of Alexandrians, an action which earned only a mild reproof from Julian (*To the People of Alexandria* 378D–380D; Ammianus 22.11.8). Yet here the conflict was not necessarily only a pagan–Christian one, but part of the Catholic–Arian (i.e. George–Athanasius) struggle as well.[21] Moreover, while some towns capitalised on their pagan loyalties,[22] there were still whole towns which remained Christian.[23]

Following the death of Julian, Christian reaction was swift. Gregory of Nazianzus saw it as evidence of a miracle[24] that the pagan gods were so speedily pulled down by the very men who had set them up (*Second Invective* 37). Less than two years was far too short a period in which to change a whole empire, and much would depend on his successors and on the loyalties and religious affiliations of the praetorian prefects of the major prefectures.

Paganism under Julian's successors

Julian was succeeded by Jovian, a Christian soldier. Immediately the new emperor proclaimed a policy of religious toleration (Themistius *Or.* 5). This general policy was followed for almost three decades and allowed the continuation of pagan cults at Rome and elsewhere in the empire. However, sporadic attacks were made on paganism, culminating in the legislation of Theodosius of 391. Undoubtedly the increasingly hard line taken by the emperors from Gratian to Theodosius must be seen as resulting from the influence of Ambrose, the powerful Bishop of Milan (374–98).

Jovian ruled for less than twelve months. His successors, Valentinian I (364–75) and his brother, Valens (364–78), also followed a policy of religious toleration,[25] but the church continued to expand. Although he confiscated temple lands (*C.Th.* 5.13.3, 10.1.8), thereby depriving them of much of their revenue, Valentinian was mostly accommodating in his attitude towards pagans.[26] He allowed the ancient *haruspicina*, previously forbidden by Constantine and his sons (*C.Th.* 9.16.9). He was equally tolerant of Christian divisions. Only the most outrageous Christian heretics, such as the Manichaeans, were banned.[27] Factions flourished within the church, and the contest in 367 for the see of Rome saw an undignified and bloody battle between the two candidates, Damasus and Ursinus, with Damasus ultimately the winner. The church itself grew in prestige and in riches, to the extent that Valentinian prohibited clerics from entering the houses of widows or unmarried girls, or receiving legacies from them (*C.Th.* 16.2.20). Even so, Christians did not regain all privileges they had held prior to the reign of Julian. Legislation was introduced to prevent *curiales* from using ordination as a means of avoiding service to the state: they were required to provide a substitute on the councils, or to make over their property to the council (*C.Th.* 12.1.59). It is clear that, by now, the Christian religion had taken hold among the governing class in the various towns of the empire, as well as among the poor and disadvantaged.

It was from the governing class that there arose a man who was to influence to a great extent the religious policies of the next three emperors. That man was Ambrose, himself a *consularis*, and son of a prefect of Gaul. In 374, according to the story, he was proclaimed

Bishop of Milan by public acclamation (Paulinus of Milan *V. Amb.* 6–9), only a year before the death of Valentinian. Valentinian had nominated his son Gratian as Augustus in 367. As a youth at Vienne, in Gaul, Gratian had come under the influence of his tutor, the poet and philosopher Ausonius – a Christian, but a liberal one, having perhaps more sympathies with the ideals of the Roman pagan senators than Ambrose would have appreciated. Nevertheless, possibly as early as April 378 Gratian issued an edict against heretics (*C.Th.* 16.5.4). He also proclaimed religious toleration (Socrates 5.2; Sozomen 7.1), but this policy was reversed the following year, in an edict issued, significantly, from Milan (*C.Th.* 16.5.5). From 381, Gratian spent considerable periods in that city, and Ambrose's influence increased as the young emperor's religious zeal grew. This was reflected in Gratian's policies from 379 on: apostates were now to be deprived of the right to make a will or to inherit; heretics (specifically Manichaeans) and those who converted to Judaism were similarly punished (*C.Th.* 16.7.1–3); and sacrifices specifically for divination purposes were banned (16.9.7; 9). Gratian renounced the title of Pontifex Maximus (Zosimus 4.36.5). He withdrew funding to the Vestals and other public cults (*C.Th.* 16.10.20), and his crowning insult to the pagan cause was the removal from the *curia* of the Altar to Victory.[28] This had by now become something of a symbol of pagan resistance. It and the accompanying statue of Victory had first been removed from the Senate house by Constantius in 356, and had apparently been restored by Julian. In 382 the pagan senators at Rome protested at Gratian's action, but a counter-petition was presented by the Christian senators, organised by Pope Damasus, and the altar did not return. Symmachus, one of the most prominent pagan senators of the day, implies (*Rel.* 3.20) that Ambrose was really behind Gratian's refusal. Gratian was murdered in 383, but already another round in that struggle had been won by the Christians.

Ambrose's influence was even greater over Gratian's successor, Valentinian II, another son of Valentinian I. He was still a child when he came to the throne in 383. His mother, Justina, had sought the support of the bishop when she feared that Magnus Maximus, the general who had usurped Gratian, might march on Italy and dislodge her son. A further attempt in the form of an eloquent request by Symmachus (*Rel.* 3) was now made to restore the Altar of Victory. This was again frustrated by Ambrose (*Ep.* 57). When the threat from Magnus Maximus materialised in 387, Justina and her son fled to Thessalonica, until Maximus was defeated by Theodosius. On his mother's death, probably in 389, Valentinian was sent to Trier to rule the western provinces, and this cleared the way for Theodosius to take control.

Following the death of his uncle, Valens, in 378, Gratian had appointed as his Augustus in the east Theodosius, an eminent Christian general of Spanish descent, and son of the Theodosius who had successfully campaigned in Britain against the barbarians in 367 (Ammianus 27.8, 28.3). The religious policies of Theodosius appear to have been somewhat ambivalent in the earlier part of his reign. His name appears with that of Gratian and Valentinian II in edicts against heretics (mentioned above), and it seems he did not intervene when Christians destroyed pagan temples in the east and in Egypt (Zosimus 4.37). Yet a law of 381 merely forbids sacrifice for the purpose of divination (*C.Th.* 16.10.7). A similar law was enacted in 385 (16.10.9), when Theodosius was virtually sole ruler, while another, of 386, forbids any Christian to act as the chief priest in Egypt (12.1.112). Evidently at this stage he was prepared to allow the pagan cults to remain. That was to change within five years, as he, too, came under the sway of Ambrose.

The first confrontation between Ambrose and Theodosius came with the destruction by Christians of a Jewish synagogue at Callinicum, on the Euphrates, in 388 (Paulinus *V. Amb.* 22). Theodosius ordered the local bishop to rebuild the structure, but Ambrose forbade it. A veiled threat of excommunication brought the emperor to heel (Ambrose *Ep.* 40, 41).[29] It was less than two years later that Theodosius played into the hands of Ambrose. To punish the people of Thessalonica for the lynching of his *magister equitum*, Butheric, the emperor had ordered a reprisal against the city, which resulted in the massacre of 7,000 of its citizens. The reaction of the bishop was as predictable as it was severe: the emperor's excommunication until a public and humiliating penance had been performed (Paulinus: *V. Amb.* 24; Sozomen 7.25). This second incident was even more significant, since Theodosius was deemed guilty of a great sin. It is likely that Ambrose was able to play on his piety (the emperor was baptised in 380) to have legislation against pagans tightened up, to the stage of banning their cults.

Thereafter, and certainly not merely coincidentally, Theodosius took increasingly severe action against paganism, having been restored to the bosom of the church at Christmas, 390. In 391 laws promulgated throughout the empire prohibited pagan cults and sacrifices (*C.Th.* 16.10.10–11). Penalties were particularly severe on provincial governors and probably other high officials. Another law (16.7.5) stripped apostates of rank, either inherited or acquired: the provisions of Gratian's laws regarding wills and inheritance were repeated, and apostates were further disqualified from giving testimony (16.7.3). Probably in the same year, the Serapaeum at Alexandria was destroyed by Bishop Theophilus, followed by the destruction of all temples there. As a result of this, we are told, many converted to Christianity (Socrates 5.16; Sozomen 7.15). In 392 domestic cults were prohibited (*C.Th.* 16.10.12).

In the struggle of wills between Ambrose and Theodosius the Church ultimately prevailed, its position strengthened. But paganism still had one final chance to challenge Christianity, at the time of the usurpation by Eugenius 392–4. Eugenius, at least a nominal Christian, had been proclaimed Augustus by his pagan *comes*, Arbogast, after the suicide (or, more likely, murder) of Valentinian II. Immediately the pagan senatorial 'party' petitioned Eugenius to restore the Altar of Victory.[30] He acceded to the request and, in addition, gave to two pagan senators, from his personal funds, the endowments which the Vestals would have received from the state (Ambrose *Ep.* 57). The urban prefect, the aristocratic Flavianus, enthusiastically applied these funds to the revival of pagan cults. But Theodosius would not lift his ban on such cults, and the whole issue escalated into a religious war. The army of the emperor met and defeated the pagan forces led by Eugenius, Arbogast and Flavianus at the Frigidus River near Aquileia in September, 394 (Augustine *De civ. Dei* 5.26; Rufinus of Aquileia *H.E.* 11.31–3). Eugenius was executed, Arbogast and Flavianus committed suicide, and organised senatorial resistance to Christianity collapsed.

Paganism at Rome

Despite this flurry of activity by the pagan element in the Senate at Rome, it is doubtful that even its strongest representatives could ever have defeated Christianity. Many Roman senators now had a vastly different background, and different loyalties, from those of earlier times. The pagan element became proportionately less influential as successive Christian emperors ruled. Indeed, it is likely that religion was not high among the priorities of many pagan senators of the day (Cameron 1993: 156).

From the time of the earliest days of the Republic, the Roman aristocracy had provided the magistrates who would carry out the government of Rome and, later, its empire. While the Senate of the fourth century was now far removed from its patrician origins[31] and from much of its traditional involvement in administration, it still carried great prestige, if not power. The emperor of the east, Constantius, had even seen fit to create a Senate at Constantinople, probably in 340. Initially that body comprised mostly men who also made up the court of the emperor and were from varied backgrounds, much less exalted than their contemporaries at Rome.[32] On the other hand, the Senate at Rome, its origins lost in the mists of the regal period, was an hereditary body drawn from the aristocratic families of the city. Both senates were, however, supplemented from time to time by adlections from the equestrian order (at Rome, especially from the time of Diocletian).[33] By c.384, membership at both Rome and Constantinople had grown to around 2,000 and, of these, an increasing number owed their positions to the emperor. Presumably they were also encouraged to adopt the religion of the emperor. In fact, Prudentius (*Contr. Symm.* 1.565) relates that Theodosius, on a visit to Rome in 389,[34] had such an impact on the Senate that hundreds of senators converted to Christianity; but the story may be apocryphal.[35] A decreasing proportion belonged to the very old, very rich and very conservative Roman aristocracy. It was these men who formed the core of resistance to Christianity in the second half of the fourth century.[36] While the pagan senators were undoubtedly influential in Roman affairs when they held high office, a study of the Fasti and the written sources for the period suggests that their influence was not as great as might be believed from the voluminous writings of Symmachus. Moreover, it is doubtful that their part in the pagan revival had any real chance of success.

If we look at the religious affiliations of these Roman families, we see that they often followed the trend towards the mystery cults of the east, as promoted by Julian. In a very useful study, Bloch (1945) analysed the inscriptions of a number of senatorial families of the period. The leading senator until his death in 384 was Vettius Agorius Praetextatus. He was in a good position to head any pagan revival at Rome as he was a noted antiquarian and, having been appointed Proconsul of Achaea by Julian in 362 (Ammianus 22.7.6), was certain to have been involved in the revival of the ancient pagan religion there. At Rome, he was a priest of three of the four traditional religious colleges, a priest of the cult of the sun, and also associated with the cults of Mithras, Cybele, Liber, Hecate, Isis and Hercules (*CIL* 6.1779). This extraordinarily broad range of religious affiliations is almost identical to those promoted by Julian. Other senatorial inscriptions show the same kinds of affiliations, though not on such a comprehensive scale. The literary evidence confirms that of the inscriptions. Macrobius, in the *Saturnalia*, sees the early gods in a cosmic sense, with the sun standing for the whole. All the gods he mentions relate to the sun in some way: Apollo, Liber, Mars (whom he equates with Liber/Dionysus), Hercules, Minerva, Pan, Jupiter, Cybele and Attis, Isis and Osiris, Venus and Adonis; the goddess of love he relates to the (re)productive power of the sun. There is, therefore, a close relationship also between the religion of Julian and that recorded later by Macrobius, who was writing at the beginning of the fifth century about a paganism which was to all intents and purposes dead. Indeed, the participants in Macrobius' imaginary symposium included the leading pagan figures of the late fourth century, notably the aristocratic Publius Caeionius Caecina Albinus, Caeionius Furius (Rufius) Albinus,[37] and Praetextatus. At about the same time or a little earlier, the anonymous *Carmen adversus Flavianum* recorded a similar list of deities. Presumably this anti-pagan composition was directed against another eminent senator, Virius Nichomachus Flavianus.

It was Flavianus who, with the usurper Eugenius, faced the army of Theodosius, supported by images of Jupiter and Hercules (Augustine *De civ. Dei* 5.26). That pagan religion was still being promoted, despite the bans of Theodosius, is confirmed by an inscription (*AE* 1948, 127 = *AE* 1941,66) dated to 393, or even to 394, the year of the defeat of Eugenius. It was found at Ostia and commemorates the restoration of an altar of Hercules by a *praefectus annonae*, who may even have been a member of the circle of Flavianus (Bloch 1945).

The last great pagan figure of the day was Quintus Aurelius Symmachus, whose father had been consul-elect around 377 but had died before taking office. The paganism of Symmachus was of the more traditional Roman kind. His petition to the Emperor Valentinian II for the restoration of the Altar of Victory (*Rel.* 3) is not so much an attack on Christianity[38] as a plea to retain what has served the state well in the past.

This senatorial pagan resistance did not, however, pose any real threat to Christianity, in part because there is no evidence that the senators at Rome took up Julian's call to proselytise, or to reform the pagan cults to make them more attractive to the masses. Julian saw himself as part of the Greek world and, at least in his adult life, never visited Rome. His asceticism would not have attracted many upper-class Romans. His proposed appeal to the masses by way of a reformed pagan religion would have repelled those same aristocrats. Although both Julian and the senators purported to worship the same gods, for those at Rome there was an exclusiveness about the cults and a harking back to the old values which automatically excluded the *plebs*. Any pagan revival could not originate in Rome.

Moreover, an analysis of the Fasti[39] shows that few of the leading pagan senatorial families were now actively involved in government outside Italy, beyond the level of continuing patronage in a particular area, presumably where a family held property.[40] Even Ammianus (14.6.1–25) is critical of the pursuit of pleasure by the upper classes. The list of consuls for the period from Valentinian I is increasingly one of men at the time, or previously, in positions of real power, as praetorian prefects or as *magistri militum*. It is noticeable that there is a growing reliance in the later period on barbarian *magistri militum*, whether Christian or pagan, for the now largely barbarian armies: Theodosius, despite his Christianity, was pragmatic in his choice of commanders. But it is unlikely that following the reforms of Diocletian the military leaders would have been in a position to influence the policies, religious or otherwise, of provincial governors.[41] These *vicarii* were answerable to a praetorian prefect, which was a civilian appointment made by the emperor himself; and a study of the religious affiliations of the praetorian prefects from 362–94 shows that they were overwhelmingly Christian.[42] Only rarely do the names of men from the (old) senatorial families appear, and when they do they too are known to be Christian.

An exception to this, but confined to Italy, is the position of Prefect of Rome. This was a prestigious position, the senior senatorial appointment, the holder of which presided over the Senate but had no power beyond the bounds of the city itself. It had long been the prerogative of the aristocratic families of Rome. It was, however, a position in a city which had become increasingly out of touch with the emperor and the real centre of power. These senators may have been able to influence religious affiliations or events in Rome itself, but they could not and did not make any concerted effort to revive paganism beyond their own immediate environs. It is interesting to note that during the stormy events at Rome in 367 the urban prefect and leading pagan Praetextatus was responsible for restoring order between the warring Christian parties headed by Ursinus and Damasus (Ammianus 27.9.8). He did not, as far as is known, take advantage of the situation to advance the pagan cause.

His only recorded public action involving paganism at that time was the removal of houses which had been attached to the walls of temples (Ammianus 27.9.10). In 384, as prefect of Italy, he is said (Symmachus *Rel.* 21.5) to have initiated an investigation into the spoliation of temples, an investigation presumably to be carried out by Symmachus, then urban prefect.[43]

The years from 360–94 should not be seen as a life-and-death struggle between Christianity and paganism. That battle had already been fought and won by the House of Constantine. If the policies of subsequent emperors gave pagans room for hope of regeneration, it was a false hope, without any real chance of success. Julian *may* have been able to stem the tide for a time, although his efforts seemed to have been a classic case of 'too little, too late'. At Rome, the efforts of the pagans of the senatorial class were concentrated on an exclusive and inward-looking religion, and they could not and did not use active government service for the promotion of their cults, even if they ever had a thought of proselytising. In the period from the death of Julian to the end of the century, the aristocratically led pagan movement at Rome would have had little chance of directly influencing changes in religion in distant parts of the empire.

In all, the pagan revival must be seen generally as a lost cause. This study confirms a definite and ultimately irreversible trend towards the Christianisation of most of the empire, with Christians in positions likely to foster the spread of the religion. It has shown, however, that although Julian's programme was not successful, the failure of his immediate successors to negate all of his measures at least allowed pagan cults to survive. In Britain, a combination of this and other factors caused the growth of Christianity to falter. There the survival of the Christian faith was not guaranteed.

The survival and revival of paganism in Britain

The survival and/or revival of paganism in Britain in the late fourth century has been postulated by various scholars over the years, although their explanations for such a revival vary. Toynbee is specific, attributing the restoration of a Jupiter column at Cirencester (*RIB* 103) to 'the pagan revival under Julian the Apostate' (1953: 3). Frend (1984: 608–9; 1992) also sees the 'final era of prosperity' for pagan cults in Britain from Julian to Theodosius, but does not directly link the revival of paganism in this period to Julian. Rather, he sees the types of cults and their longevity as factors which caused them to flourish. This view is perhaps more in line with that of Henig (1984: 13–14), who sees the restoration of the pagan cults as 'a return to "normalcy"'. Thomas (1981: 266, Figure 48), too, while proposing that the reign of Julian may have given paganism 'a limited impetus', seems inclined to agree with M. A. Murray (1921: 19) that most Britons persisted with their pagan beliefs, even long after the mission of Augustine in 597, and that such beliefs were always part of British religion, continuing into the Middle Ages. In a regional study, Rahtz and Watts (1979) reappraise the archaeological evidence from the south west, noting that two temples[44] were begun in the period from *c.*360 to the earlier decades of the fifth century and that others were 'revived' at that time or continued in use, some into the period beyond the Roman occupation. In a later publication, Rahtz (1991) suggests that disillusionment with Christianity may have been one reason for such revival of paganism. All of these views have some validity, and the answer is probably a combination of them all.

Earlier in this chapter, the attitudes of the emperors and their policies towards the pagan cults in the second half of the fourth century were analysed. If the archaeological record in Roman Britain for the period is examined in the light of historical events, it is found that there was, indeed, a pagan revival in Roman Britain, probably stimulated by the reign and policies of Julian, and continuing for at least a couple of decades after his death. In essence, what we have is a brief phase of increased overt pagan activity in rural areas, against a background of a deep-rooted but gradually declining commitment to the old native religions. Reverence for the religious sites themselves declined even more slowly. The paganism which was revived after 360, however, was mostly far removed in character from that which had been promoted by the emperor and the pagan aristocracy at Rome.

Julian had become sole Augustus on the death of Constantius at the end of 361, and immediately made public his apostasy (Julian *To Maximus* 415C). At the beginning of February 362 he proclaimed religious freedom in the empire. He sent throughout the empire dispatches designed to revive pagan cults: for example, he ordered the re-establishment of traditional honours to pagan gods (John Chrysostom *De s. Babyla* 14) and the refurnishing of temples with statues and altars; and temples which had been quarried (usually by Christians) were to be restored by reclaiming the stone (Julian *To his Uncle Julian*).

Official appointments were undoubtedly made by Julian with a view to ensuring his various decrees were carried out. It will be seen (Appendix 1) that he gave preference to pagans. In Gaul, the prefect was the pagan Fl. Sallustius, who replaced Nebridius after that worthy had been given safe passage by Julian (Ammianus 21.8.1, 5.11). Sallustius was rewarded for his loyalty by holding the consulship with his emperor in 363, so it can be assumed that Julian's policies in the west were relayed to the provinces, and therefore to the (unknown) *vicarius* of Britain.

Following Julian's death, the emperors who followed were Christian, and this was reflected in their appointments. The information is not always available, but where the religion of the prefects of Gaul from 361 to 391 is known, the incumbent was a Christian. One possible exception was for the period from ?December 379 to some time in 381: the post was held by Siburius, whose son is known to have been a pagan.

Since Julian's successors from Jovian to Theodosius I (until 391) generally followed a policy of religious toleration, the paganism unleashed by Julian was only mildly restrained by subsequent legislation. Nevertheless, Libanius, in his address to Theodosius composed around 386 (*Or.* 30), complains that in contravention of the law Christians were causing the destruction of temples, often with the connivance of the bishops. He hints that such action had at least the tacit approval of Christian prefects, if not their active involvement.[45] He also says that country temples were the most common targets (*Or.* 30.11, 9).

It is difficult, in a survey of the archaeological evidence for Roman Britain, to determine if there was immediately a response to Julian's decrees, since less than two years was then to elapse until his death. However, it is possible to detect a resurgence of paganism in the longer period from 360 to the 380s and, for temples at least, a decline even prior to 391. (See Figures 4 and 5.)

It seems that, after about 360, a number of temples were given a new lease of life by refurbishment, or reinstated as pagan cult centres after a spell of Christian use. There was also limited investment in new buildings. Some temples continued in use to the end of the century and beyond, but others which had survived the threats of Constans and Constantius lasted only another two or three decades before succumbing to the pressures of Christianity. With few exceptions, most of the renewed pagan activity took place at Romano-Celtic or native-type shrines, and in rural areas.

Initially there was some restoration and refurbishing of temples.

Site	Type of Site[1]	360	370	380	390
Bath	U?	←———————————————→			
Bourton Grounds	R	←———————————————→			
Brean Down	R	←—··			
Brigstock 1	R	←————————			
Brigstock 2	R	←————————			
Caerwent 1	U	←————————————·····			
Carrawburgh (Coventina's Well)[2]	R/M	←———————————————→			
Chelmsford	U	←————————————————·			
Farley Heath	R	←———————————————→			
Frilford 2	R	←———————————————→			
Great Dunmow	R	———————————————→			
Henley Wood	R	←———————————————→			
Jordon Hill	R	←———————————————→			
Lamyatt Beacon	R	←—·			
London Mithraeum	U	←·····—·			
Lydney	R	←———————————————→			
Maiden Castle 1	R	?———————————————→			
Maiden Castle 2	R	·———————————→			
Nettleton	R	←·····—————————·→			
Pagans Hill	R	←····—————————→			
Richborough 1	M	←————————			
Richborough 2	M	←————————			
Silchester 1	U	←————————·····			
Silchester 2	U	←————————·····			
Silchester 3	U	←————————·····			
South Cadbury	R	←———————————————→			
Thetford[3]	R	←————————————·→			
Uley	R	←————————————··			
Verulamium 1[2]	U	←———————————————→			
Verulamium 2[2]	U	←———————————————→			
Wanborough	R	←————————··			
Witham	R	←·····—————————→			
Woodeaton	R	←———————————————→			
Worth	R	←————————————····			
York[2]	U/M	←———————————————→			

Figure 4. Pagan temples in Britain AD 360–91

1 M = Military; R = Rural; U = Urban.
2 Abandoned 350–90, but pagan activity continued.
3 Temple presumed in view of evidence of hoard and Iron Age predecessor in the area.

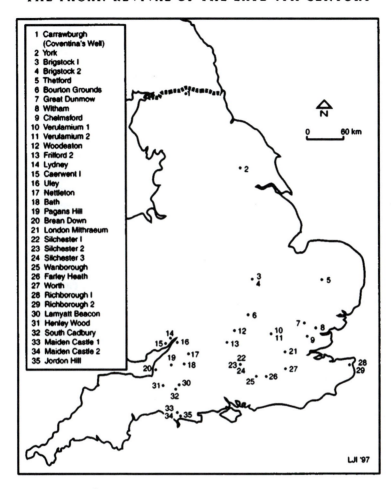

1 Carrawburgh
  (Coventina's Well)
2 York
3 Brigstock I
4 Brigstock 2
5 Thetford
6 Bourton Grounds
7 Great Dunmow
8 Witham
9 Chelmsford
10 Verulamium 1
11 Verulamium 2
12 Woodeaton
13 Frilford 2
14 Lydney
15 Caerwent I
16 Uley
17 Nettleton
18 Bath
19 Pagans Hill
20 Brean Down
21 London Mithraeum
22 Silchester I
23 Silchester 2
24 Silchester 3
25 Wanborough
26 Farley Heath
27 Worth
28 Richborough I
29 Richborough 2
30 Lamyatt Beacon
31 Henley Wood
32 South Cadbury
33 Maiden Castle 1
34 Maiden Castle 2
35 Jordon Hill

Figure 5. Map of temples surviving to AD 391

This suggests that, even if paganism had been in decline since the conversion of Constantine, with the advent of Julian not all hope was lost. At Lydney, for instance, renovation work on the temple of Nodens was carried out around 367. According to the revised interpretation of the coin evidence, the temple had been built in the late third or early fourth century.[46] At another site in the south west, pagan practices resumed after a period of inactivity following likely Christian desecration: the *cella* in the octagonal temple at Pagans Hill was given a stone reredos and its cult statue restored about 367 (Rahtz and Watts 1989). In the towns, a temple at Verulamium seems to have been renovated after 379 (Niblett 1993), and one at Caerwent, noted by Brewer (1993), had repairs which sealed a coin of Valentinian (364–75). Generally such renovation was not on a grand scale. This evidently reflected the relatively impoverished condition of the pagan cults now that they were deprived of their revenues by the legislation of Valentinian I which had confiscated temple lands.

In some cases churches reverted to temples, or even ceased to operate. The suggestion by Rahtz (above) that some Christians may have become disillusioned with the new and demanding religion could well apply here. The former shrine to Apollo Cunomaglus at Nettleton, earlier converted to a church, seems to have resumed its pagan character around 370 – again, in a very modest way. At the same time the small rectangular chapel at the site probably ceased to be used. In the east, the oratory and baptistery at Witham were dismantled, and pagan activity was revived some time around 360–70 (R. Turner, personal communication). At Bath, pagan practices were reinstituted after some restoration work following Christian desecration of the classical temple (*RIB* 152). Certainly the curse on the lead tablet which refers to Christians and pagans (Cunliffe 1988: 232–4) points to a discernible Christian presence there; yet the *defixio* itself confirms that pagan activities still persisted. There is also evidence for at least one new rural shrine and a Romano-Celtic temple in or following Julian's reign. At Great Dunmow, in Essex, a square building or enclosure was constructed on a site which included three votive pits. One or more of these pits, dated to about 350, pre-dated the shrine, which was in use from about 360 to 390 in its first phase (Wickenden 1988). The crude nature of the structure suggests a native cult. More sophisticated was the building at Maiden Castle: a square Romano-Celtic temple built some time after 367, close by a circular shrine which may still have been in use at that time (R. E. M. Wheeler 1943: 74–7; Drury 1980: 68). It has been proposed that as Christianity expanded in the towns of the south the pagan cults were forced into the country, and that this construction was the result of the growth of Christianity at Dorchester (Richmond 1963: 142).

Temples already in existence (Figure 3) continued, with some experiencing renewed activity in the second half of the fourth century. These have been documented by various scholars,[47] who have based their conclusions on increased coin loss (or votive offerings) at these sites in the latter part of the century.[48] But while pagan shrines are known to have remained in use to the end of the century and beyond, instances such as these were now in the minority, and becoming even less common as the century drew to a close. More usual was a situation where, once Christian emperors again ruled, the shrines continued for a number of years before being abandoned. In some cases at least, this might be attributed to the growth of Christianity, even when deliberate Christian destruction is not suspected. An example is the Mithraeum at London, which had been in use perhaps since the late second century. It is likely that anti-Mithraic activity led to the careful burial of the major cultic sculpture of the temple early in the fourth century. The structure itself continued in presumably pagan use in a deteriorating state until later in the century (Grimes 1968: 92–117).[49]

On the other hand, some temples which had been in existence at the time of Julian and his immediate successors may now have been deliberately closed and/or dismantled as first Gratian and later Valentinian II came more under the influence of Ambrose from about 380 on. At Silchester, temples 1, 2 and 3 went out of use in the late fourth century. Temple 3 may have been the target of Christians: the fragmentary state of its statuary suggests a violent end (Hope 1908: 208–9). Perhaps the same situation arose at Worth, where pieces of a large statue were found in the remains (Klein 1928). The two Richborough temples adjacent to the Roman fort were probably out of use before 380 (Bushe-Fox 1932: 36). Inside the fort, an apsidal church arose soon after, incorporating in its foundations a fragment of a relief of Fortuna (P. D. C. Brown 1971) likely to have come from one of the earlier pagan buildings.[50] It would have been politically expedient for the military commander there to order it, and such actions may well have been the result of the elevation of the (Christian) usurper emperor Magnus Maximus (383–8), raised to imperial status by the army in Britain (Zosimus 4.35). The temples at Brigstock (Greenfield 1963: 229–40) also seem to have been closed in this period,[51] and those at Chelmsford (Wickenden 1992) and Wanborough (O'Connell and Bird 1994) probably before 391, although in the case of the latter, because of the disturbed nature of the site the dating is inconclusive.

Other temples seem merely to have failed and their sites were taken over for Christian use. In the south west, the Romano-Celtic temples at Brean Down and Lamyatt Beacon were abandoned and their fabric partially reused for the construction of small oratory-type buildings around 360–70 (Leech 1980: 349–50). Rahtz (1991: 11) has suggested that these sites in the south west may have been eremetic and, if so, would be the earliest known sites of this type in the west of Britain. Pagan shrines seem to have continued in the same region, however. Indeed, the construction of a temple adjacent to the circular shrine at Maiden Castle demonstrates this continuity; and the location of the circular shrine precisely on the site of one which existed some three centuries earlier (Drury 1980: 64) says a great deal for the conservatism and deep-rooted beliefs of rural Romano-Britons.

Such deep-rooted beliefs were also reflected in the burials of the period 360–90. Christian cemeteries were becoming larger and, as a result, more prominent. At least one new small farmstead cemetery was also established during these years, at the Romano-British site of Bradley Hill, in Somerset (Leech 1981). But pagans continued to be buried with their own rites. More particularly, data from more recently published or excavated cemeteries[52] provide evidence that some non-Christian rites were on the rise. These occurred at both Christian and pagan sites.

The cemetery at Butt Road, Colchester, was mentioned earlier as one where there was a change from pagan to Christian practices around 320. Crummy (1993: 134–62) has carefully charted the sequence of burials and has found that by about 340 the west–east burials had shed almost all pagan characteristics (e.g. burials with footwear, pots, coins, jewellery, etc.). But the analysis of the burials after about 360 revealed the presence of grave goods of an amuletic type, which suggests the revival of old pagan superstitions. These items, which include jet beads, pierced coins, combs and even a key, an attribute of Epona in her guise of a chthonic deity, were sufficiently innocuous not to have offended Christian sensibilities had they been noticed at time of burial. However, the fact that, at Colchester, such objects were progressively eschewed by Christians after 320 but favoured once more after 360 indicates a resurgence of pagan superstitions in Christian burial in the second half of the fourth century. This was in a thoroughly Romanised part of Britain and in a graveyard which was closely associated with a church, and thus, presumably, under some kind of supervision.

At Poundbury, the evidence is not so clear cut. A sequence of sorts, based on coin evidence, has been seen from east to west, but the northern and southern parts of the main Late Roman Christian cemetery do not necessarily fit into this sequence (Farwell and Molleson 1993: 70–4). Figures 126 and 136 of Farwell and Molleson's report (1993) show a paucity, if not a complete absence, of grave goods in the central part of the cemetery, with the majority of finds from the eastern, northern and western peripheries. The exception is coins in burials, but even these, significantly, date from *c.*350–6 at the earliest; and two groups – one of four, the other of two burials[53] – seem to be closely related spatially and chronologically, suggesting in both cases a family burial practice. Of seven late-fourth-century combs found, the presence of which may indicate the introduction of a practice of pagan significance (see below, Chapter 4), none was in the central part of the cemetery: one was on the easternmost edge of the excavation, two at the south and the others in the west. Although the evidence is not so conclusive, we may be seeing here what occurred at Butt Road: an increase in grave deposits and thus in covert pagan practices in the second half of the fourth century, particularly after *c.*360.

Another cemetery where there was a demonstrable increase in particular types of burial rites is Lankhills in Winchester, a pagan site which also has a small enclosure of seventeen burials, Feature 6, identified as Christian (G. Clarke 1979: 97–9; Watts 1991: 89). In the main cemetery there were seven decapitated burials from a total of about 400. Six of these have been shown to have occurred after *c.*350, and the seventh may also be from this late period (G. Clarke 1979: 372). Postmortem decapitation and skull burials occurred in pre-Roman Britain and Ireland, and were certainly Celtic practices.[54] In Britain, decapitated burial generally occurred in rural rather than urban cemeteries. Instances are known from the third and early fourth centuries,[55] but the practice is more common in the late fourth, continuing into the fifth century and the Anglo-Saxon period (Philpott 1991: 78–9; Harman *et al.* 1981). Since the pre-350 part of Lankhills cemetery was devoid of decapitated burials and the practice was introduced there soon after 350, it would seem to confirm that old Celtic modes of burial were reinstituted in this period. This would fit comfortably with Julian's policy of revival of pagan practice. (A more detailed study of decapitated burial and its implications for a pagan revival will be made in Chapter 4.)

As the resurgence of decapitated burial coincides with the reign of Julian and his successors, so too does the practice of placing bodies in a prone position for burial. At Lankhills, the incidence of prone burials is mainly in the later period of the cemetery, after *c.*370 (G. Clarke 1979: 138–9, Table 10). Other late examples from cemeteries where a sequence of burial in the cemetery might reasonably be proposed include that at Ancaster, where a woman and child were buried prone in the western, and probably the latest, phase of the fourth century cemetery (D. R. Wilson 1968 and personal communication), and Dunstable, where the two prone burials seem to belong to the later phase, perhaps as late as early fifth century (C. L. Matthews 1981).[56] The practice does not seem to have been an Iron Age burial custom, nor was it found in cemeteries which have been identified as Christian (Watts 1991: 58).[57] Rather, while isolated instances are known from earlier than the fourth century,[58] as with decapitated burials the practice became more widespread in pagan cemeteries of the Late Roman period and beyond (Harman *et al.* 1981; Philpott 1991: 73; Watts 1991: 196). Although its significance is not fully understood, it must be seen as anathema to Christians, many of whom believed in a physical resurrection. Christians were buried in a supine and extended position, in order to rise in immediate response to the reveille of the Last Trumpet (1 *Cor.* 15.11). Prone burial seems to have been another funerary practice which reinforced the pagan identity of a cemetery, and of the people who had interred their kith and kin there, despite the spread of Christianity.

Dunstable may have evidence for the revival of another practice known from the pre-Roman Iron Age: the burial of certain animals with humans, specifically horses and dogs. While the burial of remains (skulls, limbs, ribs and various parts which might be termed 'joints') from domestic birds and animals occurred quite frequently in the pre-Roman and Roman periods, the practice became less common after the late third and early fourth centuries (Philpott 1991: 203). All of the usual domestic fauna (e.g. cattle, pigs, sheep, goats, poultry) are found in a funerary context, the larger species generally as 'remains'.[59] This would almost certainly indicate that these either were part of grave offerings (i.e. food for the deceased) or were the leftovers of a funerary feast: the creature would be sacrificed to the gods of the Otherworld (*dis manibus*), the better cuts consumed at the feast and the inedible parts consigned to the grave or the cremation pyre as an offering to the gods. Horse and dog meat was not regularly consumed in Roman Britain, however (Philpott 1991: 204), horses probably because they were too valuable, and dogs because of their use in hunting and herding, and as companion animals. Their presence in cemeteries of the Late Roman period is, therefore, of some interest, and may be connected to practices of the pre-Roman period.

The cemetery at Dunstable contained the graves of 112 humans, along with the remains of four horses and a dog. The excavator has interpreted the site as the burial ground of a town which was occupied in the last half of the fourth century and abandoned for a while before being reoccupied, perhaps under harsher conditions and sterner masters (C. L. Matthews 1981). The burials are located in an enclosure and in the ditches which form it. In the enclosure itself they are arranged in rows, often in coffins, whereas in the ditches they are less carefully laid out. Burial AQ in the 'organised' section produced a beaker with Latin graffito which, when amended, reads: *ollam dendrofororum Verulamiensium Regillinus donavit* – 'Regillinus presented the pot of the *dendrophori* of Verulamium'. This indicates a burial club at Dunstable, the Roman small town of *Durocobrivae*, whose members were associated with a cult of Cybele at nearby Verulamium. It also demonstrates the Roman influence on religion at Dunstable in the earlier years of the cemetery, probably from mid-fourth century, and perhaps even a link with the cults promoted by Julian 361–3. But the ditch burials belong to the later period. It is there that the articulated remains of the horses and dog were found, among human burials. There is every indication that they were purposely buried and as carefully laid out as any humans nearby, and represent a return to a pre-Roman rite.

Horses seem to have been important in the Dunstable area. The bones of twenty-eight were found in a Roman well in the town (C. L. Matthews 1981: 60, 71) and other bones were discovered elsewhere. The town was likely to have been established as a posting station, and this may explain the presence of large numbers of horses. It seems that here the fate of the animals was to be victims of the butcher's knife, since examination of the remains suggests 'extensive use of horse as meat'. The presence of whole animals, given special care when buried in a cemetery with humans, is, therefore, even more curious. An explanation may be the revival of a cult of the horse. That they were found in a cemetery for humans points to the cult of Epona, as a chthonic deity, protector of the dead and perhaps here even as a fertility god, associated with the earth.[60]

Horse burials, whether linked to Epona or some other nameless Celtic deity, are known in Britain from the Iron Age, and in unusual circumstances. For example, at Odell in Bedfordshire, at a ritual site which seemed to be linked with fertility rites as well as with a small cremation cemetery, the decapitated head of a woman was found cradled by the pelvic girdle of an adult horse (Dix, forthcoming).[61] In Yorkshire, at Arras, the so-called 'King's burial' contained the remains of two horses along with a dismantled two-wheeled cart (Stead 1965: 6), and at Stanwick, the head of a horse had been placed above a body interred beside the rampart (Haselgrove 1990).[62] At Deal, in Kent, the articulated remains of a horse were buried in a cemetery and aligned with the nearby graves of humans (Parfitt 1990). These examples indicate a ritual significance for horse burial.

Less detail has been published about the dog burial at Dunstable, but it appears that its presence in the cemetery was also more than a matter of convenient disposal of the body. The animal was buried above the remains of a human interred in prone position, in one of the late enclosure ditches. Dogs were a well-known feature of Celtic and Roman religion, having particular association with death and healing, but it may be significant here that the dog was also an attribute of Epona.[63] The number of instances recorded of burials of dogs with humans would seem to preclude an interpretation of merely the burial of the family pet with a member of the household. In an important article, Black (1983) has documented the incidence of ritual dog burials in late Iron Age or Roman Britain, some of which are associated with human remains. Philpott (1991: 204) also gives some examples from the Roman period, and others have been noted from time to time in archaeological reports or summaries.[64] One of the most significant for our study of religion in the late fourth century is that from Lankhills, where a coffined burial (G400) contained a dog, while the dismembered remains of another were found above, its backbone tied into a circle. This has been interpreted as a cenotaph (*kenotaphion*) for a person whose remains were elsewhere: the dog seems to have been a substitute (G. Clarke 1979: 83). While the grave itself and its contents are of great interest, so too is the proposed date, 390–400: yet another indication of a Late Roman occurrence of the practice of dog burial which was known as early as the neolithic (Black 1983).

The fact that, at both Dunstable and Lankhills, these horse and dog burials occurred amidst what have been interpreted as the later burials in the cemetery suggests the revival of ancient Celtic ritual in the last few decades of Roman occupation in Britain.

It seems that the revival of paganism in the empire resuscitated not only old Roman and Greek practices. It may also have been responsible for the fairly sudden cessation of use of at least two Christian cemeteries: Nettleton and Ashton. At Nettleton, in rural Gloucestershire, the restoration of pagan practices at the shrine of Apollo around 370 probably led to the abandonment of the west–east cemetery and of the adjacent rectangular building 23, interpreted as a cemetery chapel. The cemetery has most of the features one would expect to find in a Christian cemetery.[65] It also lacks any evidence for the gradual decline in standards for Christian burial, such as the reintroduction of grave goods or a decline in burial care. The evidence is similar for Ashton, a Romano-British 'small town'. The limited coin evidence suggests the final burials may have been as early as the 380s. Apart from the slight departure from the strict alignment of burials at the southern and western sides of the cemetery (attributable, no doubt, to the fall of the ground and the difficulty of maintaining intervisibility between earlier and later burials), there is no indication of decline in the care given to this group of burials at Ashton. There is, however, evidence of the continuation of pagan practices, such as decapitation and prone burial and burial with footwear, in the 'backyard' burials in the Roman town into the late fourth or early fifth century (B. Dix, personal communication).

The end of these cemeteries may be compared with that at Poundbury and Colchester, identified as Christian, which survived into the fifth cemetery.[66] The late burials at Colchester saw an increase in grave goods, interpreted as a return to certain pagan practices, and also included some inhumations which were uncoffined, and others which used hollow tree trunks as coffins (Crummy 1993: *passim*). At Poundbury there was a decline in the care taken with the latest burials in the main cemetery: shallow graves, absence of coffins, stone-lined or cist graves (Farwell and Molleson 1993: 74–80, 235–6). This suggests a decline of civic and/or religious order in the last decades of Roman occupation. At Nettleton and Ashton, the seemingly sudden abandonment of the cemeteries may have been connected with the revival of paganism, particularly in rural areas.

Pagan destruction of Christian ritual objects seems to have occurred in this period. This is suggested by the fate of a number of circular lead tanks, many of them decorated with unequivocal Christian symbols, and believed to have been used in the baptism rite.[67] Nineteen whole or partial vessels have been found,[68] and of those whose provenance is known, at least four seem to have been no longer in use by about 370, a fifth was found under late-fourth-century pottery and another with fourth-century pottery and tiles. The deliberate damage sustained by a number of these vessels and the abandoning of others has been seen as the result of anti-Christian activity (Guy 1981: 275). This is a reasonable premiss, especially since at least six whole or fragmentary tanks were found in some kind of watery context, which could also indicate a reversion to a Celtic nature-type religion.[69] Moreover, that they ceased to be used by Christians may have been the result of a fall in numbers of those being baptised, this the corollary of a resurgence of paganism.

Finally, from Thetford in Norfolk comes some of our most important evidence for paganism in late-fourth-century Britain, and one of the few sites to produce any connection with the cults which Julian favoured. A spectacular hoard of Late Roman gold jewellery and silver spoons and other implements was discovered in 1981 (Johns and Potter 1983). The jewellery had clear iconographical connections with pagan cults popular in the fourth century: Bacchus, Diana, Mercury, Mars, Pan, Venus and Cupid. A number of the silver utensils had inscriptions connected with the god Faunus, with Celtic epithets; and Faunus is shown to be almost indistinguishable from Pan or Silvanus (Dorcey 1992: 33–40), and his worship an aspect of the Bacchic cult (Johns and Potter 1983: 49–52; Hutchinson 1986: 136–7). But some of the spoons carry inscriptions or symbols which in another context would be taken as Christian. It has been argued (Watts 1991: 146–58) that the hoard represented a group of people which included lapsed Christians, who used their knowledge of Christian rites (and in particular the Eucharist) to create a pagan ritual. This was in honour of an old Latian deity, and in response to Julian's revival of paganism. There is little doubt that this material represents a rare Romano-British link with the pagan revival of Julian and, even more specifically, with that promoted by the aristocrats of the Roman Senate (see above). The hoard is a valuable one, so the members of the cult were wealthy. From the iconography and inscriptions it would seem also that they were Roman in outlook, but with Celtic roots.

The evidence as presented above demonstrates that paganism and the pagan cults in Britain experienced some kind of resurgence. This was beyond that which might be seen as a state of 'normalcy', given that the period under discussion, from 360–90, was one in which Christianity was expanding rapidly within the empire despite the aberration of Julian's reign. It is argued here that Julian was responsible for the initial stimulus. His Christian successors failed to restore the status quo of the Constantinian era, and the various pagan cults were resumed, reinvented or merely now continued openly, rather than covertly as when they had been proscribed. The hold of Christianity on the native people of Roman Britain seems in this period to have been particularly tenuous, and this may have been connected with the uncertainties of the political situation in the second half of the century (see below, Chapter 3). It remained to be seen whether the tough laws Theodosius would introduce in 391 and 392 would root out the pagan cults and allow Christianity to triumph there as it had elsewhere in the empire.

3

CLOSURE OF THE TEMPLES
AND BEYOND

In 391–2 the Emperor Theodosius legislated to ban all sacrifices and cults (including domestic) and to close the temples (*C.Th.* 16.10.10–12). Severe monetary penalties were to be imposed on any pagan provincial governors and members of their staff who attempted to practise their pagan rites. At that time there was no law requiring the temples to be destroyed, but as late as January 399 the Emperors Honorius and Arcadius were forbidding such destruction where the buildings no longer held cultic objects (16.10.18). This indicates that such activity had occurred, and it was legalised in July of that year (16.10.16), at least as far as rural temples were concerned. Nor did Theodosius or his sons immediately exclude pagans from government service, although it is known that at least one *vicarius* in Britain after 405 was a Christian.[1] It was not until 415 that imperial posts were closed to non-Christians, but the writing was clearly on the wall for pagans and their practices well before this date. Even so, that laws regarding paganism continued to be enacted for decades after 391[2] supports the belief that its demise in the Roman Empire as a whole, while inevitable, was a long-drawn affair. In Britain, the departure of the army meant that such an end never came, and that Christianity failed to triumph over the pagan cults.

The reasons for this are manifold, some possibly relating to the nature of Romano-British paganism, others to the fragility of the hold of Christianity in Britain, and yet others to the political events of the last three decades of the Occupation.

Paganism and its survival in Britain

In view of the gradual decline of the pagan temples in Roman Britain after about 380, it comes as something of a surprise that there is so little archaeological evidence for compliance with Theodosius' decrees immediately or even soon after their promulgation, despite their apparent severity. A very small number of shrines may have been converted to Christian use. Others were disbanded, although cultic activity seems to have continued. In many more cases the pagan cults survived into the sub-Roman period.

Examples of the possible conversion of pagan shrines or temples in Britain following the Theodosian decrees are very limited, and the evidence is not conclusive. The primitive rectangular shrine at Great Dunmow was replaced some time between 390 and 400, after the removal of what may have been cultic vessels from the structure. A further pagan shrine is unlikely, given the spread of Christianity in the Essex region. The situation had been seen as paralleling Uley (Wickenden 1988: 42, 92), but the interpretation of that site is now of the progressive deterioration of the Romano-Celtic temple at the end of the fourth century, followed by a hiatus and then, 'probably in the fifth century', by the construction of a timber basilical building, interpreted as a Christian church (Woodward and Leach 1993: 11, 316, 318). The continuity of overt religious activity originally proposed for the site (Ellison 1980) is no longer supported. The octagonal temple at Pagans Hill is another possible candidate. It too may have seen Christian use some time around the end of the fourth century, as well as similar activity in the Anglo-Saxon period (Rahtz and Watts 1989: 362–6; Rahtz 1991: 12), but such interpretation is very tentative. Identification as Christian or pagan in such circumstances can rarely be confident.

Any progress in the conversion of pagan sites to Christianity was neither rapid nor uniform, and many sites may have retained their pagan character for considerably longer than others even in the immediate area: for example, in the fifth century the desecration of the temple and temenos of Henley Wood temple with west–east (Christian?) burials occurred at the same time as Structure II at Cadbury Congresbury, c.140 metres away, was continuing the pagan traditions of the site (Rahtz et al. 1992: 242–6; Watts and Leach 1996). There is no reason to believe that such a situation could not also arise during the Roman period.

Some pagan sites under threat were apparently protected by their devotees. The dismantling of the shrine at Coventina's Well at Carrawburgh – its sculptures, dedicatory stones and altars carefully deposited in the well itself (Allason-Jones and McKay 1985: 12, 15–19) – may readily be interpreted as the work of pagans, rather than Christians, especially in view of the decree of January 399, discussed above. Deposition of the Thetford Treasure also probably occurred at this time (Johns and Potter 1983). The circumstances which led to this action will never be known but, in view of the cultic associations of the objects, it is likely to have been the anti-pagan laws of Theodosius, rather than a later Saxon threat, which prompted the followers of Faunus to hide the cult's treasure.

Such examples as these are few and far between. There is much more evidence for the continuation of pagan cults and religious activity at shrines, if illegally and often covertly. Indeed, the reinforcing legislation of Honorius and Arcadius of 395 (C.Th. 16.10.13) implies that the decrees of Theodosius which banned the cults had not been complied with. This is supported by the archaeological record, not only in the rural areas where Christianity was not always secure, but also in the towns. In some cases, because of the end of the money economy, a date for the cessation of pagan activity is impossible to determine. Paganism may, as Rahtz points out, have extended 'decades or even centuries' (1991: 7).

The evidence comes from all over rural Roman Britain. In the north, it seems that coins and other votives were still offered to the goddess at Coventina's Well, although the altars and stones were now no longer visible (Allason-Jones and Mackay 1985: 54, 73). In the south west, while Christianity had made substantial gains, it did not eliminate all pagan cults by the end of the fourth century. Structure II at Cadbury Congresbury, a circular building believed to be a pagan shrine which continued into the post-Roman period, may already have been in existence at this time. The temple complexes at Maiden Castle, Lydney, Nettleton, and perhaps Henley Wood and Pagans Hill seem to have remained in cultic use at least into the period without numismatic evidence, when most fell into decay.[3] The considerable number of coins for the years 388–95 at Jordon Hill are a good indication that the temple there continued in its original role until well after the Theodosian decrees, when it became a home for squatters (O'Neill 1935); but the site of a Romano-Celtic temple at South Cadbury (the existence of which is accepted by the present writer)[4] was deserted by the end of the fourth century.

Further east, at Farley Heath, it was not until some time in the first half of the fifth century that fire destroyed the temple there (Goodchild 1938). In East Anglia, the Witham site resumed its pagan character. There is evidence of cultic activity into the early fifth century (R. Turner, personal communication).

In the central area, a number of Romano-Celtic temples were in use until at least the early part of the fifth century, when they were finally abandoned, or met a violent end. The Bourton Grounds building, erected in the mid-third century, reached its peak during the reign of Constantius. It was in use until the first decades of the fifth century, when it may have been deliberately destroyed (C. W. Green 1966: 360). The temple at Woodeaton, built and rebuilt over about 350 years, probably survived until destruction by fire (Kirk 1949; Goodchild and Kirk 1954: 22–7); and that at Frilford, after having experienced considerable activity in the second half of the fourth century (with a marked increase in the incidence of coins for the years 360–85), continued in use until its abandonment in the first half of the fifth century (Bradford and Goodchild 1939: 35, 63, 69). Other likely temples in the area, as yet only briefly reported, include a further example from Oxfordshire, at Lowbury Hill (M. Fulford in Esmonde Cleary 1993: 299), which produced finds down to the early part of the fifth century, and one from Northamptonshire, where a small temple built c.300 amidst a villa complex at Cosgrove also continued in use until early in the fifth century (D. R. Wilson 1970: 288).

More curious is the evidence of the towns, given their long connection with Rome and, presumably, their susceptibility to religious trends at the imperial court. At Verulamium, coins up to Arcadius were among the surface finds in the theatre adjoining the temple in Insula XIV, and in the midden associated with the triangular temple, although the temple itself was probably abandoned mid-fourth century. With regard to the finds in the theatre, these coins cannot with certainty be said to be votive (Niblett 1990, 1993). Even so, as noted earlier, there was a strong connection in classical times between the theatre and religion. The evidence from York is more secure: while the temple outside the fortress ceased to be used by about 350, coins to 402 and other votives continued to be left there.[5] At Bath, latest accounts indicate that the grand classical temple of Sulis-Minerva was modified to a meaner, less public shrine, still in use until well into the fifth century, and that coins, votives and curse tablets also continued to be deposited (Cunliffe and Davenport 1985: 184–5; Cunliffe 1988). It seems that, in the towns as well as in distant Carrawburgh, pagans still left offerings to the gods, despite the counter-influence of Christianity and the threats of imperial lawmakers.[6]

The nature of the pagan revival in Britain

There is clear evidence that in Britain during and after the reign of Julian there was a resurgence of paganism and that pagan cults survived to the end of the fourth century and beyond, though in a restricted and less visible way. The reasons for this are related to the nature of the paganism that was revived: the kinds of cults, the location of the shrines and the date when cultic practices began at the various sites.[7]

Although the associated deities are not always certain, sufficient evidence remains to suggest that the paganism which survived or revived after 361 and that which was not eliminated by Theodosius' laws more frequently involved native-type cults than Roman. If we look at the epigraphic evidence for temples, shrines or cults which were in existence or began life after about 360, we have little sure detail of dedications: Apollo Cunomaglus at Nettleton, Sulis-Minerva at Bath, Nodens at Lydney, Mercury (or Mars or Silvanus) at Uley, Coventina at Carrawburgh and Faunus (with Celtic epithets) at Thetford. Archaeological finds give some hints as to other gods worshipped, but no certainty: perhaps Sucellus (= Jupiter-Taranis) at Farley Heath; another Celtic Jupiter-type deity at Witham and Wanborough; Mars at Lamyatt Beacon; a Mars-type god at Silchester 3; Mars, Cupid or even a deity associated with childbirth at Woodeaton; a Mars- or Minerva-type god at Worth; a healing-type deity at Caerwent 1; Apollo Cunomaglus or similar at Pagans Hill and Maiden Castle, at the latter site associated with Diana. In addition, there may have been a composite native-type deity at Maiden Castle. The votive material at Great Dunmow also suggests a native cult, perhaps a *genius loci*, although there is no indication of a long religious tradition at the site. The octagonal temple at Chelmsford had a large quantity of ovacaprid remains, and it has been suggested these indicate a link with Mercury (Wickenden 1992: 136). Such interpretation is not backed up by any other archaeological material, however, and is very tentative.[8] There was no archaeological evidence at all for the dedication of the temple at Brean Down. The site seems to have been cleared of votive material (Leech 1980: 334). Frilford 2 and Bourton Grounds temples were similarly devoid of dedicatory evidence, although there may be some hint from associated cultic buildings. A circular shrine about 25 m south of the square temple at Frilford revealed a foundation deposit of a ploughshare, which probably indicates that the whole site was in honour of a fertility deity. A similar deity is

56

suspected at Henley Wood; and an ancillary building at Bourton Grounds had a threshold burial of a horse's skull ringed with oyster shells, perhaps indicative of a connection with Epona.[9] The presumably votive deposits of military fittings at South Cadbury near the late Iron Age shrine suggest some kind of war god, but there were also animal burials, including a number of new-born calves and a full-grown cow (L. Alcock 1972: 82, 164). In Celtic mythology, the war goddess the Mórrígan owns a magic cow (Ross 1992: 389). We may have a shrine to such a deity here, the tradition continuing into the late Roman period.

Add to this the evidence of those towns where no temple survived but perhaps votives continued to be offered. The Verulamium triangular temple was probably dedicated to Cybele, since Italian pine seeds had been found there (Wheeler and Wheeler 1936: 113–20); the temple in Insula XIV possibly to a Celtic manifestation of Mercury (Niblett 1993). There was no indication of the dedication for the temple at York.

In every case but one, known deities have names which are Celtic or a blend of Roman and Celtic, although that does not necessarily indicate a blend of Roman and Celtic beliefs. On the *defixiones* at Uley, which date from the late second century on, the god invoked is usually the Roman Mercury;[10] but in view of the early votive activity at the site (Woodward and Leach 1993: 305–10) the god(s) here must originally have been native. There is little doubt that even when the name is not known the gods which were worshipped at rural sites were generally a conflation of Roman and Celtic deities, or Celtic only. At urban sites one might well expect Roman or eastern gods.[11]

At least thirty-five individual temple sites[12] or locations of pagan cultic activity are known to have existed between 361 and 391 (Figures 4 and 5). Nineteen of those were probably officially out of use before 391: nine urban, two military and eight rural. While up to five of the remainder have few or no clues as to the dedication, the association with native gods is an outstanding feature of the others. If we now look at the twenty sites, as opposed to actual structures, where pagan activity continued or probably continued after 391 and/or into the fifth century (that is, for at least some time after the legislation of Theodosius), this trend continues (Figures 6 and 7): seven sites seem to have been associated with healing and/or hunting, two with a war god (although Mars could also be associated with fertility), two with Jupiter-type gods, perhaps associated with the weather, one fertility-type goddess, two sites (one urban)

Site	Type of Site¹	Type of Temple²	390	400	410	Iron Age Predecessor	Deity or Type of Deity Worshipped
Bath	U?	C	←————→			√	Sulis-Minerva (healing)
Bourton Grounds	R	RC	←————→			√	? (Epona? River god?)
Carrawburgh (Coventina's Well)³	R/M	?	←———			?	Coventina (healing)
Farley Heath	R	RC	←————→			√	Sucellis? (Jupiter type)
Fritford 2	R	RC	←————→			√	Mars type (military/fertility)
Great Dunmow	R	S	←··			x	? (native deity?)
Henley Wood	R	RC	←————→			√	Native goddess (fertility?)
Jordon Hill	R	RC	←——— ····			√?	?
Lydney	R	RC	←————→			?	Nodens (healing)
Maiden Castle 1	R	S	←————→			√	⌈Hunting/healing/ ⌊fertility
Maiden Castle 2	R	RC	←————→			√	⌈composite ⌊native deity
Nettleton	R	RC	←————→			√?	Apollo Cunomaglus (hunting/healing)
Pagans Hill	R	RC	←————→			?	Apollo C'maglus type? (hunting/healing)
South Cadbury	R	?	←··			?	? (war god?)
Thetford⁴	R	?	←			√	Faunus (salvation type)
Verulamium 1³	U	RC	←—— ···			x	Mercury (god of merchants)
Verulamium 2³	U	RC Δ	←—— ···			x	Cybele (salvation type)
Witham	R	S	←————→			√	Jupiter/weather god type
Woodeaton	R	RC	←————→			√	Mars/Jupiter/ Cupid type (war/fertility/healing)
York³	U	C	←—— ··			x	? (Roman deity?)

Figure 6. Pagan temples surviving and pagan activity after AD 391
1 Type of site: M = Military; R = Rural; U = Urban.
2 Type of temple: C = Classical; RC = Romano-Celtic style; S = Simple rectangular, circular or polygonal.
3 Abandoned, but pagan activity continued.
4 Temple presumed in view of hoard evidence.

with a salvation cult and another urban site with perhaps a god of trade and merchants. The five sites with virtually no evidence for dedication are omitted. [13] Dedications such as these do not generally indicate a high degree of sophistication or Romanisation; nor do they indicate a heightened awareness of the political and

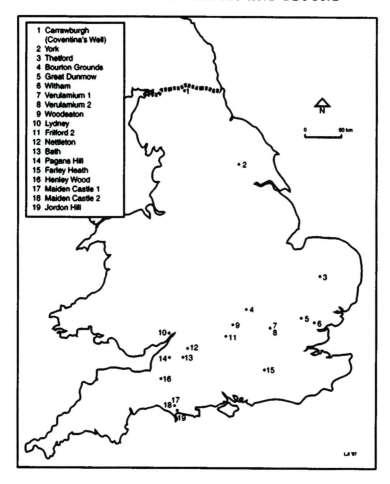

1 Carrawburgh
  (Coventina's Well)
2 York
3 Thetford
4 Bourton Grounds
5 Great Dunmow
6 Witham
7 Verulamium 1
8 Verulamium 2
9 Woodeaton
10 Lydney
11 Fritford 2
12 Nettleton
13 Bath
14 Pagans Hill
15 Farley Heath
16 Henley Wood
17 Maiden Castle 1
18 Maiden Castle 2
19 Jordon Hill

Figure 7. Map of temples surviving and pagan activity after AD 391

economic problems of the late fourth century which might have
been manifested in the spread of salvation-type cults to the country
from the more Romanised areas.

The virtual absence of these types of cults (e.g. of Bacchus,
Orpheus, Mithras, Isis and the Magna Mater) in rural areas suggests
that religion there had not progressed far beyond its pre-Roman
origins. This may be explained by the evolution of early British religion. Weather and chthonic gods, which were also common in the
civilisations of the ancient Egyptians, Mesopotamians, Hittites and
Persians, to name a few, were among the most primitive of deities,

relics of the days of hunter-gatherers. They were only displaced in pre-eminence by fertility deities as the emphasis changed to agriculture and the building up of herds, and by war gods, with the staking out of tribal lands. A further step was to invest birds and animals and natural sites within the tribal lands (springs, trees, shafts, caves, etc.) with spirits, and then, as survival became no longer merely a matter of dependence on the elements, to attempt to prolong life by seeking the assistance of these spirits. Healing cults must be seen as a later development in the evolution of religion in pre-Roman Britain. But the native people did not take the further step of creating salvation cults. The Celtic view of an afterlife was at best hazy[14] and tied to a belief, fostered for military purposes, in the transmigration of souls,[15] or in some vague afterworld. The horses buried with humans in the fourth/fifth century AD cemetery at Dunstable would have represented Epona in her role as the protector of the dead. There is little reason to suspect that this extended to belief in salvation.

The salvation cults in Britain which promised an afterlife were Graeco-Roman or eastern in origin, and were generally found in Britain in the towns or villas, and in military areas.[16] Their message did not spread into the country in the same way that Christianity, also a salvation cult, did; and Christianity in the fourth century had, except in the reign of Julian, the support of the imperial family, and undoubtedly many ambitious army commanders in Britain. Yet the advance of Christianity into the countryside was not as rapid as it was in the urban areas, and even in the towns vestiges of paganism, including salvation-type cults, remained.

Not all of those sites where paganism continued had a temple in use into the fifth century beyond the period of Roman occupation. Apart from Bath,[17] those that did so were only in rural areas; and, where the information is known, all but three of the thirteen sites (Coventina's Well,[18] Pagans Hill[19] and Lydney[20]) almost certainly had Iron Age cultic predecessors; the three less certainly so. Thus the paganism which is known to have survived after the laws of Theodosius and even after the departure of the Romans in almost all cases had its beginnings in the pre-Roman period. This is a strong indication of the conservatism of Romano-Britons in rural areas. It is difficult to argue against the view of Rahtz and Watts (1979: 183) that the cults that survived probably did so because they were native, not Roman.[21] In view of the failure of Christianity to organise and evangelise (Frend 1992: 126), and the twin disasters of the Saxon incursions and the Roman withdrawal, continuation of

60

the native pagan cults into the fifth, sixth and seventh centuries, and even beyond, was inevitable.

The evidence from the towns and of the Thetford Treasure must now be considered separately. It is here that one feels a closer affinity to the pagan revival of Julian. The evidence is varied. Finds from Verulamium/Dunstable and Thetford demonstrate the continuation, resumption or introduction of salvation-type cults in the second half of the fourth century. Other material from Verulamium and also from Bath shows that, even in such long-Romanised centres, paganism continued; Julian's order to resume the traditional honours to pagan gods clearly included native deities, such as Sulis-Minerva, as well as those originating in Rome or further east. The abandonment of the York temple mid-century did not eliminate covert pagan practices there.

These examples might be more closely examined. At Verulamium, the triangular temple, probably dedicated to Cybele, seems to have been frequented and coins lost (or offered) long after the building had ceased to be used about the middle of the fourth century. This suggests the continuation, if not the revival, of covert devotion to the eastern goddess promoted by Julian and addressed by that emperor in a hymn (*Or.* 5). The inscribed pot found in the cemetery nearby at Dunstable confirms that at least one guild honouring Cybele was still in existence in Verulamium in the late fourth century. Doubtless these organisations fulfilled a social as well as a religious role. Amidst the turmoil and uncertainty of the late fourth century, disrupting life in the towns probably more than in the country, salvation-type cults would have provided both companionship and solace; and, based as they were among the lower echelons of society, their members would have been relatively inconspicuous.

The temple near the theatre in Verulamium also seems to have had some activity in the late period, and renovation after 379. (The theatre itself was closed before the end of the century.) It has even been suggested that the building may have been converted to a church, or it may merely have become a rubbish dump (Niblett 1993). Either is possible, but, in view of the evidence of similar coin losses in the triangular temple, both are unlikely. More likely the building had a period of renewal, until the closure of the temples by Theodosius in 391. The continued deposition of coins after that date, perhaps to a Celticised version of Mercury, bears witness to the staying power of the old religions in the face of what is sure to have been a strong Christian community there.

Votives at the abandoned temple at York were probably to a Roman god, given the prominent position of the temple. In view of the fact that it contained a number of altars or statue bases, the temple may even have been for the Imperial Cult.[22] An inscription attests to the existence of the cult in the town (*RIB* 678). The modest offerings found at the site would not have been noticed, and could hardly have caused offence to the casual observer. A similar view may be taken of the offerings and *defixiones* which continued to be deposited at Bath after the partial dismantling of the main temple and the construction within the precinct of a small room, interpreted as a shrine. Here the god was a native deity, and probably a very ancient one. Nevertheless, even if the temples had fallen into disrepair and almost total disuse, their statues and altars removed or overturned, the law was not being observed.[23] The votives at Bath, York and probably Verulamium must be seen as the work of urban or military folk who retained their beliefs amidst a community with growing numbers of Christians. This kind of covert pagan devotion would have been very hard to stamp out.

The Thetford hoard, on the other hand, indicates a cult which may have had a more obvious presence and been seen as a greater problem once imperial policy became more actively anti-pagan. The members of the cult were obviously wealthy, so presumably influential in their community. It would be such a group who would have had sympathy with the resistance to Christianity as demonstrated by the pagan senators at Rome. Its members could well have felt threatened by the anti-pagan laws of 391–2, not only for openly practising pagan rites, and perhaps parodying Christian ones, but also because they may have represented a political threat. The events of 394 and the battle at the Frigidus River (above, Chapter 2) showed that not all wealthy Roman pagans were pacifists.[24] Some, such as the aristocratic Flavianus, were prepared to die for their beliefs. Moreover, throughout its history, the government of Rome had used religion as a political tool for manipulation and conformity. The fourth century AD was no exception. Scores could still be settled in the name of religion.

In a different category is the evidence of pagan practices in cemeteries of the late fourth century. This was not, as in temples or ritual objects, paganism for all the world to see, and perhaps influenced by that. It is evidence of adherence to practices which remained private, and related only to the deceased and to the relatives or friends who interred the body. Such practices must be regarded as a true reflection of the revival or survival of paganism, even in areas which to all intents and purposes had converted to Christianity. That many of the practices seen as reintroduced or on the increase (see above, Chapter 2) were Celtic in origin leads us to conclude that the paganism which survived in burial practices was more Celtic than Roman.[25]

This conclusion is reinforced by the analysis of evidence of the temples and shrines, above, where it was shown that the gods worshipped were most frequently Romano-Celtic or Celtic; that generally only rural temples or shrines survived beyond 391, although there was still some (?Roman) pagan activity in towns; and that almost all of the surviving shrines had Iron Age origins.

In other words, what we have in Roman Britain in the late fourth century is a Celtic pagan revival rather than a Roman one. The influence of Julian's favoured religions was limited; his revival of paganism was, after all, a 'very highbrow affair' (Cameron 1993: 156). What he did was to check for a time the spread of Christianity, to prompt some half-hearted Christians to abandon their faith and, most significantly, to give the signal for the resumption of old Celtic religious traditions. The withdrawal of direct Roman control early in the fifth century meant that the elimination of paganism, which would have led to the ultimate triumph of Christianity in Britain in the Roman period, was never effected.

By the end of the Roman Occupation, Christianity probably dominated in those civilian areas which were most highly Romanised, although this involved but a small percentage of the total population. In rural areas throughout Britain, despite the growth of Christianity, paganism held out against imperial legislation;[26] our evidence is mostly from sites where there had been a long visible religious tradition, and undoubtedly there were hundreds of other sacred places where no structural evidence remained or had ever existed. That native pagan gods kept their hold on the hearts and minds of so many Britons, particularly in the rural areas, says as much for the shallowness of Romanisation as it does about the conservatism of the inhabitants.

As a footnote to the study above, it could well be that some Romano-British temples were still standing when Gregory sent Augustine to England at the end of the sixth century. Bede (*H.E.* 1.30) tells us that Augustine was instructed to destroy idols but to leave the temples and convert them to churches. This has generally been taken to refer to the religious structures of the Anglo-Saxons, but in a recent study of Anglo-Saxon paganism (D. Wilson 1992: 44–66) the author concedes that, with the possible exception of

Yeavering, there is to date no evidence in Britain for any building which might fit the description of 'temple' from the Anglo-Saxon period. Moreover, it is very likely that the early Germanic people in Britain had shrines and sanctuaries similar to those of the pre-Roman British: trees, hills and groves (Hutton 1991: 270). It is proposed here, therefore, that the buildings to which Bede was referring were, in fact, temples from the Roman period, relics of cults which had their origins long before the Conquest and which outlasted the conqueror.

Christianity and its fate

Christianity, now the official religion of the empire, continued in Britain. But its prominent status is not matched by the archaeological record for the period 390–410. There are no known examples of new churches or cemeteries in these years and, although there must have been Christians of considerable wealth (such as the owner of the Hoxne Treasure (Bland and Johns 1993)), there is little evidence that such wealth was actually shared by the Church. Even before 410, what we seem to have is a contraction of Christian influence to the towns, where, as late as 429, there were still sufficient numbers of informed Christians to be involved in the Pelagian controversy. But in the face of Saxon incursions and without the support of the Roman administration and the Roman army, Christianity withered and all but died on the vine. It was sustained only in some urban centres and in those parts of the countryside away from the influence of the Germanic invaders.

In the previous chapter, mention was made of probable new Christian structures in the period 360–90: the apsidal building and baptistery[27] at Richborough, and the two oratory-type buildings at Brean Down and Lamyatt Beacon. To date, these constitute the only likely new Christian churches in Roman Britain after the rule of Julian, since the Christian phase at Uley has now been reassessed and assigned an indefinite time, probably in the fifth century. The tantalising evidence recently uncovered at Lincoln, however, suggests an earlier church at the site of St Paul-in-the-Bail than had been published previously (M. J. Jones 1994). It, too, could conceivably date from the late Roman period (c. 390 is suggested), as had been proposed, it now seems incorrectly, for the apsidal building (Watts 1991: 119–21); much of that argument still holds for the earlier building, however.

Existing churches continued after 391, at least for a time.

Examples are from highly Romanised areas: the complexes at Butt Road, Colchester and Icklingham probably lasted until the end of the Roman period, and the Silchester church until the end of the century.[28] The house-church at Lullingstone was destroyed by fire c.400, and the Stone-by-Faversham building abandoned also about this time, only to be once more used (and extended) as a Christian church in the early Saxon period. The church at the site of St Pancras, in nearby Canterbury, may well have been the direct ancestor of a series of churches lasting into the Middle Ages. To this list we might add buildings whose existence is attested in the literary sources but whose archaeological remains have not yet been uncovered: the church at Canterbury, noted by both Bede and Eadmer, and the shrine to St Alban on the outskirts of Verulamium, also described by Bede.[29]

The evidence of the Christian cemeteries seems to reflect that of the churches, although it must once more be pointed out that there is great difficulty in assigning final dates. Their very nature means that they have little, if any, datable evidence. There were no new cemeteries, but most begun earlier in the century continued; exceptions were probably Ashton and Nettleton, which may have been abandoned even before 391. Those at Butt Road, Colchester and Icklingham probably lasted as long as the churches with which they were associated (above), and others, such as Poundbury and Shepton Mallet, at least until the end of the century and most likely later; the last phase of the small farmyard cemetery of Bradley Hill probably continued, along with the farmstead, until the early fifth century, c.410–20. The Cannington cemetery in Somerset is exceptional in that it was in a rural area and that it survived for at least a further three centuries with the same rites. The cemeteries at Henley Wood, Lamyatt Beacon and Brean Down are best located in the sub- or post-Roman period.

There is thus no evidence for a flowering of the faith following the decrees of Theodosius in 391–2. Christianity had, in the years after 312, or at least from c.320, when we have our first archaeological evidence in Britain, progressively expanded. Over a period of eighty years or so, there were few parts of Roman Britain where there were no Christian finds.[30] But the picture from 391 to 410 is one of stagnation and possibly decline even before the Romans left.

The question to be asked is why Christianity failed in Britain, when across the Channel and at the same time it was flourishing in Gaul and in the rest of the Roman world.

The problem has, to date, attracted little attention. Frend (1979) first posed the question and proposed that reasons for the failure of Christianity in Britain were internal, rather than external: lack of popular appeal and of a developed parochial system.[31] In later studies Frend expands on his earlier theme. In a 1982 work he suggests two additional reasons: the absence of any missionary effort, such as that of Martin of Tours in Gaul (Sulpicius Severus *v. S.Mart.* 13), to convert the pagan population by force, if necessary; and the continuation and the revival of paganism. He holds that effectively the destruction of 'episcopally based Christianity' in Britain occurred in the period 430–50. In his most recent work (Frend 1992) he proposes that the floruit of the Church in Britain was from 330–60, after which it went into decline. He suggests that the 'barbarian conspiracy' of 367–9 (Ammianus 18.2.3) was the factor, not common to Gaul and Spain, that caused the religion to falter and ultimately to fail in Britain.

Frend's suggestions are logical and most can readily be accepted as contributing to the failure of Christianity in Roman Britain. While his connection between the barbarian conspiracy and Christianity may be drawing too long a bow, one cannot discount the effects of the political situation on religion, whether pagan or Christian. The matter will be considered further below.

Other factors which are likely to have had an adverse effect on Christianity have been proposed by the present writer in an earlier work (Watts 1991: 215–16) and above. These might be again considered briefly. The first involved the conscious or unconscious admission of pagan elements into Christianity, which, while broadening its appeal, may well have diluted and weakened it. Ignorance of or connivance at burial practices which may have seemed innocuous to the uninitiated occurred with greater frequency in Christian burials after 360: coins in the mouth or in the grave (Poundbury), grave goods with amuletic or other significance (Butt Road, Colchester), for instance. The survival of the Church had been dependent on strict orthodoxy; any practices which departed from this line, even the surreptitious deposition of grave goods, would weaken its image and its hold on followers. One has only to recall the injunctions of early Christian figures such as Paul[32] and Clement of Alexandria,[33] stressing the need for converts to conform to standards of behaviour, dress and so on.

While the 'paganisation' of Romano-British Christianity could well have had a diluting effect on the religion, the departure of the Roman army and the end of Roman administration must have been far more devastating. We know that in the fourth century the towns were already in decline,[34] yet it was the towns which kept Christianity alive. Moreover, by now Christianity must have been seen as a *Roman* religion (Watts 1991: 8–9); and Pope Julius (337–52) had taken advantage of Constans' gaining control of two-thirds of the Roman Empire in 340 to reaffirm the supremacy of the See of Rome[35] in the Christian world. With the withdrawal or expulsion[36] of a Roman administration ready to uphold the emperors' and the state's religion, and of an army able to reinforce the efforts of zealous missionaries such as Martin of Tours (*c.*330–97) against paganism, the Church in Britain must have suffered a colossal blow. The devastation within the Church would have been greater in the country than in the towns, where a Roman-type administration might still maintain order and ensure patronage for Christianity for a time.[37]

Saxon, Pictish and Irish incursions must also have contributed to the problem of maintaining Christianity. Attacks on towns and the subsequent disruption to civic order, and marauding bands in the countryside affecting the stability of villas would all contribute to loss of control and finally of Roman institutions. The progressive withdrawal of the Roman army compounded the situation, and there was little now to arrest the slide back to the old pagan ways.

The strength of the pagan cults in Britain, or, conversely, Christianity's lack of appeal to the masses, has been demonstrated by sites which reverted to paganism or continued to exist openly in the face of the Theodosian decrees. It is tempting to speculate on the fate of the Gaulish Church if Martin had not had the might of the army behind him in his conversion of the heathen. If we also take into account that for many of the pagan sites which can be identified there was a long history of cult from the Iron Age, it seems clear that the commitment to Christianity was, at best, an experience closely associated with Rome, manifested more often in the towns, where only a small percentage of the total population of Roman Britain lived.[38] At worst, it was but a transient affair, an experiment with a new religion which required the renunciation of all other gods, a long apprenticeship and a personal code of conduct which for many would have been too demanding. The tug of the old religions, superstitions and traditions, perhaps still now transmitted by Druids,[39] was too strong.

Political events in the late fourth century and their effects on Christianity

As noted earlier in this chapter, it had been suggested (Frend 1992) that political events, and specifically the barbarian conspiracy of 367, may have contributed to the weakness of Christianity from the 360s on. Although the idea has merit, it might be argued that the political events that were more likely to affect Christianity in Britain occurred later in the fourth century and that the decline, too, began at a later date.

If we are to look for external pressures on the survival and growth of Christianity in Britain, we need to begin before 391. A starting point could be around 380, since it has been proposed (above) that it was in the period 380–91 that the last expansion of the Church occurred there in the Roman period. In the West, a youthful Gratian had, the year before, called upon Theodosius to be Augustus in the East. In 383, while Theodosius was dealing with the Visigoths, Gratian had earned the ill will of the army by favouring a new bodyguard of barbarian troops. They failed to come to his aid when the Spaniard Magnus Maximus invaded Gaul; Gratian was deserted by his own soldiers and killed, and Maximus, previously elevated to the purple by his troops in Britain, claimed status as co-Augustus.[40] The others were Theodosius, the senior Augustus, and Valentinian II, Augustus since his father's death in 375. Magnus Maximus prevailed until his defeat by Theodosius in 388. It is known that he returned to Britain, probably in 384, for a successful campaign against the Scots and Picts,[41] and was evidently popular there.

Following the defeat of Maximus, Valentinian II was sent by Theodosius to Trier in *c.*389, ostensibly to govern the West, but probably to keep him out of the way. Theodosius dispatched as *comes* the Frankish general Arbogast; he was a nephew of Richomeres, consul in 384, *magister militum* in the East in 383 and 388–93 and, like his uncle, a pagan. Arbogast had been appointed *magister militum* in the West in 385, and the young emperor came to be more under the sway of his advisor with the appointment of the philosopher Eugenius as his *magister scriniorum*. This man had been recommended to the post by Richomeres. The other strong influence in Valentinan's life after the death of his mother, the powerful Justina, was that of Ambrose of Milan; and the struggle between Christian and pagan to manipulate the emperor led ultimately to his death in 392, presumably at the direction, if not the hand, of

Arbogast. Arbogast promptly installed Eugenius, a nominal Christian, as emperor, serving (and probably manipulating) him until the showdown with Theodosius at the Frigidus River in 394.

Theodosius did not live to savour his victory. He died in January 395, and his sons Arcadius and Honorius failed miserably in any attempt to live up to their father's memory. It must also be said that their father himself had failed to train them in any form of statecraft or military activity. Arcadius, the eastern Augustus and the more competent of the two, was content to be manipulated by the eunuch Eutropius, his *magister officiorum*, and later by Eudoxia, his wife, in Constantinople; his brother, the feeble-minded Honorius, was only about twelve years old when he became Emperor of the West, his court now at Milan, although the Prefect of Gaul was still based at Trier. They were fortunate to have, as *magister militiae utriusque*, the Vandal-born Stilicho, who was son-in-law of Theodosius and loyal to the dynasty. Stilicho aspired to unite the eastern and western parts of the empire, but he also wanted to protect its 'heartland', Italy, Africa, Illyricum and the East; the rest, including Britain, was presumably non-essential.

In the spring of 395 he put his own appointees in place in the West and hurried east to meet a threat by the Visigoth king and general Alaric, with a combined army of eastern and western field units. Because of opposition from the Prefect of the East, Rufinus, Stilicho was unable to complete the mission; he was forced to withdraw to the Rhineland, leaving Alaric to sack the Greek lands. The loyalty of the combined army may also have been questionable (Williams and Friell 1994: 146).

Between 397 and 403, East and West moved further apart, and while the fortunes of Stilicho fluctuated, he survived; a revolt by the *magister et comes* of Egypt, supported by the East and threatening the grain supply to Rome, was overcome; Stilicho was for a time declared a public enemy by Arcadius and Eutropius; and, to top it off, the sacker of cities in Greece, Alaric, was appointed by Arcadius *magister militum* in Illyricum and threatened Italy while Stilicho was dealing with a threat to Gaul from across the Rhine. To counter this, soldiers were withdrawn from other areas, and it is probably this crisis that led to the further depletion of forces in Britain at that time.

In 404 an invasion by the Goth Radagaisus, at the head of a combined barbarian army, led to an alliance between Alaric and Stilicho, and ultimately the defeat of Radagaisus and the absorption of many Huns into the army. But this campaign necessitated the recall of more troops from the provinces, especially from the upper Rhine. Italy was now vulnerable, and the court moved to Ravenna. Early in 407 many major centres in Gaul were attacked. Stilicho's position became increasingly precarious with the death of his daughter, the wife of the Emperor Honorius, and his subsequent loss of control over the emperor. On the death of Arcadius in 408, Stilicho travelled to Constantinople in one last vain attempt to unite East and West. He was arrested and executed, and many of his barbarian army deserted to Alaric – to sack Rome two years later.

It has been suggested (Williams and Friell 1994: 156) that the neglect of the provinces in the West led to the alienation of the native aristocracies there. This could well be so, and would account for the unrest in Britain which resulted in three usurpations in the years 406 and 407. The Britons were beset with troubles of their own, notably the Picts, Irish and Saxons, yet Stilicho had withdrawn troops for the defence of Italy (Claudian *De bel. Goth.* 416–18). The first revolt was by Marcus (Zosimus 6.3.1, 2.5), a disaffected general who was probably stretched to his limit defending Britain with reduced resources. We are told that he lost the army's support, and was replaced by Gratian, a British aristocrat, who, although aware of the worsening situation in Gaul, refused to engage in forward defence and take the fight across the Channel. He was in turn replaced by Constantine (III), who responded to the barbarian threat and crossed with the bulk of his army to Boulogne, leaving behind an administration appointed by himself and an armed force of native Britons. He never returned to Britain, having met his death after four years as Augustus. Nor did his army return. Order was restored in Spain; but Britain was left with an army little better than a militia, some kind of limited native administration (Zosimus 6.5.2–3) and, by 411,[42] no longer any direct Roman influence, apart from the Church. As far as the Church was concerned, in thirty years the prospects for Christian dominance in Britain had been reduced from promising to impossible.

In the 380s, despite the usurpation of Magnus Maximus, or perhaps because of it, Christianity in Britain had seemed to flourish in a last round of Christian building activity during the Occupation. The number of operative temples was falling, and new churches (if only modest ones) were being erected. The prefects of Gaul for the three years 384–6, at least, were his appointees, and it would thus be reasonable that his commitment to Christianity would be translated into policy. This would occur in Britain, where he was undoubtedly popular (to the extent that he later appears in Welsh king-lists),[43] as well as nearer afield. Such obvious imperial patronage must have had some impact on Christianity in Britain in the short term. A church at a military site such as Richborough[44] would be a fitting symbol, since Maximus had been baptised soon after his elevation to the throne and from that time on would have made much of his allegiance to Catholic Christianity. His defeat by Theodosius in 388 marks the end of effective influence by any emperor or prefect of Gaul on religious affairs in Britain.

Although the reign of Maximus was followed by virtual sole rule by Theodosius, we do not have any evidence that, with the emperor's anti-pagan legislation, Christianity in Britain received any boost at all. The reason may lie in what was happening in the corridors of power elsewhere in the Western Empire. It would appear that from 389 to 394 control of the Gaulish prefecture and the Western Empire, while still at Trier, was effectively in the hands of Arbogast rather than the Emperor of the West and the various prefects.[45] Arbogast had evidently been given a free rein as far as Valentinian was concerned; Theodosius could not have anticipated the death of the young emperor or the events that followed. Moreover, it is highly unlikely that Theodosius would have involved himself in the day-to-day administration of his decrees, especially in the western provinces. He had, after all, a trusted lieutenant based there and had troubles of his own in the East.

In Britain, the effects on religion of the events from c. 389 to 394 can only be speculated, but the presence of Arbogast at the court of Valentinian would explain why the severe decrees of Theodosius of 391–2 do not seem to have had any marked effect at the time. Theodosius had left Italy for Constantinople in 391, still further removed from the western provinces.[46] That his decrees were not carried out in Britain indicates either that he did not know, that he did not care or that, already, that part of the empire was seen to be expendable: the troops which would have been withdrawn by Magnus Maximus in 383 had not been replaced;[47] their absence was felt later, when, in 396–8, it took two years for Stilicho (or, more likely, a subordinate) to restore order in Britain against the Irish, Picts and Saxons.

Another reason for the neglect of Britain and the slowing down of Christianity before 410 must be the inadequacies and ineptness of the sons of Theodosius, Arcadius and Honorius. Stilicho, a Christian, had been *de facto* ruler of the West from 395, but his focus had been Italy and the East. His constant preoccupation with Alaric and other barbarian invaders must have left little time, if he had indeed been so inclined, to take an interest in the progress of Christianity in Britain. His death in 408 spelt the end of any remaining mild concern for the western diocese. The emperors were incapable of acting resolutely without prompting, and Ambrose, the towering figure of the late-fourth-century Church, had died in 398. True, Arcadius and Honorius re-enacted Theodosius' decree closing the temples and other earlier decrees concerning cults and temple funds; they even brought in decrees of their own.[48] But these re-enactments merely make it quite clear that the laws were not being observed. It is interesting to note that now not only the provincial governors were to be held responsible, but also the local *decuriones* (*C.Th.* 16.10.13). Apparently more force was necessary to see the law was carried out.

Such legislation at the end of the fourth century would have been virtually unenforceable in Britain. The *vicarius* could certainly have applied pressure on local administrations in the towns, but the problem of persisting paganism was far more a rural one. A law is one thing; to carry it out is another. The situation in Britain was not the same as in the Gaul of Martin of Tours. Parts of the army were in Wales, or defending the Saxon shore, and others (perhaps even now an 'irregular militia' (Frere 1987: 344)) were far away along the Wall; Stilicho withdrew more troops in 401,[49] and the usurper Constantius III took the remainder with him to Gaul in 407. What hope for law enforcement?

A further factor affecting control of the empire and the fate of Christianity in Roman Britain is that the centre of gravity of the empire had shifted irrevocably to the east; Constantinople was continually enhanced while shanties appeared on the Campus Martius at Rome (*C.Th.* 14.11.1). The capital of the Western Empire had moved with the court variously to Trier, Milan, Aquileia and finally Ravenna; all except Ravenna would have been threatened by the barbarian hordes; none was likely to have a great deal of interest in, or sympathy for, Britain once its resources (i.e. armed forces) had been exhausted. For the years 407–11, Gaul had been nominally ruled by Constantine III (who also, it seems, cared little for Britain); but in reality control of much of it was now in the hands of the barbarian invaders. Honorius' letter in 410 to the cities in Britain merely formalised what had virtually been the situation for the previous four years.

It should not be surprising that Christianity failed to overcome paganism in Britain when, at the same time, it was expanding elsewhere and had become the dominant religion in the empire.[50]

72

What is surprising is that it survived at all, given the strength and longevity of the pagan cults, their hold on the native Britons in rural areas and the chaotic political situation from the mid-380s onward. Christianity continued for some decades into the sub-Roman period, petering out in many towns, but surviving in places such as Lincoln, Canterbury and St Albans, and in those rural areas little affected by the incoming waves of Anglo-Saxons, in Somerset, Wales and southern Scotland.[51] At its peak, although Christians were still in the minority in Britain, their religion is likely to have been the largest of the individual cults and to have attracted adherents from much of the Romanised area. But while many townsfolk may well have been Christian by the end of the century, the majority of the people, still living in the country, remained untouched or had reverted to their pagan cults and practices after a brief flirtation with the religion of the emperors.[52]

4

FURTHER EVIDENCE FOR THE REVIVAL OF PAGANISM

The revival of paganism in the second half of the fourth century was manifested in various ways, not least in the rise in burial practices which were not Christian. Of these, one, the burial of bodies decapitated post-mortem, is readily recognisable in late fourth/early fifth-century cemeteries. Another, the practice of placing combs in burials, is less recognisable as a deliberate burial rite but, it is proposed here, also has links with pagan religions and practices. Both occurred with increasing frequency after c.AD 360.

Decapitated burials

In British archaeology, the term 'decapitated burial' is usually given to an inhumation, mainly of the Roman and Anglo-Saxon period, which is normal in other respects (that is, in a dug grave, with or without coffin, with or without grave goods, etc.), but where the head has been detached presumably post-mortem and prior to interment. We are not discussing execution, that is, decapitation as a *cause* of death.[1] Usually the head has been removed with care, with a sharp blade and with little damage, if any, to the bone. The cut is high, often between the second and third or third and fourth vertebrae. The body is then interred, with or without the head. If the head is present, as it usually is, it may be placed between the knees, the feet, the upper legs, outside the knees or feet, or on the pelvis. In a couple of published cases the head has been found outside the coffin or in the fill above it.[2] Only rarely is it replaced in its correct anatomical position.[3]

Decapitated burials have been found in Roman Britain supposedly from the first century, but such finds are rare. The practice is far more common in the late Roman period. Nonetheless, it can be

seen as having a close connection with the 'skull burials' of the pre-
Roman period, both in Britain and in Ireland.

A number of examples of skull burial or votive deposition[4] are
known from Ireland[5] dating from the Early to the Late (Irish) Iron
Age. In one, in a souterrain at an Early Iron Age triple-rampart site
at Cahercommaun, Co. Clare, a skull was found resting on top of an
iron hook; the mandible was missing. It is believed that such a
burial was ritualistic, and that the hook may have been used earlier
for displaying the head (Rynne 1992).

A second example, also dated by the archaeologist to the Early
Iron Age,[6] came from a small cemetery at Ballinlough, Co. Laois. It
comprised five whole burials and one discrete skull. The five were
supine, extended and west–east. The skull, of an adult female, was
found in an undisturbed patch of soil, propped upright against a
large piece of human hip bone and flanked by three pieces of rib
bone. The mandible was also missing here, causing the excavator to
propose that the skull had been deposited after the flesh had fallen
away. The careful arrangement of the remains suggests a 'planned
skull-burial' (Rynne 1974–5).

A later burial, with a radiocarbon date range of 100 BC to AD
130, comes from Raffin Fort, Co. Meath, a Neolithic foundation
which extended into the Iron Age and appears to have had a ritual
function from at least the Bronze Age. The Iron Age level had a
central feature of a round 'building' surrounded by free-standing
posts. The whole was enclosed by a circular earthwork with an entry
to the south. Just inside this feature, to the north-west, was a pit in
which a partial human skull had been placed face upwards. It was
set on a bed of charcoal, and was accompanied by part of an animal's
pelvis and a rib bone (neither identified at time of publication). The
burial was marked by an upright stone, 0.63 m high (Newman
1993a, 1993b, personal communication; Raftery 1994: 80).

The Raffin Fort Iron Age feature seems to have some resemblance
to the great Neolithic monument at Newgrange, where at the
winter solstice the rising sun shines through a gap in the roof box
and along the entry passage to the burial chamber (O'Kelly et al.
1983). An examination of the plan of the Raffin Fort site shows that
the standing stone was directly opposite the entry, in a line through
the central circular structure. The orientation seems to resemble
closely that at Newgrange. The stone, with the partial skull beneath
it, may well have been the focal point of cult at the site in the Iron
Age. The skull itself seems to have been an important ritual feature,
paralleling another, but much earlier, Late Bronze Age (900 BC)

find at King's Stables, near Navan Fort, Co. Armagh: here an artificial lake yielded, among other finds, the front of a human skull, deliberately cut off from the rest of the head (Lynn 1993). About a kilometre to the east, a 'ritual lake' at Loughnashade yielded more human skulls (Raftery 1994: 185).

The practice of skull burial may have developed into decapitated burial in the middle part of the Irish Iron Age. An example from Knowth, Co. Meath, dated 40 BC to AD 100 is of two adult males, lying head to toe in the one grave and accompanied by grave goods which included beads, bone dice and other 'gaming pieces'. Both had been decapitated: the skull of one had been replaced upside down, that is, with the lower jaw away from the body, and the other lay at an angle with the face towards the feet (Raftery 1974).

Although depositions of skulls in clearly votive contexts such as shafts, wells and lakes are also well known from the Iron Age in Britain,[7] detailed published examples of skull burials are rare.[8] In his study of Iron Age ritual, Wait (1986: 83–121, 357–84) collates examples from British hillforts and settlements. He demonstrates that there are fewer instances in settlements than in hillforts, but those in hillforts are concentrated in only a very small number of sites. The skulls are generally male (probably the heads of enemies taken in battle). The incidence of skull burials in settlements increases in the Late Iron Age, but the deposition of human remains generally increases as well. Wait also notes that in his sixth category of human remains, 'single bones', there is a predominance of skulls and long bones which, he says, 'makes a random process (of selection) very unlikely' (1986: 117). We shall return to this point later in a discussion of the Rushton burials.

British Iron Age sites with skull burials range from the eighth/fifth century to the late first century AD. A few examples from more detailed reports will suffice here.[9]

The La Tène site of Garton Slack produced a series of pits associated with the well-known cart burial. One of these pits contained an inverted human skull (Brewster 1971; Challis and Harding 1975: 169). At the Iron Age hillfort at Danebury there were, in addition to three burials of skulls with other fragmentary remains, eight discrete skull or partial-skull burials, seven of which had no mandible. These too were all in pits, with domestic material; in five instances this material included animal bones: cattle, sheep, pig and horse. Six skulls were of adult males, one female[10] and one child 7 to 9 years old. The condition of most of the skulls suggests that they had been buried after decomposition of the flesh and tissue; only the child's skull had a mandible. On the ceramic phasing of the pits, these burials ranged from the fifth/third century to the end of the second century. Winklebury, another Hampshire hillfort, produced a small number of burials of which two, both females, were headless and another two, both males, were represented only by skulls. One of these was without a mandible. The burials are dated to the late phase of the site, third to first century BC (K. Smith 1977: 74–9).

There is also an unpublished example from Odell, Bedfordshire (mentioned briefly earlier, Chapter 2), which has some similarity to the Irish skull burials described earlier. Here, in a small cremation cemetery, fragments of burnt skull were placed outside vessels containing other cremated remains, and an unburnt head was given a separate burial. Nearby, at what seems to have been a ritual site associated with fertility as well as with the burials, the head of a woman was found cradled in the pelvic girdle of a horse. This burial was dated to the third quarter of the first century AD (Dix, forthcoming).

One further site provides a link between skull and decapitated burials. Whimster (1981: 60–9, 74) gives hitherto unpublished details of a cemetery from Harlyn Bay in Cornwall. One hundred and fifty burials were recorded in the excavations of 1901–5, and the position of fifty-three of them has now been plotted. Amongst these were two small graves, each containing only skulls, five in one and three in the other. Another two graves contained decapitated burials, one at least with the head placed close to the feet. In view of the limited grave goods, a chronology was difficult to establish, but Whimster believes the cemetery was operating by the second century BC.

Such examples demonstrate that in certain, and presumably special, circumstances rituals and burials in the Iron Age placed special emphasis on the head. The evidence for Britain, though only slowly emerging and as yet limited, seems to indicate that skull burials and even decapitated burials did occur in the Iron Age, perhaps around 3 per cent of all known Iron Age inhumations,[11] and that there were similarities to those in Ireland.

The coming of Rome was to have a considerable influence on British burial practices. The importance of the skull continued to be demonstrated, not now so much in the burial of discrete skulls, but more often in burial of complete bodies, with the head detached. While skull burials all but disappear, there is a second-century example from the Racecourse cemetery at Derby which has some similarity to one of the skull burials at Odell (above): an unburnt skull was found at the edge of a large cremation pit containing other calcined remains (H. Wheeler 1985). A skull deposition of second-century AD date is also known from St Albans. This example is of particular interest because the skull appears to have been deliberately defleshed and perhaps exposed (or put on display) for some time before being placed in a pit with the body of a young dog and an iron blade (Mays and Steele 1996). Skull burials reappear late in the Roman period: one, believed to be of fourth-century date, was recently reported from a small cemetery in Newarke Street, Leicester (Esmonde Cleary 1994: 271).

There are, in addition, some undated Romano-British skull burials from Oxfordshire: Barton Farm, Abingdon (skull); Barford St Michael (an inhumation with an extra skull); Millstream, Horley (a skull in the silt deposit of a pond); Churchill Hospital, Oxford (skull); Park Crescent, Oxford (four skulls); and Stadhampton (skull).[12] Such examples are few. There were far more decapitated burials in Oxfordshire, and, indeed, in much of the province.

The dating of the earliest decapitated burials in Roman Britain cited by Philpott (1991: 78) is far from conclusive: at Cuxton, in Kent, a burial dated by pottery evidence to AD 50–100; a cemetery at Radley in Oxfordshire tentatively second/third century, although none of the decapitated burials there had any grave goods; a cemetery at Orton Longueville, with a decapitated burial which may be first/second century, or fourth century (D. R. Wilson 1975: 252; Philpott 1991: 78). The evidence from the Derby Racecourse site is more closely datable and thus more conclusive: here, five decapitations spanned the period from the late second century to the late third/early fourth century. Since cremation was still the preferred rite in Britain until the third century,[13] early decapitated inhumations are somewhat unusual. In view of the evidence of Derby, however, they should not be entirely discounted.

The headless bodies of two infants buried in the foundations of a mid-second-century Romano-Celtic temple at Springhead are also more securely dated, and apparently had a votive function, but there is no record of the whereabouts of the heads, the main subject of our enquiry. Presumably they, too, had a votive and probably even more important role elsewhere. The water source at Springhead is a likely place for such deposition.

During the period from the middle of the second century to the middle of the third, cremation was phased out and replaced by inhumation throughout the Roman world. It is only from this time that most decapitated burials are dated with some confidence. The evidence put together by Philpott (1991: Tables 24, 25 and 26) clearly shows an increase in the practice by the fourth century. This can, in well-documented cases, be narrowed down to the second half of the fourth century, and into the early fifth century. For example, at Lankhills, Winchester, at least six of the seven decapitations date to after c.350, and the seventh probably so; the whole Dunstable cemetery, including its twelve decapitations, appears to be late fourth century to early fifth century; and at least one of the five decapitations in the 'backyard' burials at Ashton was considered by the archaeologist to be very late, since it belonged to a group of four outliers cutting derelict or dismantled buildings in the town (B. Dix, personal communication).

From the evidence presented so far, it appears that while decapitations were most numerous in the late Roman period they do have a close connection with earlier skull burials which, in turn, have particular significance in the earlier religious cults of Iron Age Britain and Ireland.[14] Decapitations are also found mainly in rural areas (with a few notable exceptions) where, as was shown above (Chapter 3), the old Celtic beliefs survived.

The classical literary evidence for the importance of the head to the Celtic-speaking people of Europe, especially the Gauls, has been often rehearsed,[15] but it can with benefit be once more summarised here. It was a Celtic practice to take the heads of enemies slain in battle. The heads were tied to the horses, or impaled on spears, after which they were exhibited at the victors' houses or at temples. Those of the most distinguished victims were highly prized and might be embalmed in cedar oil and displayed to visitors or made into drinking cups lined with gold for use on special or religious occasions.[16]

Early Celtic literature[17] confirms and adds to the evidence from the ethnographers of the classical world. In *Mac Dá Thó's Pig*, the story from the *Ulster Cycle* which gives the origins of the emnity between Ulster and Connaught, Cet Mac Mágach of Connaught boasts of carrying off the head of the eldest son of an enemy. In the same tale, Conall Cernach, the Ulster hero, tells Cet that, since adulthood, he has never slept without the head of a Connaughtman under his knee. He then produces from his belt the head of the Connaught champion Anlúan. Clearly the status of the victim was as important as the head itself.

The severed head was also able to speak, and was imbued with magical or apotropaic properties. In the Irish *Finn Cycle* the head of

Finn's fool, Lomnae, or perhaps of Finn himself, speaks to those who had killed and decapitated him,[18] and in the Welsh *Mabinogion* the king, Bran, on being mortally wounded, instructs his companions to remove his head and ultimately to bury it at Gwynfryn in London. This mission takes the next eighty-seven years, during which the head entertains them at their feasts and protects them from their foes.[19] A similar situation is depicted in the *Saga Englynion about Uryen's Head*, in which the poet carries his patron's head away from the battle and it accompanies him on the army's travels. In both of the Welsh examples there seems to be a reluctance to bury the head, either because of the protection it offered or because the fact that the head was still with the army may have symbolised that the chief was still leading them: the Welsh *pen(n)* and Old Irish *cenn* mean both 'head' and 'chief'.[20]

One further example may be relevant to our discussion.[21] In the Irish story *Cath Almaine*, the head of Donn Bó, a young man in the service of Fergal Mac Maíle Dúin, is brought back to the enemy's camp, where it is placed on a pillar and sings. It is then taken back to the battlefield, where it is presumably united with the body, and nothing more is heard of its sweet song. The inference here is that the head could only perform its magical feats when detached from the body.

Emphasis on the head was not restricted to burials but was also demonstrated in ritual practices and in what might be termed 'art', but which obviously had a cultic purpose. The subject has been extensively treated by Ross (1959, 1967, 1992: 94–171), who demonstrates that there was, at least in parts of the Celtic world, a 'cult of the head'. The stone pillar decorated with human heads, from Entremont, is perhaps confirmation that the practice of displaying on stakes the heads of enemies taken in battle had rather more than propaganda value. While evidence for such cults is harder to find in Britain than at Entremont (and also Roquepertuse) in France, a recently published find in Britain suggests they did exist. A sizeable skull fragment from a sixth-century AD context at the site of Cadbury Congresbury, Somerset, was found, by radiocarbon dating, to be from the mid-first millennium BC. From its location in a 'rock tumble', it is believed to have been of ritual significance (Rahtz *et al.* 1992: 185, 242, 244). We also have the curious evidence from the fourth-century Christian complex at Icklingham, in Suffolk. Here the site had been cleared of earlier structures and the whole covered with a layer of chalk before the construction of a church and baptistery and the creation of a cemetery nearby.

Material from the earlier structures dumped in a large pit included a small limestone pillar, fragments of decorative roof tiles, and six human skulls. Two of the skulls were without mandibles and one showed signs of decapitation. It was suggested that they may have come from a pre-Christian sanctuary (West 1976).

To date, such examples in Britain are rare. On the other hand, there is a considerable amount of evidence for votive deposits of skulls, the retention of skull fragments and the portrayal of human heads in native art, practices which continued right through to the end of the Roman period.

Wait (1986: 51–82) documents, *inter alia*, skulls in ritual shafts and wells in the Iron Age; Rahtz *et al.* (1992: 242) list two skulls with second-century AD finds from Caerwent, found close by a carved stone head; skulls as well as complete human skeletons were in the fill of the pits at Newstead, a Roman fort of Antonine date in the Borders region (Ross and Feachem 1976); and a late Romano-British example comes from Coventina's Well at Carrawburgh.

Pieces of human skull were also retained for apotropaic purposes. There are examples from Iron Age Britain and Gaul of pieces of skull bone worked into amulets to protect the wearer (Whimster 1981: 185), and the practice seems to have continued into the Roman period: analysis of the skeletal material from a late first/early second-century AD cremation cemetery at Skeleton Green, between Puckering and Braughing, on Ermine Street, indicates that there was a dearth of cranial remains because, it was suggested, the recognisable skull fragments had been gathered up by relatives of the deceased to be distributed to individuals (Wells 1981: 292–3). A further example is the 'oiled skull fragments' in the latest levels of the excavations at Wroxeter (Rahtz *et al.* 1992: 242).

In the native art of Britain and Ireland, portrayals of the human head are not as common as in continental Europe, although examples given by Ross (1992) and Rynne (1972) include many which must have been pagan Celtic idols. But heads alone obviously had particular significance, as is shown by the numerous examples from the Celtic world and the careful deposition of the head only from a full sculpture of Mercury under the sub/post-Roman foundations of a presumed Christian church at Uley, Glos (Woodward and Leach 1993: 70–5).

On the archaeological and literary evidence, therefore, it seems that, in the Iron Age at least, the removal and possession of a skull and/or its subsequent deposition did not necessarily have sinister connotations, and that there was a belief that the skull could have a benign influence. At the most basic level, it could be seen as a sign of martial prowess, a trophy to be displayed perhaps until it was no longer recognisable, after which it was buried, with or without ceremony. Since it was a Celtic belief that the head was the source of all power, possession of a head or skull allowed the strength or power of the victim to flow on to the victor. Here the identity of the victim seems to be significant. Along with this transmitted power, there seems to have been a belief in the apotropaic qualities of the head: protection for the possessor, or perhaps even for the tribe or land as a whole.[22] Finally, there is a fertility aspect: this is suggested by the two women's skulls buried with pelvic bones[23] (the one at Ballinlough with a human hip bone, the other at Odell with the pelvic bones of a horse), by deposition in wells, shafts and lakes, and by burial with certain animal remains. In this context the horse is especially relevant, since the Celtic horse goddess, Epona, had a chthonic and fertility or regeneration aspect, as well as being protector of the cavalry. It could well be that any shrine focusing on the head would incorporate more than one of these facets and that over the centuries different emphases would prevail.

This now brings us to the crux of this discussion: the reason for decapitated burial in Roman Britain. The matter has been discussed by many scholars, with as many interpretations.[24] In one of the more recent works on the subjects, M. Green (1976: 49) suggests that the decapitated burials she analyses (in Dorset), mainly middle-aged women, may have been queens, or alternatively witches or medicine women. In a later publication, she postulates that the loss of the mandible may have been a deliberate act 'to prevent the women talking after death and casting spells' (M. Green 1992: 78). There are a number of points raised here which may be countered by reference to other decapitated burials in Roman Britain. The implication from this interpretation is that decapitation is seen as some sort of punishment, yet Green sees the rite generally as a means of 'easing entry to the Otherworld' (1986: 78). Wait (1995) takes a negative view of decapitated burial, and sees it as a punitive measure reserved for 'abnormal' deaths, a means of *preventing* the move to the Otherworld after death and thus avoiding any pollution of the Otherworld and subsequent breach with earthly society.

A rather more positive view is taken by Harman *et al.* (1981), who analyse burials in the upper Thames Valley, and conclude that, most probably, in burials which are otherwise normal, decapitation is a ritual associated with beliefs concerning the fate of the body in an afterlife – but what, they do not postulate.

The study by Macdonald (1979: 414–21) is more detailed, and his interpretation more complex. He maintains that at least some of the seven decapitated burials at Lankhills were sacrificed by the slitting of their throats, and then decapitated. They were each placed in the cemetery near the elaborate burial of an individual who had died prematurely. The power of the decapitated person was then transferred to the 'special' burial. Decapitation, in effect, destroyed the soul. There are considerable difficulties and contradictions in this solution, not least that the Romans would not have countenanced human sacrifice, particularly in urban sites such as Lankhills, Poundbury and Cirencester, where decapitated burials have occurred. Nor would it have countenanced human sacrifice in what has been estimated to be around 2.5 per cent of all burials in Roman Britain (Philpott 1991: 80). We are told quite distinctly that the Romans put a stop to human sacrifice and divination (Diodorus 4.4.5; Pomponius Mela 3.2.18; Livy 30.13). Even in the unrest which occurred in the second half of the fourth century, an unrest which may have caused anxiety about the fate of the dead (Macdonald 1979: 423–4),[25] there is no reason to suspect a breakdown so serious that this kind of practice would have been reintroduced or condoned.

In the most recent work on the subject (Philpott 1991: 77–89), the author has presented a thorough analysis of the published examples of the ritual, and has also assessed the earlier interpretations. Philpott, too, rejects Macdonald's view of sacrifice and of the destruction of the soul by decapitation of the body. He accepts the view that the power of the decapitated bodies at Lankhills was transferred to those apparently deliberately associated with them, but suggests that, rather than this resulting in the destruction of the soul of the decapitated person, the potency of the head (and the soul) was increased. The healing capacity of the severed head might have been used to counteract premature death and to assist the 'associated' body to the Otherworld. He concludes that there is little evidence to suggest that decapitated burials were of low status.

With the publication of more evidence than was available to Macdonald, and building on Macdonald's thesis, Philpott has been able to make considerable progress in an acceptable interpretation of decapitated burials in Roman Britain. His explanations can be refined and expanded. There are, however, one or two points which cloud the issue, and these will be dealt with briefly. The first is his recourse to the sixth book of the *Aeneid* to demonstrate that the souls of those who experienced a premature death were destined to wander the Otherworld until their time was come to cross the Styx. This concept is Graeco-Roman and presupposes a considerable degree of sophistication and Romanisation on the part of the average Romano-Briton. The fact that most of our decapitated burials of the fourth century are from rural areas suggests that such a belief would be unlikely to have had much currency.

Philpott also proposes that bodies and severed heads were displayed. He appears to suggest that bodies were on display (presumably in the grave?) before being covered with earth, and cites Ashton formal cemetery to illustrate this. He adduces no evidence for this claim, apart from the fact that biers were apparently used instead of coffins. The use of biers was perfectly normal in Roman burials. In the funeral procession, the body was carried on a bier to the grave, with the face visible. Mourners and spectators would thus be able to identify the deceased. If it were a person of note, the young men of the family would wear masks (*imagines*) of their ancestors in the procession. In the case of Ashton a less elaborate ritual might be expected, but there could well have been a simple funeral procession in any case. More than likely the bier would then have been used in the grave as a cover over the body, since coffins were not used in the formal cemetery. Furthermore, if, as has been proposed (Watts 1991: *passim*), Ashton cemetery was Christian, there would be even more reason to cover the body. Christian burials normally took place within twenty-four hours of death. To the writer's knowledge, there is no record in the classical or Christian sources of any viewing of a body *in the grave*.[26]

With regard to the display of severed heads, it is quite possible that this took place in the Roman period, in view of the number of instances where a skull was found minus the mandible. But it is extremely unlikely, especially in a place like Winchester, that it was a public display. Further examples will be considered shortly.

We have looked at Iron Age British and Irish archaeology and the relevant literature, and it was proposed that skull and decapitated burials were closely related and probably had a significance which was positive, rather than negative. For a reason for the practice of decapitated burials, let us look again at the classical writers. Strabo (4.4.4) tells us that the Celts believed the soul was imperishable; Caesar (*B.G.* 6.14) that the Druids inculcated the belief in the transmigration of souls to encourage bravery in battle; Pomponius Mela (3.2.19) says much the same thing; and Lucan (1.455–8) also writes that Druids believe that at death the spirit moves on to another person and that death is not the end of life, but merely a mid-point in it. Ammianus (15.9) confirms the belief in the immortality of the soul and the role of the Druids in transmitting these kinds of ideas.

What is proposed here is based on the premiss that there was a Celtic belief in the transmigration of souls, and in the soul's being located in the head: the head is more powerful/apotropaic/talismanic when detached. If the head is removed, then the spirit is released and is free to move to another body or person (a parallel being the ritual bending or breaking of votive objects, as frequently found at temples). If the head is placed away from its anatomically correct position there is no chance that head and body will be reunited:[27] reunion negates the removal of the head.[28] The placement of the head at different positions around the body may also be significant, but such significance will never be known.

The practice was always limited, and may have been restricted to, say, people who had died on a particular, perhaps auspicious, day (or days) in the year, or some other similar small proportion of the population. There is no archaeological evidence that the rite was limited to one sex or age group, nor does it seem as if there was any underlying intention of punishment, degradation or debasement. On the evidence from Ashton (as yet unpublished), two instances of 'paired' decapitated burials among those outside the formal cemetery (the 'backyard' burials) suggest there may have been some family tradition or particular set of beliefs involved.

Indeed, what we may have is a *memory* of the importance of the head, and of the (admittedly limited) manifestation of this importance in burials prior to the Occupation. We are reminded (R. F. J. Jones 1987) that, even in days before the mass media, fashions in burial (and Jones refers particularly to the move from cremation to inhumation) could change fairly quickly, and right across the whole Roman Empire. Perhaps the situation was the same in Roman Britain in the second half of the fourth century.

If, as noted above, the incidence of skull burials in Iron Age Britain is calculated at around 3 per cent, and of decapitated burials in Roman Britain at something less than 2.5 per cent, it would seem, on the face of it, that in over three centuries of Roman influence there had been little change in the ways that native Britons regarded the head and treated it at death. But most of the instances of decapitated burial come from the late Roman period, and this suggests that there had been a resurgence of old Celtic practices. The meanings of these rites may have been transmitted orally over the years, or, alternatively, they had been lost over time, to be reinvented in the closing decades of Roman occupation. In other words, the reasons for the practice in the fourth century and later may not have been the same as in the first; nor, for that matter, need they have been the same in Dorchester, Dorset, as they were in Rushton, Northants.

It to the latter site that we now turn, in an effort to produce a reasonable explanation for this puzzling burial rite.[29] Rushton Mount, or Rushton Mound (SP 86088380), was a flat-topped conical mound c.37 m in diameter and 4 m high, part of an Iron Age to Roman settlement in Northamptonshire. It was completely excavated in 1964, ahead of roadworks. The site was briefly reported in the *Journal of Roman Studies* 55 (1965: 210). From the pottery remains,[30] the mound was apparently of late Roman date, built over a penannular feature which appears to have been Iron Age. The mound was cut at its base by a series of burials, twenty or twenty-one inhumations and three apparently unrelated skulls. The burials were found late in the excavation, so there was considerable damage done by earth-moving equipment and by previous ploughing and quarrying. Although the remains were poorly preserved, all were provisionally identified as male. One, with lighter bones, may have been sub-adult or female. There were also the teeth of a child about 9 to 11 years old. The burials were, with one exception, carefully laid out supine and extended, and all but one south–north: this last was north–south. There was some disturbance of earlier graves, suggesting that there were no grave markers. This is an important point.

All the bodies appear to have been decapitated, with only one skull placed in a position above the shoulders. Because of plough damage, there is some doubt as to whether it was in its correct anatomical position. Two decapitations had evidence for the actual cut. Eight had the skull or skull fragments between the knees or between or on the femora, one face down. There were five cases of bodies with no associated skulls, and three separate skulls, two of which were some distance from any body.

There is clear evidence that the skulls and bodies of individual burials were not interred at the same time. Two skulls without mandibles were found in the fill well above the bodies: one appears to belong to the body beneath it; the other, placed upright and facing east, was in the fill above two more burials, which, although decapitated, seem complete. One of these skulls was aged 'over thirty', the other was 'elderly'. In another grave the head of a male in his forties lay between the knees of another in his twenties. In a fourth instance a right femur had been removed and replaced by a skull, but because of the condition of the bones it was not possible to tell if the skull and body belonged together. It is very likely that they did not, since there was a mandible with the skull, whereas presumably the femur had been removed when the skeleton had become disarticulated. The skull was considered 'elderly'.

If the evidence above is set alongside the suggested interpretation of the classical sources, what we may have here is some sort of local belief in the transmigration of souls from the dead to the living, perhaps to the newly born. It may be that the skull of the dead person was retained by relatives (Posidonius' cedar oil embalmment comes to mind at once, but that is probably too fanciful) and buried finally when a new member of the family or social group was born. In the meantime the family would benefit from the power and protective properties of the head.

This would explain some unusual aspects of the cemetery: for instance the lack of mandibles, which suggests that a considerable time had elapsed before those skulls were buried, and the seemingly indiscriminate burying of individual skulls, which was due to confusion over who was buried where, or if anyone was buried in a particular place at all. Alternatively, these burials may have taken place covertly at night. The missing femur poses a problem, but it might be recalled that in his sixth category of Iron Age burials, 'single bones', Wait (1986: 117) records that there was a predominance of skulls and long bones: there were more of these from the right side than the left. Perhaps femora had particular significance in the Celtic world. There is, after all, the evidence from the huge Gallo-Roman sanctuary at Ribemont-sur-Ancre in Gaul, where about 2,000 human long bones (mainly femora, tibiae and humeri) were constructed into a one-metre-high stack. The interpretation is of 'funerary dismemberment' (Brunaux 1988: 19). It may be that, at Rushton, on finally burying the head, the person responsible took the femur to be yet another talisman in what may have then been a fairly uncertain existence.

What is even more remarkable about this cemetery is its date: two samples range from AD 880–1150 to 970–1170.[31] The cemetery was undoubtedly in existence by the time England was ostensibly Christianised, yet the burials were clearly pagan (that is, south–north orientation and with disturbed and decapitated burials) and individually indistinguishable from decapitated burials of the fourth century. The gap in dates for the two burials analysed suggests a long tradition of what must have been by then a covert practice, perhaps carried on only by one family or group.[32] The longevity of the rite once again reinforces the strength of the commitment of the native Britons to their old religious practices.

It is emphasised that the interpretation above applies to the site of Rushton only, and that the details would not necessarily apply to, say, the fourth- and/or fifth-century decapitations at Lankhills or Dunstable. Yet even at Lankhills there was one example of the placement of the head outside the coffin and at Dunstable a head in the fill above the body. The skulls must have been placed in the grave after the burial. The fact that in the Lankhills case it was the burial of a 2-year-old girl does not negate the argument. There are, moreover, other examples from Roman times where the mandible is missing. Suffice to say that decapitated burials do appear to have a connection with the Celtic view of immortality and that, while the rituals of the Iron Age may have been lost over the centuries, the memory of the importance of the head was retained, even well into the period of Saxon domination.

It remains now to demonstrate the connection between decapitated burials and the resurgence of paganism in Roman Britain in the second half of the fourth century.

Decapitated burials were not found throughout the whole of Roman Britain, but, paradoxically, in those areas most highly Romanised. Exceptions were the region north of the Humber to Hadrian's Wall, and west of the Pennines. There was a particular concentration in the upper Thames Valley (Philpott 1991: Figure 23), and it is interesting to note that it is this particular area that has been shown by Thomas (1981: Figure 16) and the present writer (Watts 1991: Figure 28) to be, to date, devoid of evidence for Christianity.

This is not coincidental, and the absence of the practice in fourth-century burials is one criterion for the identification of a cemetery as Christian.[33] At Icklingham, for example, the site of earlier cultic practices seems to have been purged by the dismantling of a temple and the removal of skulls to be discarded in a pit, after which the ground was covered with a clean layer of chalk (West 1976). An apsidal building and a west–east cemetery followed, both identified as Christian. Another example comes from Ashton, where there were five decapitations in the 'backyard' burials but none in the contemporaneous formal west–east (Christian) cemetery.

It seems reasonable, therefore, to connect the occurrence of

decapitated burials with the pagan cults of the late fourth century.
In Chapter 3 it was shown that there was a revival of paganism in
Roman Britain in this period, that it occurred mainly in the rural
areas and that it involved rural cults. This ties in with the evidence
from the cemeteries, which are also mainly from the country. The
major exceptions are of particular interest. At Poundbury the body
of a woman buried with two infants had the head of a man between
the feet; it was in what is considered the Christian cemetery, and
seems to have some particular significance (C. J. S. Green 1982: 74)
not discussed in the final excavation report. The other decapitation
was at the extremity of the main cemetery, and was probably not a
Christian burial at all. At Lankhills, as noted earlier, six of the seven
decapitations were after c.350, and probably the seventh also. They
were in the non-Christian main cemetery. It has been suggested that
at the Bath Gate, Cirencester, decapitations were executions. There
were no decapitations in the other major fourth-century urban
cemetery published, at Butt Road, Colchester.

If, therefore, we accept the rite of decapitated burial as a development of earlier Iron Age skull burials, and indeed linked with the
votive deposition of skulls, the increase in the practice is best seen
as part of the pagan revival in the second half of the fourth century.
It was argued that this revival in Roman Britain was of native cults.
The increase in decapitated burial would appear to confirm this.

Combs in late Romano-British burials[34]

The incidence of combs in Romano-British graves is not high and
most of the evidence comes from the fourth century.[35] Combs are
found in cemeteries which have been identified as Christian as well
as in those which it is convenient to label 'pagan', that is, non-
Christian. It may be merely an accident of archaeology that our
evidence is from the late period, or it may be that the inclusion of
combs in graves is a burial 'fashion' which fluctuated in popularity
as inhumation did as a means of disposing of the dead; however, it
may also be that combs had a particular significance as grave furniture, especially in the second half of the fourth century, and that
this, too, reflects a resurgence of pagan practices.

All the combs that have been found in this period, with the
exception of the one from Grave 155 at Lankhills, Winchester (G.
Clarke 1979: 44–5, 246–8), are made of bone. The Lankhills
example, of wood, is from the best-preserved burial in the whole
cemetery, and its survival suggests that other wooden combs might

have been found had soil conditions allowed. The grave is dated to 310–50/70, and it has been speculated (Macdonald 1979: 413–14) that the increased occurrence of combs in graves from about the middle of the century is due more to a change in material for their manufacture than to the sudden introduction of such a practice. That would not be totally incompatible with Macdonald's preferred interpretation that a higher incidence of combs would indicate 'an increasing anxiety about the . . . fate of the dead' (1979: 414). The evidence for combs in burials in late Roman Britain is probably skewed. It is, however, all we have, and this study can be based only on the surviving evidence.

The burials in three large published cemeteries, Lankhills, Poundbury Camp and Butt Road at Colchester, will be considered in detail here, as well as material from other published and unpublished sites.

An analysis of cemeteries primarily of the fourth century shows that, while combs are not often found in graves, they occur in both Christian and pagan contexts, in male and female graves and in burials of all ages except infants. Their positions in relation to skeletal remains and other objects indicate either that they were worn in the hair at burial or that they were deliberate grave deposits.

The three large cemeteries have produced a total of thirty-six combs. The largest number, twenty-one, came from Lankhills, a cemetery of almost 500 burials. Three were of children under ten, four were of adult females and one, possibly three, were of adult males; the rest were unsexed adults. Far fewer combs came from Poundbury. Here the main late Roman cemetery of 1,114 burials yielded seven combs from the graves of five adult females, one unsexed, and one which was initially identified as female (no. 485), and then identified as male (no. 485a). The Butt Road, Colchester, Period 2 cemetery had eight graves out of 669 with combs: two females, four unsexed adults and two children, one 4 or 5 years old, the other aged 7.

A few isolated instances of combs in cemeteries from the fourth century and relevant to later discussion might also be noted: at Bath Gate, Cirencester, with the remains of a female aged 50–60 years; Lynch Farm, Peterborough, with an adult female (R. Jones 1975); Queensford Farm, Dorchester, with an adult female 30–40 years (Chambers 1987: 58); and Ashton, with an adult female 17–25 years (B. Dix, personal communication).

The placement of the combs may well be of significance. At

Lankhills, in fourteen instances the comb was found somewhere near the skull, 'by right shoulder', 'under skull', 'in front of left shoulder', 'under neck', 'against left side of skull', etc., so it would be a reasonable assumption that these combs were worn in the hair when burial took place.

Yet a closer examination shows that this was not necessarily so. For example, it is questionable whether the fine hair of young children 3 and 4 years old would be able to hold a heavy bone comb. More likely the combs were placed against the head on burial. Furthermore, at least another six burials in this cemetery had combs which were apparently intentionally placed away from the head: in the rib area, by the hip, knee or ankle. There can be no doubt that these, and probably those of the two children, are examples of the deliberate placement of combs as grave furniture.

Butt Road presents a similar picture, with only one comb, found near the shoulder, likely to have been worn. Of the other seven, one may have been residual, one was found about 200 mm from the head, one under the right foot, and four deposited with other unworn objects. Three of these burials had the combs at the head end of the grave, the other about the middle.

Of single instances of combs in cemeteries, at Bath Gate and Lynch Farm the comb was away from the head: in the first case it was placed across the sternum, while in the second it was near a hip. At Queensford Farm it was found under the head. In the Ashton burial the comb was found about 25 mm from and at right angles to the left side of the skull. Clearly, in the first two burials the comb was not worn in the hair. At Ashton it may have been.

This leads to a consideration of the Poundbury burials, where all combs found could also have been worn in the hair. The report does not give full details of all the seven relevant graves, but from the available sketches and descriptions it seems that all combs were found near the head. Burial 517 might be more problematic as it seems that there is no sketch of the skeletal remains and, although it lay at the head end of the grave, the comb was found with a copper alloy ring. These may have constituted an intentional grave deposit, with parallels at Lankhills and Butt Road.

Burial 517 from Poundbury resembles no. 194 and perhaps no. 396 at Lankhills and 109, 174 and 647 from Butt Road. In all these cases the comb was accompanied by jewellery of various types, bracelets, rings, beads, etc., placed near the head. Only in Butt Road no. 519 were comb and jewellery found elsewhere, along the middle north side of the body.

Of the thirty-six burials with combs, ten also had jewellery. There was a considerable variation in the ages of those in this group, but the number included four of the five children, as well as adults, female or unsexed.

Discussion on combs and their purpose in Romano-British burials has been fairly limited. Macdonald (1979: 411–14) first addressed the problem in the Lankhills report, suggesting that unworn personal ornaments were offerings to gods. The presence of combs in graves was linked to the Celtic inhabitants of Britain, and was indicative of their admiration of long and well-groomed hair. An alternative but related suggestion is that hair was related to classical beliefs about death and afterlife, and that the presence of a comb would indicate to the gods of the dead that the deceased person had died at the appointed time and thus his or her soul would be sure of travelling to the Otherworld.

In his study of Romano-British burial customs in south-east England, Black (1986) seems to agree with Macdonald. He gives the example of a pot accompanying some cremations at Rainham Creek which contained a length of plaited human hair, and suggests that the hair was either an offering made by a relative of the dead person, or one from the deceased to an Otherworld god.

Philpott (1991: 181–2) quotes Macdonald's interpretation but expands this by suggesting that a comb in a grave may have symbolised that the proper rites of burial had been observed. His valuable collection of evidence of combs in graves is weighted to the fourth century, but he does give examples from sites possibly as early as the first/second century. He also believes that the practice reflected a native practice, since there was no evidence from Roman York or London. The present writer has taken a contrary view (Watts 1991: 194–5), that the practice reflects Roman influence, since there was no evidence for combs from the Iron Age burials of Britain and Ireland.[36]

In the light of the above interpretations, the question of combs as grave goods might be explored a little further. In the discussion which follows, cemeteries will be classified as pagan (Lankhills, Bath Gate, Lynch Farm and Queensford Farm) and Christian (Butt Road Period 2, Lankhills Feature 6, Poundbury Main Cemetery, Ashton), according to criteria developed by the author (Watts 1991: 38–98).

Combs in pagan cemeteries may be seen on at least two levels: as part of the preparation of the body for burial and for the journey to the Otherworld, or as a votive offering. An offering to whom is uncertain – to the gods of the Otherworld, probably, although that other well-known grave deposit, hobnailed boots, would seem more likely to have a purpose connected with the deceased, not the gods. It is worth noting that few of the burials studied here had also a coin in the mouth or grave. Perhaps the Otherworld could be appeased, and the Styx crossed, with objects other than a coin. Graves with both coins and unworn personal items were rare.[37]

The incidence of combs in pagan cemeteries seems to be greater in the second half of the fourth century. This occurs at Lankhills, with all but two of the twenty-one burials with combs dating from 350. The Queensford Farm burial with comb dates to after 365, while the one from Bath Gate is similar to another in a Lankhills burial dated 390–410. The Lynch Farm example is probably after 350, but dating evidence here is scanty.

With regard to Christian cemeteries, the presence of combs is more complicated. Christians, after all, did not need material possessions in the New Jerusalem. We have the distinct impression that even combs worn in the hair were not favoured in the burial rite, but that their incidence, too, increased in the latter part of the fourth century. The single example from Ashton, the only definite grave furniture in the cemetery, supports this argument. This burial came fairly late in the development of the cemetery and, from the meagre dates available, was probably after 350–60. At Poundbury, it is likely that all combs found in the large Christian cemetery were worn in the hair. Sparse evidence once more precludes a firm date for these, but late fourth century is likely, on stylistic grounds. The comb near the right shoulder of a burial in Feature 6 at Lankhills may have been worn. (This burial also has hobnails.) Feature 6, an enclosure considered an early Christian group in an otherwise pagan cemetery, was probably set up by a family which converted to Christianity, but evidently some of the old pagan customs prevailed. The date suggested for this particular burial is 365–90.

Our last Christian cemetery, Butt Road Period 2, is of particular interest. In her sequencing of the site, Nina Crummy has shown there were two periods when the cemetery saw grave deposits: in the early transitional period from pagan to Christian 320–40 (i.e. in the move from north–south to west–east burial), and in the second half of the century particularly after about 360 (see above, Chapter 2). All combs are considered to date to the last third of the century, and only one was worn. The grave groups which included the unworn combs could well have been deposited covertly, but if seen they would not have been likely to cause comment.

From all this it is seen that, when worn, combs in pagan cemeteries might be regarded as preparation of the body for the journey to the hereafter; when clearly a grave deposit, as offerings to an other-world deity, or perhaps for the use of the deceased in the next life. In Christian cemeteries they were rarely worn in the hair. Presumably church authorities intended that the body went to the grave completely unadorned. As unworn objects, they must be seen as covert deposits which, even if found, might not cause any mightily raised eyebrows. They had, after all, no obvious connection with pagan cults.

But that may not be the full explanation. Combs may have links with ancient mystery cults from Rome and the East. In his exhortation to the pagan Greeks, Clement of Alexandria (c.150–c.215) condemns the mysteries of Demeter, Dionysus and Cybele, and refers to the 'unmentionable' symbols of Themis (who came to be equated with Demeter and Cybele): marjoram, a lamp, a sword and a woman's comb (*kteis gynaikeios*) (*Protr.* 2). This last, he says, is here a euphemism for the female pudenda. The Latin *pecten* can also mean a comb, a shell(fish) and the pubes. If we take into account the general ignorance of the average Roman Briton in Greek and Latin (exemplified by frequent misspellings in graffiti and even in inscriptions), then it is only a small step to see the *kteis* or *pecten*, by the fourth century, as having its usual sense of a comb for the hair rather than its erotic meaning. A 'comb' then becomes an attribute of Cybele, now one of the most prominent of the mystic pagan cults. The placing of a comb in a grave may therefore reflect a belief in the cult of Cybele and Attis, with the promise of a life after death, or, in the case of Christians, a means of having a bet both ways.

This, of course, is only speculation. We can, however, be fairly certain that the presence of combs and personal ornaments generally in late-fourth-century graves means rather more than simple grave deposits for the deceased to enjoy in the afterlife.

Finally, an explanation for the rise in the incidence of combs in late-fourth-century burials must be attempted. Macdonald (1979: 406–24), in his discussion on pagan religion in relation to Lankhills cemetery, believes that the increased incidence of grave goods in the second half of the fourth century was due to a growing concern about the dead and their ultimate fate, and that propitiation of the gods by means of various grave deposits would go some way to ensuring a happy afterlife. This is a reasonable interpretation, given the chaotic state of the empire and even religion in the period (above, Chapters 1–3).

It has been shown that, in Britain, there is evidence for a revival of paganism in the second half of the fourth century. In the main it is relatively low key: a few instances of refurbishment of temples, renewed pagan activity and some new shrines, for example. Much of this activity was in the country and seemed related to Celtic religion rather than Roman or eastern. Nevertheless there is evidence that in the larger Romanised towns the cult of Cybele was active in the mid-fourth century, and probably later, when Julian came to the throne. There is evidence of a burial club at Dunstable whose members were associated with a cult of Cybele at nearby Verulamium; and until early fifth century, votives continued to be offered at the triangular temple in Verulamium despite its abandonment mid-century. This cult at least did not die easily even when Christianity had triumphed.

The increase in grave goods and particularly combs in Romano-British graves may, therefore, be due not only to an increasingly dark outlook on the future and a perceived need to appease the gods, but also to the actual revival of paganism in the years from c. 360–90. Even Christianity was not immune to this influence.

5

THE ECONOMY AND RELIGION IN THE LATE PERIOD

Earlier in this study (Chapter 2) a decline in the visible symbols of paganism, the temples, even before 391 was noted; and, while the growth of Christianity may have been a contributing factor, it is very likely that other more potent forces were involved. Indeed, if we look at the progress of Christianity in the last decade of the fourth century we see that it, too, was by now failing to make ground. From 391 to 410 it may have been static or already weakening. Possible reasons for the failure of Christianity to achieve the dominant position it held elsewhere in the Roman Empire have been advanced (Chapter 3). In view of an apparently similar state of affairs for the pagan cults, however, it seems that it is necessary to look further: the deteriorating economy of Roman Britain in the late fourth century provides both a common background and a common cause.

The economy in the fourth century

Because of the widespread political unrest in the empire in the third century there had been a general decline in the economy, particularly in trade and in agricultural production. Farms lay abandoned or uncultivated, and emperors used various measures to encourage people back on to the land. By the end of the third century some recovery had taken place. In Britain, since this part of the empire had been spared the worst excesses of invasion and usurpation, recovery was strong (Rees 1987: 485). The villas, the mainstay of surplus production, were able to build on their relative prosperity, and the first half of the fourth century saw unprecedented displays of wealth. The 'small towns', some of which were perhaps providers of official services in relation to the surrounding countryside (Burnham and Wacher 1990: 316), had also flourished in the third and early fourth century, reflecting the prosperity of the villas. The large towns, *coloniae* and *civitas* capitals, on the other hand, seem in the main to have reached their peak before the end of the third century. This was followed by a gradual decline: in a number of towns, large and impressive houses were still being built, but by *c.*350 the most obvious symbols of Romanisation, public buildings such as fora and basilicas, theatres and baths, were in decay or had even ceased to operate.

In the second half of the fourth century, and perhaps concomitant with the military problems in the empire, the whole economic situation in Britain deteriorated. The evidence is not always consistent, and certainly the decay was more marked in some areas than others, but it can be observed in all aspects of the Romanised way of life, both in town and country.

Let us look first at those manifestations of *romanitas*, the large towns,[1] which most scholars now agree were already failing before the end of the Roman period. In the second half of the fourth century many of the features of a Roman town were lost, yet civic administrations still seemed to carry on. By the mid-fifth century the remnants, too, had disappeared. It is difficult to generalise in a study such as this, but it can be said that while most Romano-British towns survived in some fashion until about the middle of the fifth century their character in the preceding century, and particularly after 410, was considerably changed: what came to be experienced was 'life in towns', rather than 'town life' (Wacher 1995: 421). There is little doubt that this process began decades before 410.

The evidence varies from place to place, but although the reasons for decline probably also vary, the end results are similar.

Colchester, the first officially established *colonia* in Britain, was never really a large town by continental European standards. It has been estimated that there were perhaps only about 300 houses and a population of 'a few thousand' for the entire walled town (Crummy 1993). The walls enclosed an area part of which was never built on, and even at the peak of prosperity in the third century this land seems still to have been under cultivation. Yet over fifty floor mosaics have been found (Wacher 1995: 123), indicating at least for some of the period of Roman occupation a fairly high standard of living. Towards the end of the third century the suburban settlement shrank drastically. There does not appear to have been a corresponding growth in the urban population, and in fact by *c.*325

whole streets of houses had disappeared: at Culver Street only a fairly ordinary building, perhaps a barn, remained. By the late third or early fourth century Colchester may already have been under attack by Saxon raiders. Little is known of the public buildings in the town, or their fate.

Unlike Colchester, London began as an unplanned settlement, around AD 50, and experienced its period of expansion in the second/early third centuries. At this time the town had the largest enclosed area of any in the province. It had all the trappings of a prosperous provincial capital. There was a large forum and basilica, an amphitheatre outside the walls, a fort for the provincial guard and a thriving waterfront. Within a hundred years, however, while the town still had many substantial private buildings and there was development in the suburbs, the basilica had been demolished and not replaced; by around 350 the amphitheatre was derelict; and by the end of the fourth century a far smaller area was enclosed by new walls, running along the river bank and tied to landward defences. Significantly, the quays were no longer being maintained (G. Milne 1993; Wacher 1995: 88–111). If the basis for London's prosperity had been its strategic commercial position, then interruption to trade may have been the cause of its decline. The disruption of long-distance trade within the empire occasioned by the political upheavals of the third century would have certainly been felt: international trade all but ceased at this time, to be replaced in regard to many items by regional self-sufficiency (Parker 1987; Fulford 1991). Wacher has proposed that a rise in sea levels from c.300 would have had a deleterious effect on the port installations, thus contributing to a deteriorating economic situation. More difficult to assess is his suggestion that the weight of government administration may also have had an inhibiting effect on the residents (Wacher 1995: 110–11).[2]

Lincoln and Gloucester, the other *coloniae* created in the first century, had differing histories in the last century of Roman occupation, mainly because Lincoln became a provincial capital. The resultant influx of government officials and administrators at the beginning of the fourth century gave that town a boost at least until c.350. A number of large private houses are known from the end of the third century or later, although there is no evidence for new public buildings in the period and the baths may have been out of use early in the fourth century. The construction in the forum some time around 390 of what seems to have been the first Christian church on the site of the later St Paul-in-the Bail (M. J. Jones 1994) suggests either that, by that date, the forum was no longer in use, or that the civic fathers had no objection to this structure in such a prominent position. By the last quarter of the fourth century, however, the town had contracted, and some if not all of the grand houses of the civic fathers were no longer in use. In the lower town, to where there may even before this time have been a shift in population, there seems to have been a concentration of reclamation efforts along the banks of the River Witham, where trade was still being carried on despite rising water levels. Trading establishments also operated along the road leading to the south entrance to the town. The economic downturn probably began around 370, although pottery kilns may have operated until the end of the century. Despite the strengthening of fortifications, presumably to protect the town against invaders from the sea, the last years of the Roman period saw an emptying out of the town and a return to agricultural-type pursuits. As Jones has pointed out, fortifications are no defence against a collapse of the economy. Even so, organised civic life may yet have continued into the early fifth century (M. J. Jones 1991, 1993).

At Gloucester, too, the town contracted towards the river from the third century on, with a considerable population now outside the defences. While public facilities such as the forum ceased to be used before the end of the fourth century, town life seems to have continued into the early fifth. Fragments of North African amphorae of the late fourth or early fifth century and a mosaic in Southgate Street under which lay a coin of Valens are indicators of a reasonable standard of living in the late period, despite the fact that Gloucester was quite clearly eclipsed in wealth and importance by nearby Cirencester. A conservative population of veterans, perhaps supplemented from time to time from the legionary fortress at Caerleon, is likely to have contributed to the relative stability of Gloucester when other towns were already in an advanced state of decline (Wacher 1995: 165).

Because of its different character and economic base, attributable to a large active military presence throughout its existence, the *colonia* of York also suffered in the late period. A legionary fortress in the Flavian period, it later became the home for Legion VI Victrix (Holder 1982: 105). Such an army base would naturally attract traders, and the civilian population seemed to comprise mainly members of the native upper class and their clients, craftsmen and those engaged in industry and commerce. There is little evidence for a sizeable, unskilled population (Ottaway 1993:

66). The prosperity of York was thus tied to a large extent to the presence of the army, since there were fewer (and less opulent) villas in the surrounding region than in the south. The town became the capital of Britannia Inferior early in the third century, but its status as a provincial capital seems to have had little positive effect on housing standards until Diocletian's reforms. In the early fourth century there were substantial, well-appointed houses both inside and outside the city walls, probably the homes of provincial or local administrators and retired army officers (Ottaway 1993: 107). Trade was vulnerable to attacks by sea raiders and pirates, and it is significant that the *Dux Britanniarum* was later based at York. From about mid-fourth century, rising sea levels seem to have affected port installations (Wacher 1995: 188). But the economy of the town would have been even harder hit by the large-scale withdrawal of soldiers to Gaul in the second half of the century, a process accelerated by Magnus Maximus *c.*383. Certainly the character of the fortress changed from *c.*380, with a rapid build-up of rubbish there (Ottaway 1993: 111). Although living standards in the civilian part of York deteriorated, some sort of order was probably maintained until the end of the Occupation. Burials within the city walls appeared early, however, some at least dating to mid-fourth century.

Of the *civitas* capitals, Verulamium was the earliest to be laid out as a Roman town, and may have been one of the last to collapse. There is evidence that it remained fairly well populated, with continuing prosperity in the fourth century. Unlike the situation in most Romano-British towns, public buildings seem to have continued to be used in the latter half of the century (Wacher 1995: 235). A temple near the theatre was renovated as late as 379, although the theatre itself was abandoned. Even though houses were more widely spaced (suggesting a reduced population), they were of high standard, with hypocausts, mosaics and wall paintings. A stone house was built in insula XXVII next to the forum some time around 380 (Niblett 1993). A timber water pipe functioning well into the fifth century has been taken to indicate the continuation of civic amenities, if not town life, at Verulamium.[3] It may, on the other hand, be explained merely as a sign of continuing authority, the water serving some powerful individual, rather than as a continuation of Roman-style urban administration (R. F. J. Jones 1991b). Even so, when Germanus came to Britain in 429 (Bede *H.E.* 1.18) it is likely he venerated the shrine of St Alban in a still recognisably Roman town.

Cirencester also appears not to have suffered early decline to the same extent as did those towns threatened by raiders from the sea or by the rising sea water itself. The town, probably the largest and certainly the most prosperous of the tribal capitals, had from an early date been a wealthy centre. It is very likely that it became a provincial capital early in the fourth century, and this period saw the forum and basilica remodelled. It also saw town houses and nearby villas even more luxuriously appointed. This was matched by commercial establishments: for example, at the same time that houses were becoming more opulent, all the shops in insula V were rebuilt in stone. It has been suggested that commercial life may have continued almost to mid-fifth century (Wacher 1995: 164), which would be exceptional for Roman Britain. This does not mean that civic administration also continued. If Cirencester was a provincial capital, however, presumably government officials remained in the town until at least 407, the time of the usurpation of Constantine III. Activity in the last decades of the fourth and early fifth centuries has been difficult to assess. It appears that there was now more agriculture carried on within the town's walls, a situation which was not without parallel elsewhere.[4] There is the suggestion that the amphitheatre ceased to be used for performances by the third or early fourth, and that it came to be used as a market. At some later date, in the fifth or even sixth century, the amphitheatre may then have become a refuge for the remaining inhabitants, sheltering from some threat, perhaps Anglo-Saxon (Wacher 1995: 322; McWhirr 1993). Yet the Bath Gate cemetery is dated only to fourth or early fifth century (McWhirr *et al.* 1982; McWhirr 1993). Whatever its fate, from the limited evidence it seems Cirencester may have been one of the few Romano-British large towns to be functioning more or less 'normally' at the end of the fourth century.

The situation in the other *civitas* capitals varied, but some common features may be detected. Where the evidence is available, public buildings such as fora, basilicae and baths are often found to be out of use by mid-fourth century or slightly later (e.g. Canterbury, Dorchester and Leicester). In some towns, such as Silchester, this occurred earlier. In others, such as Caerwent, Exeter and Wroxeter, the facilities seem not to have fallen into disuse until the end of the century (Wacher 1995: *passim*). It is significant that these centres were further removed from the Saxon shore.

Nevertheless, virtually all walled towns – *coloniae* and *civitas* capitals alike – strengthened their defences in mid/late fourth century. Furthermore, while population density often decreased within the town walls,[5] there are numerous examples of large and impressive residences, often maintained until quite late. This occurred even in distant Carmarthen (James 1993). Such houses are now generally interpreted as those of provincial or local government officials,[6] the latter in particular performing their civic duties by providing for essential services such as defences, water supply and street maintenance, rather than putting their money into public buildings. Administration could, after all, be as easily carried out in a private building as in a basilica.

There is little evidence for violence and destruction in Romano-British towns after 410. In most cases the end came with a whimper rather than a bang. Wacher (1995: 416) suggests flight, famine, disease and economic collapse as possible final causes. The remnants of the urban population dwindled until, by c.450, little or nothing remained to recall the days of Roman rule. In a number of cases this end of Roman towns had initially little to do with the Saxons, and much more to do with the situation in the last fifty years of Roman occupation (to be discussed in more detail below).

The state of affairs in the large towns is paralleled by that in the less organised, smaller towns.[7] Following a period of development in the third century, generated no doubt by the expansion of villas in that period,[8] they too experienced a contraction in the fourth century, particularly in the suburban or extramural areas (Esmonde Cleary 1989: 134). There were exceptions, and some continued to prosper until quite late. This was especially so for towns connected in some way with officialdom, and for those with a clear economic focus such as an industry or market (Burnham 1995). Indeed, some may have replaced the larger *civitas* capitals as major markets. But overall the picture was one of declining population and contraction or abandonment of settlement.

In some instances the focus for the town disappeared, such as the *mansio* at Godmanchester burnt down c.300 and not replaced (Burnham and Wacher 1990: 316). In others the focus lost much of its attraction: for instance, the temple at Bath was in disrepair by mid-fourth century (Cunliffe and Davenport 1985). On the other hand, a new or increased military presence might give a boost to the local economy for a time. Examples suggested include Catterick and Dorchester-on-Thames (Burnham and Wacher 1990: 317).

A number of small towns in the east were fortified, mirroring the uncertainties of the larger towns. Towers were added to the walls of towns in a line from Ancaster to Water Newton (Burnham and Wacher 1990: 316). Presumably there was still something to defend. As with their larger counterparts, however, fortifications did not prevent decline.

The end of the small towns in Roman Britain is in many cases not clear cut. Some may have been ultimately abandoned.[9] Others had evidence of Germanic settlers from the early fifth century.[10] In many more there was continued, if contracted, occupation and, with the end of the villas and large towns, the growth of self-sufficiency. This process, it has been proposed, brought about the end of any urban continuity, that is, continuity along traditional Roman lines (Burnham and Wacher 1990: 319; Burnham 1995).

The prosperity of the small towns was to a large extent dependent on the surrounding countryside and the villas which dominated the rural scene, particularly in the lowland area. But they, too, ultimately reflected the decline in the Romano-British economy in the late period. Their fate varied: many failed, but some survived into the Anglo-Saxon period to become hamlets or villages, and others religious sites (Percival 1987: 544–6).[11]

During the third and early fourth century villas in Roman Britain had reached their peak of prosperity. This was especially so in the west, where there were a number of quite palatial houses built or extended.[12] These villas, in Hampshire, Dorset and Gloucestershire, probably benefited from the less stable conditions pertaining elsewhere. In the south east, for instance, signs of economic decline were evident before mid-third century.[13]

Some villas in Britain may have been victims of the disruptions and political upheavals of the 350s and 360s: it has been proposed that the villa at Gadebridge Park, Hemel Hempstead, was deliberately demolished around 353, a casualty of the ill-fated rebellion of Magnentius (Neal 1974: 98). Frere (1987: 345) believes a further seven villas in Somerset, five in Hampshire and one each in Hertfordshire and Yorkshire may have been affected by the series of raids in 367 known as the 'barbarian conspiracy'.

Others survived to the end of the Roman period and sometimes beyond, but the general impression is one of declining standards, with fewer repairs being carried out and reconstruction in timber rather than in stone (Higham 1992: 57). As far as is known, there were no new villas in the last quarter of the fourth century.

In fact, there seems to have been a drop in the number of villas in the later fourth century and a small decrease in the average villa size (Millett 1990: 186). Yet there does not seem to have been any decline in the productivity of the land (Esmonde Cleary 1989: 136), and the drop in the number of villas may mask the aggrandisement of some, at least in terms of area, if not in luxury. Millett (1990: 202–4) believes that on these large estates there was increased production because of advances in technology and husbandry. But he also follows M. K. Jones (1982) in suggesting that the introduction of the colonate system would have helped to weaken the villas, since this would have produced a 'market-based' economy rather than a 'socially embedded' economy, which would in turn have depressed markets. Any improved productivity generated by the colonate system without a corresponding increase in demand would have helped to push down prices.

There is, therefore, evidence for abandonment of some villas in the last quarter of the fourth century; in more cases they were allowed to run down to little better than squatter occupation.[14] Yet the land was still worked and, from the limited pollen analysis available, there is nothing to suggest that there was a widespread return to woodland, although marginal lands may have reverted to pasture (Esmonde Cleary 1989; de la Bédoyère 1993: 129; Higham 1992: 61). People still had to eat, and food still had to be produced. This could be done without the luxury of hypocausts, mosaics and baths suites. One might now envisage in the sub-Roman period a countryside which came to resemble that of the pre-Roman period, with former dwellers of towns and villas becoming almost indistinguishable from their rural brothers, but with control of large tracts of productive land still being the determinant in any hierarchy. These leaders would, no doubt, have been the same people who had lately been involved in local administration and had had considerable investment in large-scale operations, whether agricultural or industrial.

Little is known of any organised industry in Roman Britain apart from pottery. From the limited evidence available, it appears that the decline in the economy was reflected in the production of pottery in the late fourth century. Around mid-century, the products of the New Forest and Oxfordshire potteries came to replace the black-burnished ware which factories in Dorset, Somerset, East Anglia and the Thames estuary had previously supplied to the army. This has been attributed to the disruption caused by the events of 367, resulting in the shift of the market into the hands of a few large-scale factories (Frere 1987: 284, 364–5). But the new suppliers did not survive much beyond 400 (at the latest 410–20) and Frere concludes that it was economic difficulties which were the main cause of their failure.

Reasons for decline in the economy

A picture has been drawn of the Romano-British economy in the second half of the fourth century and the first decade of the fifth, up to the withdrawal of the Romans. The impression is one of general deterioration. Although the situation in some areas remained relatively buoyant for longer than in others, by c.410 the town-and-market-based society was but a shadow of its former self, and Britain quickly retreated to a cashless and largely subsistent economy.

The reasons for this economic failure are manifold, not least being the position in which Britain now found itself in relation to the rest of the empire: a backwater, still good for supplying taxes in kind, especially grain (as attested by the large granaries still operating in the south east (Black 1987: 56–60, 83)), perhaps also woollen cloth or other requisites for the army (a possible explanation for the Hoxne Hoard), and, for as long as they were available, replenishments for the army itself. Britain was not of any strategic importance. Except as a springboard for usurpers, it never had been. The self-promoting policy of Claudius in the first century AD had led to the conquest of its untamed people. Now the struggle against the barbarian was taking place in central Europe, and Italy itself was at risk. The army was needed elsewhere. Most Roman investment would long ago have been withdrawn. Britain, together with its contribution to empire, was expendable.

That is not, of course, the whole story. Factors within Britain itself must have contributed, but many of these were also connected with the army and its lifeblood, taxes; and Millett (1990: 213) has demonstrated, from figures extrapolated from A. H. M. Jones (1964: 1,449), that the tax burden was proportionately heavier on the Western Empire.

There is no doubt that there existed a nexus between taxes, the army and the economy.[15] From the second half of the third century until Valentinian I (364–75), taxes were paid in kind,[16] and thereafter gradually commuted to gold.[17] Much of the produce acquired would be distributed to the units of the army stationed relatively near by. Soldiers received the balance of their pay and additional payments such as donatives in cash, which in turn circulated within a community.[18] With the withdrawal of the army there was less money in circulation. There was also a lowered demand for goods and services. In such a downward spiral it did not take long for the centres of trade, the towns, to fail. The trend would extend to the producers of surplus, the villas. It is not surprising that after the official supply of bronze coinage to Britain ceased in 402 there is little or no evidence of counterfeiting. In other words, coins were no longer essential.

There was also the cost of collecting taxes in kind, and it has been pointed out (Hopkins 1980) that such a system requires more supervisory staff than the collection of taxes in cash. This additional burden would have to be borne by the provinces, as part of the cost of administering them. Furthermore, with the division of Britain into four provinces early in the fourth century, there was an increase in the number of officials on provincial payrolls.[19] This was in addition to existing obligations to provide upkeep on roads, *mansiones* and other state buildings and maintain the *cursus publicus*. These expenses, too, had to be paid from landholders' taxes, no doubt with the weight falling inequitably on the poorer, rather than on the rich. Taxes had to be paid on land whether under crops or not. The smaller, poorer landholders, with less choice for ploughing or fallow, would thus have been driven to overproduction, and likely soil degradation. But the effects may not have been all negative, and such taxes may have helped to delay the end of Romanisation in some parts of Britain. There is a suggestion that in the west Magnus Maximus handed over responsibility for urban defence to the towns, that is, that the towns now had to pay for their own defence forces (Frere 1987: 355; B. Jones and Mattingly 1990: 307). This may have given rise, in the next century or so, to petty kings in the west and Wales. It would also help to explain why some towns in the region, such as Cirencester, Gloucester and perhaps Wroxeter, appear to have had a longer 'town life'.

One further connection between military affairs and the decline of the economy should be explored: the invasions of the fourth century. These had not begun overnight, and the Saxon shore forts and other coastal defences were built from the early third century on, a visible reminder of the long-standing threat by the Germanic tribes from the east. To the north the Picts had been troublesome early in the fourth century, and in the west the Scots increased their seaborne raids on villas and towns via the Bristol Channel. Finally, in 367, worst fears were realised when a concerted attack east, west and north was made by these groups, aided by deserters from regular army units stationed in Britain.

This 'barbarian conspiracy' undoubtedly caused havoc, and even greater nervousness once it had been put down. While the disruption was probably relatively short-lived, there seem to have been some long-term effects on the economy. As noted above, it is likely that the disruption to the pottery trade caused small producers to fail. For some villas, those which seemed to falter in the second half of the fourth century, perhaps the raids were the final blow in a general decline of the economy (Percival 1975: 168). For towns, the outcome may have accelerated their end: Colchester, it was seen, had probably been exposed to barbarian attacks from an early date; and towns on waterways, such as York and Lincoln, were especially vulnerable. Virtually all walled towns, large or small, continued to strengthen their fortifications, and many built towers. This seems invariably to have been at the expense of public buildings. If, as is likely, the wealth in Britain was declining, the limited amount which might be spent as fulfilment of one's civic duties had to be put where it was most needed – in the defence of one's town. Some trappings of *romanitas* were not necessary. Those which represented survival were.[20]

Trade and industry were the heart of the town. But demand for goods and services was declining, in part because of the withdrawal of the army. Demand also decreased as overseas trade declined. When imported goods were no longer available, because of disruption to trade routes, problems with transport overland internally or other reasons, then people either did without or began producing a local alternative. This had happened earlier with the pottery industry and the import of Samian ware. As local producers became more confident and competent there was now less need to go to the towns. The countryside had become more self-sufficient from the third century on. A good example is the villa or small settlement at Gatcombe, at which a variety of activities was carried on beyond the usual pastoral and agricultural pursuits (Branigan 1977). The reason for this self-sufficiency has been questioned: was it a deliberate policy of villa owners to reach this state (Percival 1975: 48), or was it the result of a decline in the standard of living and of villa production, with capital put into corndryers and workshops rather than mosaics and baths? In view of the fall in population in the towns, and thus in demand, the answer is likely to be the latter.

The economy of Roman Britain was, it is clear, in decline by the second half of the fourth century. The reasons were diverse, and connected to the general economic decline in the empire,[21] which was in turn related to military threats, particularly in the West. Britain was already under stress from the pressures of taxes raised to support an enlarged provincial administration and the army stationed there. The withdrawal of the army may not have lessened the tax load greatly, since any local militias would still have to be paid, but it did mean the loss of markets for surplus production, and ultimately the end of the circulation of coinage. There was still the threat of invasion, and reduced resources had to be put into fortifying towns and constructing watchtowers. There was little money left over to build, renovate or restore public buildings.

Such buildings included temples and churches, and it is to these that we now turn to determine the effects of a declining economy on the religions of Roman Britain in the late fourth century. The evidence is, as is often the case for Roman Britain, almost exclusively archaeological.

The effects on religion

Paganism, we have seen, had experienced a resurgence in the reign of Julian and his immediate successors. This renewed activity was demonstrated in the continuation and even refurbishment of existing temples, the building of new shrines and a return to pagan use of others. Although many of these sites which were in existence after 360 are not fully published, where the evidence is available it can be seen that the cults and their followers were now, in the main, becoming impoverished.

From the towns there are few examples, and even fewer details. In London, a Mithraeum built perhaps at the end of the second century survived until at least mid-fourth century. It underwent much remodelling, necessitated by the waterlogged nature of the soil. In the latest phases of the temple a makeshift altar had been created from a reused stone column and capital, evidence of the decline in the temple's fortunes (Grimes 1968: 105) and reflecting that of the town itself.

At Verulamium, where the decline seems to have been later, large numbers of late coins were found at the site of two of the Romano-Celtic temples in the town and in rubbish tips associated with them. It has been postulated that the temples themselves had also become rubbish tips (Niblett 1993); but the fact that one temple is known to have been renovated some time after 379 suggests that it may have still been in cultic use even up to 391, when Theodosius closed all temples. The association with rubbish suggests a decline in standards, however.

One further example is the elaborate temple complex at Bath, which, like the London Mithraeum, underwent many repairs because of its unstable location. It deteriorated in the late fourth century to the extent that its cultic focus was considerably reduced. All that was left operating into the fifth century was a small room, about 6.8×5.5 m, which incorporated reused material from the temple. Later building was in timber (Cunliffe and Davenport 1985: 184–5; Cunliffe 1988). This is a far cry from the opulent structure of the Flavian era and its extensions of the late second/early third century. The dilapidation was presumably the result of the ravages of the River Avon, a shrinking number of cult followers and the poverty of the inhabitants of the town.

While we have only a handful of pagan religious sites which continued after 360 in the towns, there is much more evidence from the rural areas, and it has been pointed out by more than one scholar[22] that there was a close connection between the prosperity of the villas and that of the temples. It was shown above that, in the last quarter of the century at least, many villas declined. As the amount of disposable wealth decreased, so there was less to spend on non-essentials within the villas and certainly on buildings beyond them. Upkeep on rural temples would have had to be reduced or to cease altogether.

The best-known example of a refurbished temple in the late fourth century was at Lydney, which was an elaborate and richly appointed complex, probably associated with a god of healing. It was built in the late third or early fourth century, and when part of the floor of the temple subsided the building was renovated and remodelled. This included new mosaics. Some time after 367 repairs were again necessary to the temple and to the 'long building' (Wheeler and Wheeler 1932; Casey 1981). The repairs in this latter building were rough and makeshift, those in the temple now without the addition of ornament such as mosaics, and nowhere in keeping with the quality of the original building. There has been an attempt in recent times to redate the phases at Lydney (Woodward and Leach 1993: 317), and it has been proposed, *inter alia*, that the last mosaics were laid in the fifth century. But given the lack of evidence for any similar construction or reconstruction in the fifth and the collapse of the Romano-British economy generally, and even allowing for the relative wealth of the villas of the area in the late period, it is considered that such a date for costly renovations is much too late. The dating of Lydney remains inconclusive until a full re-examination of the site and of the Wheelers' records can be undertaken.

More conclusive is the evidence from Pagans Hill, where the octagonal temple complex was desecrated some time after its floruit in mid-century. There was also rubbish deposited in a well which may have been sacred. Around 367 the temple was refurbished, a stone reredos was added and probably a stone sculpture group restored. The well may have resumed its earlier character, but it was not cleared (Rahtz and Watts 1989). The somewhat crude reuse of the sculpture and the failure to empty the well of the deposit which had profaned it suggest that the refurbishment of the Pagans Hill temple was a fairly modest operation.

Some 30 km or so away to the north-east, the temple of Apollo at Nettleton experienced a similar revival as a pagan cult centre. The octagonal temple had been modified earlier for use as a Christian church. This fell into disuse, but some time after 360 the north–west section was changed once more to create an improvised shrine, reusing a small column and bases from the original building. The life of this mean little focus may have been brief, however: part of the roof of the now derelict building collapsed and buried it. The excavator writes of the 'squalor and . . . changed building standards' of the late period (Wedlake 1982: 109).

Two further temples from the south-west, at Uley and Henley Wood, might be considered together. Both had Iron Age activity, probably religious. In both cases in the late Roman period there appears to have been limited resources for repairs and renovations. The Romano-Celtic temple at Uley was first built in the second century, and was improved and added to until around 353–60, when the front fell and was replaced with a projecting portico. Further collapse between 380–400 did not lead to rebuilding, and a section of the ruined temple was severely modified for continued, if limited, pagan rites. The building was then demolished and the site remained unoccupied for a couple of decades, if not longer, until it was adopted for Christian use (Woodward and Leach 1993: 10–11). The Henley Wood temple, built over an earlier cultic building c.270–90, was modified around 367–75 or later. The changes seem to have been quite unremarkable: a new floor in the ambulatory, perhaps of sandstone slabs, some strengthening of the east *cella* wall, and an improvement to the *cella* entrance (Watts and Leach 1996: 22–5).

In the east, in Essex, examples of building on a modest scale occur at Great Dunmow and possibly Witham. At the former, a small (6.75×6.60 m) shrine was erected c.350–60. It was a simple structure, perhaps of timber, and had votive pits associated with it which may even have predated the shrine. There was no evidence of any wealth here, either in the building itself or in the votive finds. Similarly, at Witham the pattern of limited expenditure on religious buildings may have continued. The original Iron Age focus had been replaced around 330 by a small oratory-style Christian church and octagonal font, but by 360–70 the site reverted to paganism. There was a considerable amount of votive material from this phase, but no certain evidence for any new building. Pit F3681, however, yielded scorched daub and charred wood (Turner 1982 and personal communication), which suggests a utilitarian building of little pretension, perhaps a simple wooden shrine. On the other hand, it may be that in a rural area such as this the need for a religious building no longer existed. The spirits of the place may not have required it.

While there seems to have been a decline in the standard of building and renovation of pagan buildings in the period, there were exceptions, as one might expect. But perhaps they merely serve to prove the rule. An example is the temple near the forum at Caerwent. It was a fourth-century creation, built around 330 on an alignment which paid little respect to earlier streets. It was later extended with extra rooms and niches, presumably for statuary, and continued to be well maintained until late in the fourth century (Brewer 1993). Clearly the temple goes against the trend for the late fourth century, but it will be remembered that Caerwent itself seems not to have declined as early as towns in the east.

The example of Caerwent notwithstanding, the evidence as presented above indicates that, on the whole, pagan religious buildings in Roman Britain did not have large amounts of money expended on them in the second half of the fourth century. The corollary of this is that members of the cults did not have the money to spend, and that this was in large part the result of a deteriorating economy. If this was so, then it is to be expected that a similar situation would exist in regard to Christian churches.

There is no doubt that there were wealthy Christian communities in the first half of the fourth century. The Water Newton hoard is eloquent testament to a rich community which adopted Christianity around 330 and was constrained, some two or three decades later, to hide its treasured communion plate from some menace, presumably one which threatened members' wealth as well as their faith. The villas at Hinton St Mary and Frampton, with their Christian mosaics laid down c.325–40, reflect the prosperity and optimism of the period. Similarly, two short-lived rural churches on opposite sides of the country, at Nettleton and Witham, were graced with features which later small churches such as those at Brean Down and Lamyatt Beacon would lack: at Witham

111

masonry walls, plastered and painted, a tiled floor and perhaps window glass (Turner 1982 and personal communication);[23] and at Nettleton, a cruciform church created from an octagonal stone temple, with walls brightly painted and a freshly laid floor of blue pennant limestone (Wedlake 1982: 61–3). Yet despite this early display of relative wealth, it is clear that as the century progressed churches became more, rather than less, modest, even if their numbers increased. This may be the result of a failing economy.

Using the chronology developed in Chapter 1, we find that the first identifiable Christian buildings appeared around 330. The Butt Road, Colchester, cemetery church was of some pretension, built of stone which was not local, and adorned with a veneer of Purbeck burr. It had a tiled roof and probably a rammed earth floor. Originally rectangular, it soon acquired an apse and nave.[24] A further extension took place when the western wall was rebuilt following subsidence. From the report (Crummy *et al.* 1993: 166, Figure 3.5) there does not appear to have been any decline in the standard of construction. Yet it seems that by the end of the Roman period the building was derelict. It is proposed, therefore, that the decay of the Colchester church was the result of a lack of maintenance or care, or both, in the second half of the century, brought about by the straitened circumstances of the inhabitants. The limited evidence from the Period 2 cemetery at the site appears to bear this out. There are five certain examples of uncoffined burials, and three of burials in tree trunks. Where dating is available, they all come from the late period.[25]

The churches at Icklingham and Silchester probably appeared soon after the Colchester church, around 340–50. There is not enough evidence in the report of the former (West 1976) to assess the quality of the construction. The Silchester building, however, was better preserved, and it seems that it was well built, with flint walls, a floor of red tesserae with a feature black and white mosaic on the chord of the apse, and walls plastered and painted (Frere 1975). The later history of the church is much debated: it fell into disrepair and may have been a squatters' refuge as early as *c.*360, or, more likely,[26] it declined along with the town towards the end of the century.

Another church likely to have been built *c.*340–50 was that at Verulam Hills Field, St Albans. Like the Colchester church, it too was associated with burials, but probably was not in use by the end of the century. It appears to have been of fair, if not remarkable, construction, with walls of flint, a tiled roof and a floor of red tesserae (Anthony 1968). This would not have been the only church in or outside Verulamium. Undoubtedly a far more elaborate church existed in the Roman period (Bede *H.E.* 1.7.19), on the site of the martyrdom of Alban, the same church visited by Germanus in 425. According to Bede, it was built soon after the Peace of the Church (313).

This period of building activity was not restricted to formal churches. Around the same time the house church at Lullingstone was built in an existing villa. A group of three rooms was set aside with a separate entrance, and decorated with Christian motifs and figures of *orantes*. The church continued to exist until early in the fifth century, but the owners of the villa had long ceased to maintain the living quarters. The situation reflects that of many other villas in Britain in the late period. What is of particular interest is the continued use of the house church, despite the now squalid conditions nearby (Meates 1979).

A deterioration in the standard of building may be detected from about this time. Perhaps around mid-century, the first church at the site of St Pancras in Canterbury was built. Detail is scant and dating evidence is very slight here, only a coin 'of the House of Constantine I' (Jenkins 1976); but the fact that reused bricks, few of which were complete, were employed in the construction suggests that new bricks were no longer available, or that they were too expensive for those who built the church. Either way, it points to a date well into the century.

Some time between 360 and 390, there seems to have been another period of church building activity. The standard of construction, however, reflects the worsening economic situation in Britain. Little detail is available, but it seems that the churches at Richborough (P. D. C. Brown 1971) and Lincoln (M. J. Jones 1994) were of timber, and the small oratories at Lamyatt Beacon (Leech 1980, 1986) and Brean Down (ApSimon 1965) of masonry; at the latter site at least, the stone came from a dismantled Romano-Celtic temple. The Richborough building reused, as bases for its uprights, masonry blocks which also seem to have come from a dismantled temple near by. None of these sites has produced any evidence for tesserae, roof tiles, painted plaster or other decorative features.

The reduced wealth of Romano-Britons in the second half of the fourth century is apparent from their towns, their villas and, it has been seen, their religious buildings. It might be expected that their straitened circumstances should also be reflected in burial practices of the period. This can be demonstrated, despite the lack of well-published cemeteries.

Christians normally eschewed elaborate burials and grave goods, so it is difficult to draw many conclusions from their cemeteries. It was possible, however, to show (above) that poor burials, such as those without coffins or in tree trunks, occurred in the later burials at Butt Road Christian cemetery in Colchester. Similarly, at Poundbury, of the forty-three burials considered to be 'late', only four were coffined, while the others were without coffin and/or had stones as grave liner or lid. Moreover, it seems that the majority of more expensive burials of bodies in lead-lined wooden coffins occurred during the first half of the fourth century, after which they were much rarer (Farwell and Molleson 1993: Table 5, 128).

If we look at Lankhills pagan cemetery, which, like Butt Road and Poundbury, spans much of the fourth century, we find a similar situation. Burial standards declined. The proportion of coffined graves in the latest period was 52 per cent, compared with an average for the whole cemetery of 83 per cent. The incidence of grave goods also fell, but not to the same extent: 51 per cent of graves in the late period, compared with 67 per cent in the earlier part of the cemetery. The occurrence of hobnailed burials, which might be a better gauge of economic circumstances, fell from 43 per cent to 26 per cent (G. Clarke 1979: 147, Tables 14 and 22).

Because dating is not as firm at the Dunstable cemetery, it is more difficult to assess trends there. But if a date for the formal cemetery of, say, mid- to late-fourth century is accepted, and the ditch burials still later, then it will be seen that a similar situation to that above exists. There were at least thirteen wooden coffins, only two of these in the ditch burials, and of seven graves which had 'offerings' (i.e. deliberate grave deposits), only two came from the late burials (C. L. Matthews 1981).

In previous chapters it was shown that the religions of Roman Britain had been subjected to forces which caused them to change direction and which were often beyond the control of the inhabitants of the province. Christian or pagan emperors, imperial (and, implicitly, army) patronage, political upheavals and usurpations all played their part in the advance or decline of the various cults. The one force which worked to the detriment of all religious cults in Britain was the decline of the economy. Perhaps it was the overriding factor, bridging the Roman and the sub-Roman worlds, which caused Christianity almost to disappear from lowland Britain, along with other vestiges of *romanitas*. The pagan cults, we have seen, were made of sterner stuff.

6

THE QUESTION OF
SYNCRETISM

A feature of religion in Roman Britain which has frequently drawn comment by scholars is its syncretic nature, that is, the conflating of native cults with those of Rome. Such a process is found in many aspects of Romano-British religion: in the gods worshipped,[1] in the temples built for the gods, in ritual and burial practices and in artistic representations of deity. Yet although Romano-British society lasted for over 350 years, it is doubtful whether the influence of Rome on Celtic religion was ever more than superficial – unlike the situation in southern Gaul and, to a lesser extent, the rest of Gaul and Germany, where the Roman religions came to dominate (King 1990: 235–6, Table 15.2).

While it is generally accepted that Romano-British religion was a blend of Celtic and Roman traditions, what has not been agreed is whether the result was the domination of the Roman religions (the *interpretatio romana*)[2] or of the Celtic (the *interpretatio celtica*).[3] As with many such problems in interpreting the past, the reality is probably somewhere in the middle. In an important study of early Romano-Celtic religion in the empire, King suggests that, for the early empire at least, Roman-Celtic religion became 'culturally Roman while remaining ethnically Celtic' (1990: 237). Such an interpretation, it is proposed here, applies to religion in Britain for the whole of the Roman period.

Inscriptions and temples

Although there are exceptions in some instances, a number of patterns can be discerned from a study of formal inscriptions relating to religion (altars, tombstones, dedication stones, etc.): where datable, they are mainly from the first three centuries of Roman occupation, at a time when the army was at its greatest strength in Britain, rather than at a time when, with the creation of four provinces, there was supposedly the largest number of government officials in Britain; the provenance of these inscriptions is the Romanised area of Britain (that is, the *coloniae*, *civitas* capitals, etc.) or areas where units of the army were permanently or temporarily based; there are more inscriptions from the frontiers than from the civilian zone; the gods addressed or to whom dedications are made are mostly Roman,[4] Roman with a Celtic equivalent,[5] Celtic with a Roman equivalent,[6] or foreign.[7] Where there is a dedication to a Celtic deity or deities, the dedicator is usually a Roman,[8] commonly an army detachment or an individual soldier;[9] if the dedication is by a member of a local group[10] or by a Celtic-named person[11] to a Roman god, these people are often of some status, that is, it can be assumed that they form part of the native élite, or of some socio-economic group which is Roman in origin;[12] alternatively, they belong to a community which is in close contact with Roman ways.[13] There are, however, very few inscriptions to Roman gods by individuals who have Celtic names (i.e. native Britons),[14] or to Celtic gods by people with Celtic names.[15]

Conclusions can be drawn, and the results compared with those drawn from other evidence. It is clear that the practice of making dedications to gods, whether Roman or Celtic, was never widely adopted by the native Britons during the Roman period. This may reflect the failure of Roman culture to spread throughout the province, or merely stem from the fact that the commissioning of an inscribed altar, dedicatory slab or tombstone would have been within the means only of the more wealthy members of the community. It was this same stratum of society which actively sought Romanisation, and it is likely that it was on this group that Rome relied to carry out provincial government in the fourth century, rather than, as in earlier centuries, seconding serving army officers to civic administration.[16] The very small number of inscriptions from what appear to be ordinary Romano-Britons, folk who have no indicated status or whose names do not hint at Roman citizenship, seem to come mainly from heavily Romanised areas, that is, large towns and settlements near army establishments.

The evidence from informal inscriptions, such as the *defixiones* from Bath and Uley, presents a different picture. While the temple of Sulis-Minerva at Bath[17] was built in the Flavian period and remained in use throughout the Occupation, several factors lead one to believe that the loyalty of the ordinary Britons was directed to the native, rather than Roman, focus of religion there. Of the tablets where the dedication has been preserved, most are to Sulis. Others are to Sulis-Minerva or Minerva-Sulis, but there are none to Minerva alone. In fact, the only known reference to the goddess at Bath as Minerva is from an early-third-century Roman writer Solinus.[18] It has already been noted (Chapter 1) that the names of the petitioners were those of ordinary Romano-Britons, not of the Roman legionaries and officers who frequented the place and recorded their more elaborate addresses to the goddess in stone.[19] Moreover, the dates proposed for the tablets are late, in comparison with the early date for the construction of the temple: the third century for those inscribed in capital letters (with three possibly from the second century), late second to late third for the Old Roman Cursive tablets and probably fourth century for the New Roman Cursive examples.

Although the temple of Sulis-Minerva at Bath has been used to illustrate the supposed early Romanisation of the native religion,[20] it is proposed here that the very opposite is the case. The lack of evidence for the use of the name Minerva by itself in dedications and the fact that the supplicants were of the lower levels in society suggest that the ordinary native Britons even by the fourth century saw themselves as approaching a Celtic[21] rather than a Roman deity at the temple.[22] Moreover, the relatively late introduction of the practice of depositing *defixiones* with a deity to avenge a wrong indicates the correspondingly late adoption of a religious practice which came from the Graeco-Roman world, not the Celtic.

The evidence from Uley is much more complex.[23] This temple, too, was built very early. The first period lasted *c.*100–310, after which the temple was extended and renovated. Two noteworthy features of the building even in this early stage were the Romano-Celtic plan and the construction in stone. The original dedication is unknown, but there was evidence of votive offerings of goats, sheep, cattle and pigs from the prehistoric phase of the site, with a high proportion of goats. Perhaps it was the association with sheep and goats which led the Romans to believe the god honoured was Mercury. Domestic fowl (the cockerel was also an attribute of Mercury) came to be offered as votives in much greater numbers from around the time the Romano-Celtic structure was built, the numbers peaking in the early to mid-fourth century.

Full-sized weapons were also found from the prehistoric and early Roman phases, to be replaced only in the late period by weapons in miniature,[24] ritually bent before deposition. It may be that the presence of weapons caused the confusion amongst early Romans over the identity of the god at the site, a Mercury- or Mars-type deity. Most commonly the god addressed in the *defixiones* is Mercury, but this may initially have been merely the identification by the newcomers of an unnamed Celtic god (as Caesar *B.G.* 6.17). Uley tablet 2 was originally addressed *deo Marti Silvano*, then overwritten *deo Mercurio*; *Silvano* occurs later in the same text; tablet 3 is addressed *deo Marti Mercurio*; and nos. 24 and 84 are addressed to Mars only. The native god apparently had characteristics which allowed him to be equated with Mars and Silvanus, as well as with Mercury (Tomlin 1993: 115–22).

The *defixiones* contain a mix of Celtic names and Latin *cognomina*. Some of the 'Latin' names may even have had a Celtic etymology. There are, however, no names of Roman citizens, and this has been taken to indicate that most of the tablets belong to the period before 212, when Caracalla granted Roman citizenship throughout the empire (Tomlin 1993: 117). More than half of the tablets so far recorded are written in Old Roman Cursive style, which dates from *c.*AD 175–275. In the light of the various goods lost or stolen, the petitioners of the god(s) at Uley do not appear to have been of the lowest stratum of Romano-British society: while there are a few items which compare with those lost at Bath, a cloak, money, and household goods, the rest of the property – such as a 'draught animal', sheep, cattle, a bridle, a gold ring, pewter plates, a pair of wagon wheels (these stolen along with two cows and various household items from the same person), linen cloth, wool and a crop of standing grain – gives the impression of considerably more wealth than that indicated by the tablets at Bath.

Interpretation of the evidence above would seem to suggest a community of native Britons who, soon after the coming of the Romans, adopted a Roman name for their local god[25] and the new temple architecture for his shrine. We are, however, not talking about the rural poor, as represented by the tablets at Bath. Here we have a relatively wealthy community, led by a tribal élite who could afford to build a stone temple and who aspired to emulate Roman ways. If the presence of such a group seems odd in this location so early in the Roman period, it must be remembered that Uley is close (*c.*20 km) to Gloucester and about the same distance from Cirencester. Bath is about another 5 km further away. Some of the Dobunni, at least, were among the first Britons to surrender to Rome, even before the arrival of Claudius (Dio 60.20–1) and would thus have enjoyed Roman patronage (and protection from their erstwhile Catuvellaunian overlords) from the earliest days of the

Occupation. Gloucester, Bath and Cirencester were all settled by
Romans by the late first century, and it is reasonable to assume that
the native leaders in the surrounding countryside were anxious, as
were their fellows in the eastern part of the province, to adopt the
Roman way of life (so Tacitus *Agric* 21).

There is no doubt that at Uley such ways were adopted with
enthusiasm, and there is clear evidence of a syncretism which might
be seen as an *interpretatio romana*. But this would seem to involve
primarily the wealthier members of local society; and the fact that
when the front of the temple collapsed around 380–400 the
building was not reconstructed but merely modified, with a small
part used as a shrine, suggests that an imposing stone edifice was
not necessary to the religion of the local people, some of whom, at
least, for a long time yet clung to their old beliefs despite the
advance of Christianity in the area. That these old beliefs were
related to the Celtic rather than to the Roman element of Romano-
British religion is demonstrated by the later deposition of part of
the cult statue of Mercury early in the sixth century, ahead of an
extension of the Christian phase of the site. The head was of great
importance in Celtic belief,[26] and in this case the head of the statue
had been carefully buried, although other parts of the cultic group
were broken up and used in the foundations of Structure VIII, interpreted as a small stone church (Woodward and Leach 1993: 324–5).

A study of the votives at Uley shows that one Roman practice at
least was adopted late by the local population and that Celtic practices were not forgotten. The offering of votive leaves and plaques
did not begin until the fourth century. Clearly this was one Roman
practice which was not rapidly taken up by the inhabitants of the
area. On the other hand, it is perhaps significant that the reintroduction of votive weapons, this time in miniature, also occurred in
the fourth century. As noted above, full-sized weapons had been
among the votive offerings in the prehistoric phase. Their re-
appearance in the late period suggests the revival of a Celtic ritual
at the site.

Votive leaves and plaques similar to those at Uley were offered at
other Romano-Celtic temples in Britain. These were not a native
innovation, but were found throughout the Western Empire, often
in military areas, and dedicated, as in Britain, to both native and
Roman gods (Toynbee 1978). In Britain they were introduced probably in the second and third centuries (Henig 1984: 147), and were
found in military contexts and at temples in town and country.
They are probably related in purpose to the metal letters of the

alphabet and the small figurines of deities also found at temple sites. While they were votives, and votives had been offered to the gods long before the Romans ventured into Britain, they were of a new type which suggests a change in – or rather a refining of – belief, or a personalising of the offering, in the same way that offerings from about the second century on came to include items such as toilet articles, spoons, jewellery, dress pins and brooches which the god might identify with the votary.

The Romano-Celtic temple itself could be interpreted as a manifestation of an independent architectural style: late British Iron Age shrines such as those at Heathrow (Drury 1980),[27] Hayling Island (King and Soffe 1994) and Thetford (Gregory 1991) seem to have the ingredients for the later development of the Romano-Celtic form. But it has been argued (King 1990) that it was the Graeco-Roman influence, emanating originally from southern Gaul, that led to the *development* of the Celtic religion from its earlier forms of architecture, ritual and anthropomorphic representation of deity. The *cella*-tower, a typical feature of the Romano-Celtic temple, may have been an integral focus for the religion, and this would account for the relatively early stone phases of temples, the towers having a particular religious significance. If that is the case, King suggests that Celtic religion only reached its floruit architecturally under the Romans, and that the period saw a marked advance in the development of Romano-Celtic religion: it was no 'mere veneer' of Romanisation.

To a large extent these views can be accepted for the Roman world generally, and Gaul in particular. But Britain was not Gaul. As King points out, Gaul lacked a strong local culture, having been long exposed to the Hellenised world and, most importantly, having been subjected to a period of intense Romanisation in the first century AD, during which most Roman institutions were firmly set in place. This might be compared with Britain, where a well-developed local culture preserved and cultivated by the Druids, little exposure to Roman and even less to Hellenised civilisation, and a slow and piecemeal Romanisation made the broad imposition of Roman institutions an impossibility. Romanisation was restricted to the towns and villa belts and, to some extent, to settlements associated with the military.

It has been noted (Horne 1981: Figure 3.1) that Romano-Celtic temples generally appear in the towns much earlier than in the country,[28] built by those who aspired to be 'Roman'. Temples then appeared in the country, no doubt paid for by villa owners with the same aspirations, and the villas were themselves associated with the towns. But towns and villas represented only a fraction of the total Romano-British population. The temples were built in the highly Romanised areas, or along the Wall. For a large part of Roman Britain and the majority of its native inhabitants the Roman influence on existing religion must have been minimal; and even when touched by Rome, the ordinary people felt the need to continue the old rituals. For example, it has been shown (Woodward 1992: 66–7) that, although there were additions which were typically Roman (see above), within the limitations of Roman law offerings at Roman temple sites replicated those of the Iron Age.

Furthermore, there is evidence either that the identity of gods worshipped at various temples (such as Lamyatt Beacon, Harlow and Maiden Castle) was unclear or that many gods were in fact worshipped there. This suggests that the name or identity of the god was unimportant and that the ordinary Romano-Briton had not progressed far beyond worshipping the *genius loci*. The development which King proposes for religion in Gaul did not occur in Britain. Romano-Celtic temples came with the Romans, and began to close even before the Romans left. By *c*.450 they may all have been closed. Yet it is certain that the native cults continued for decades, or even centuries. From the evidence of the temples it seems that in much of Britain the Roman element in religion had indeed been a veneer.

The evidence of the cemeteries

The same conclusion can to some extent be drawn from an analysis of Romano-British cemeteries, and particularly those of the late period. The outward and visible elements of burial, that is, dedicated burial grounds, methods of disposal of the body and its position if inhumed, very early reflected the adoption of Roman ways. In aspects such as grave goods, some typical Roman inclusions were rare and restricted to the more Romanised centres, but others existed along with the Celtic. Purely Celtic practices also continued, especially in the rural areas, and some increased by or in the fourth century.

Pre-Roman Iron Age cemeteries were rare, even in the late period. In a pioneering study, Whimster (1981: 4–128) defined four local burial traditions, applying to limited areas and to a limited time span. Both cremation and inhumation were practised, with cremation the method of disposal employed in the La Tène area of the south east. In a more recent work, Wait (1986: 83–121) showed that, despite the regional traditions defined by Whimster, the overwhelming number of Iron Age burials were in ditches or pits. C. E. Wilson (1981: 141–3) found that, while there did not seem to have been formal 'cemeteries', human remains tended to be located in specific areas away from habitation; although in the Early Iron Age they were more frequently in the perimeter areas of a settlement, in the Late Iron Age they were more likely to be found in pits inside the settlements.

All that was to change with the coming of Rome. Roman burial practices were regulated by law and custom, and came to be adopted throughout the empire, often surprisingly quickly. Formal or dedicated burial grounds became the norm, following the Roman practice of locating them outside the towns, alongside the major roads to settlements or army establishments. At the time of the Conquest, the dominant Roman rite was cremation, and this continued in Britain, spreading to areas previously practising inhumation but now under Roman influence. In some rural areas and smaller settlements, however, inhumation continued (Philpott 1991: 8). The Durotrigian site of Jordon Hill is an example of an early Roman cemetery which contained both cremations and inhumations.[29] Some of the inhumation burials contained hobnails, a feature which will be discussed below.

The arrangement of the body in an Iron Age inhumation varied to some extent, but burials were more often than not oriented north–south. The body was frequently placed on its side in a crouched or foetal position, although examples of extended burial in the Iron Age are also known.[30] Any dug grave was a simple affair, but occasionally, as in the south west, graves lined and covered with stones might occur. There were even a few instances of coffins (Whimster 1981: 43; Philpott 1991: 53), but, as far as is known, no sarcophagi or mausolea. Iron Age Britons relied on the barrow for 'status' burials. Cremations in the south east, of the so-called 'Aylesford Culture', probably reflect direct influences from the continent (and thus, indirectly, Roman influence) from about 50 AD, rather than a native tradition,[31] but others in the south and those in the north may be considered to represent a native rite. In practically all cremations recorded from the Iron Age, the human remains were buried in pottery vessels. This is, of course, not to suggest that most Iron Age cremations used urns. Many more cremated remains must have been buried without such a vessel, the bones collected and interred in a cloth, basket or skin, nothing of which remains. The discovery of such burials is even more fortuitous than the finding of an urned cremation.

The burials from the Roman period are, undoubtedly, much easier to find and to recognise. Not only might cemeteries be looked for in obvious locations along major roads, but many more burials occurred together. Cremation was not replaced by inhumation until the second century, so the effects of Romanisation on actual burial practice would not be immediately apparent. Once inhumation again became common, from the mid-second century onwards (Philpott 1991: 57), the most obvious changes from the Iron Age were in the position of the body, in the use of coffins and sarcophagi for interment and the use of tombstones to mark the grave. The change from crouched to supine and extended did not occur overnight: the late-first-century inhumations at Jordon Hill, for instance, were crouched, and such burials occurred sporadically even up to the end of the Roman period. In some areas where the rite had not changed to cremation, crouched burials now became extended (Philpott 1991: 223). Specific orientation was not as apparent, but there was still a preference for north–south. West–east became more common in the fourth century.[32]

The move to coffins would seem to be a natural progression from the urned cremations of the previous century. Coffins were made of planks nailed or pegged together. The latter type would have been that used in the few attested Iron Age examples (see above). In Roman times it is likely that most burials in urban cemeteries, at least, were in coffins,[33] although in the fourth-century west–east cemetery at Ashton, Northants, biers may have been used, first to transport the deceased to the burial ground, and then to act as a cover for the grave. The more elaborate burials, in stone or lead coffins or sarcophagi, were mostly restricted to the towns, presumably status symbols of the more wealthy members of the community. There was a slight trend noted earlier (Chapter 5) to uncoffined burials or burials in hollow logs in the last decade or so of the Roman period, but this was probably due to the increased poverty of the inhabitants rather than a change in burial practice.

If we are looking at this point in the discussion for evidence of an *interpretatio romana* in Romano-British burial practices, it is somewhat difficult to find. Certainly the introduction of formal burial grounds was a Roman innovation, but that can hardly be said to constitute the absorption of Roman beliefs. There were, after all, plenty of examples of communal burials from the Iron Age. Other practices, such as cremation, and later supine and extended burial and the use of coffins, were not unknown in the pre-Roman period. Again, a general move to those rites cannot demonstrate a change in belief. The move away from cremation to inhumation occurred throughout the Roman Empire, and no eschatological reason can be advanced for such a change.

The introduction of tombstones is important, not only for the stones themselves, which proclaimed to all and sundry the Romanisation (and presumed wealth) of the deceased, but also for what they might tell us of the deceased. Unfortunately, tombstones for civilians set up by civilians are rare in Roman Britain, and those which record dedications are usually only to the gods of the Otherworld. It is, however, significant that these tombstones come from highly Romanised areas or those with a strong military presence. Two inscriptions which may be positively identified as native British are of particular interest. *RIB* 621, found at Templebrough fort, Yorkshire, reads: 'To the spirits of the departed: Verecunda Rufilia, a tribeswoman of the Dobunni, aged 35; Excingus, her husband, from his own resources set this up to his beloved wife.' *RIB* 639, from Ilkley, also in Yorkshire, reads: 'To the spirits of the departed: Ved[.]ic[..], daughter of . . . , aged 30, a tribeswoman of the Cornovii, lies here.' Both these tombstones are for members of tribes which were friendly to Rome, the Dobunni certainly and the Cornovii probably having been among the eleven kings who submitted to Rome in AD 43.[34] The implication is that at some time after the Conquest the families of the dead women had adopted the Roman custom of providing tombstones for graves. It may be also that they saw no problem in dedicating them to Roman gods, but to what extent this involved belief, rather than custom, cannot be said. It is also pointed out that the letters 'D M' occur on two tombstones, one from Brougham (*RIB* 787) and the other found at Carlisle (*RIB* 955), believed by some to be Christian. Such a legend may well have lost its meaning over time.

The evidence so far is, therefore, best interpreted as examples of the dominance of Rome and the adoption of Roman methods of organisation and standardisation of burial practices. We must look further for genuine syncretism in Romano-British burials.

If there is to be evidence of a change in religious beliefs, or absorption of those of another culture, there is greater likelihood that it will be manifested in the more private aspects of burial, in the grave furniture found with the dead. Even then this will not necessarily reflect the religious beliefs of the deceased, but rather those of the relatives or friends who buried them. But grave goods can at least be a pointer.

In contrast to the wealth of the spectacular 'king's' and 'queen's' burial of the Arras culture, most Iron Age graves were furnished modestly, if at all. Studies such as those by Whimster (1981) and Woodward (1992) show that grave furniture, where it was present, might include pottery vessels (which presumably held food or drink), weapons, jewellery, various equipment and utensils, or joints of meat. One or two items seems usual. Occasionally the body was interred with a whole or partial animal, such as a dog or horse.

Following the conquest of Britain, cremation was widely adopted until the middle of the second century, but grave furniture did not appear to undergo dramatic change. With only a few exceptions, all types of grave goods from the Iron Age can be paralleled in the Roman period, even if occasionally of more exotic material and of higher aesthetic value. In his detailed study of Romano-British burial practices Philpott (1991: 191) lists items which he sees as peculiarly Roman: small glass perfume phials, phallic amulets, lamps and coins. To these may be added combs and figurines of deities (J. P. Alcock 1980). A study of these in Romano-British graves might be made with profit.

Glass vessels in pre-Roman burials were rare, and confined to the cinerary urns in wealthy cremations of the Welwyn type of La Tène burials. In the Roman period glass containers as grave furniture continued to indicate status burials. The small phials (*unguentaria*) which occur in the Roman period soon appeared in cremations in areas which had the earliest contact with Rome, and later in inhumations, their deposition declining up to the fourth century (Philpott 1991: 116, Tables A8 and A29).[35] If, as is thought (J. P. Alcock 1980), these phials contained perfume, oils or other substances used for anointing the body (or sprinkling over cremated bones),[36] then we have here an undoubted example of a burial rite which was very quickly adopted by wealthy Romano-Britons and which may have reflected some new or more sophisticated religious belief. The distribution of graves containing the phials was the same as for glass cinerary urns, almost exclusively the south-eastern part of Britain. Around fifty cremations from the mid-first century to the beginning of the third have been found to contain the phials, and half of these come from Colchester. They were much rarer in inhumations. Philpott lists only thirteen examples from the second to the fourth century. Two points are significant: first, these *unguentaria* were found in graves which, from other indicators, were of the more wealthy members of the population; and, second, they were restricted to military locations and to those areas of Britain which had had long contact with the Roman world.

A similar point with regard to distribution might be made regarding the phallic amulets which Philpott sees as a Roman introduction into Romano-British burials. They are very limited in their distribution and also few in number. There is no doubt that the phallus was a symbol of fertility and good fortune for the Romans. Three inscriptions, *RIB* 631, 872 and 983, all from military locations, have phallic references and depictions. One (*RIB* 983) quite clearly demonstrates the belief in the talismanic properties of the symbol: *{I}NVIDIO {S}IS MENTVLA* – 'A phallic charm against the envious'. The occurrence of phallic amulets in Romano-British graves at military locations or highly Romanised centres such as Colchester is, therefore, not surprising. What is surprising is their rarity. Only five are known from Romano-British burials: two of these are from the graves of children.[37]

More common are lamps in graves, but even they are not found in burials after the early third century. Most of those from cremations come from Colchester, Chichester and Southwark (Philpott 1991: 191–3). The decline in the use of lamps in burials seems to have coincided with the reintroduction of inhumation. The interruption to trade in the third century may have accelerated the decline, with the unavailability of imported pottery and oil.

Coins, on the other hand, were available and circulated until the end of the Roman period, although no new bronze coins were brought into the country after about 402. They were found in a handful of cremations from the pre-Roman period, but these are probably best regarded as grave goods with no specific religious significance. With the coming of Rome, coins were found in cremations and burials throughout Britain, the earliest being with burials which were almost certainly connected with the army. In the second century, however, they were found in non-military zones, in native cremations and inhumations. It seems that the practice of placing Charon's fee with the burial had been adopted by ordinary Romano-Britons. Although there were fewer coins in graves in the third century, there was a resurgence of the practice in the fourth, especially from about mid-century (Philpott 1991: 226). Most of the coins recorded from inhumations have been found in the mouth, or in a position which indicates that originally the coin had been placed there. They have been found in the mouth even in cemeteries which are very likely Christian: Icklingham (one instance) and

Poundbury (twelve).[38] Coins were also placed on the chest, as at
Butt Road, Colchester; over the eyes, at Bath Gate, Cirencester; in a
group which suggests that they may have been in a purse or bag, at
Ancaster (Watts 1991: 67); or apparently, as in a number of examples, tossed into the grave or in its fill. The persistence of coins in
graves, particularly the insertion of coins in the mouth, over the
whole of the Roman period suggests that this was a Roman ritual
adopted by ordinary Romano-Britons. Once again, we cannot say
with certainty that there was belief associated with ritual but, given
its long and consistent history in the province, we should perhaps
on balance accept the practice as a genuine instance of absorption of
Roman belief. It may be that the increase in the practice reflected
an anxiety about the future as a result of the political and economic
problems of the second half of the century (J. P. Alcock 1980). In
view of the examples from presumed Christian cemeteries in
particular, it was probably a form of double insurance, to ensure a
happy afterlife in one form or another.

The presence of statuettes of classical deities was, unlike that of
coins, a rare occurrence in Romano-British burials. Most of the
small pipeclay figures of pseudo-Venus known from Britain come
not from graves but from *aediculae* in private shrines. Those found
in graves were at Carlisle, Verulamium, York and at St Paul's Cray,
Kent, and partial figures were found with human bones in an
amphora at Hawkedon, Suffolk (J. P. Alcock 1980).[39] They were
made in the first and second centuries in Gaul or Cologne (B. Jones
and Mattingly 1990: 285). They are also found in graves in Gaul. It
is believed that the images represented a fertility goddess with
protective powers in the Otherworld. Other deities represented in
graves included Hercules, at Colchester and York, and possibly
Minerva, at Canterbury (J. P. Alcock 1980). The practice clearly
was very restricted.

A further grave deposit is dealt with here as one introduced
during the Roman period: the bone or wooden comb. The subject
has been discussed in some detail above (Chapter 4); suffice to reit-
erate that there are no known examples of combs in Iron Age
burials, either in Britain or Ireland, and that the deposition of
combs specifically as grave furniture seems to have developed in the
fourth century. It is argued that the practice was Roman, rather
than Celtic, and may even have had some connection with the cult
of the Magna Mater.

We have, up to now, looked at the incidence of grave goods
which appear to have been introduced after the coming of Rome

and which it is reasonable to attribute to Roman influence. Most were very restricted in distribution and in number, but another type of grave furniture, attributable to Celtic beliefs, was much more common and widespread. Footwear containing hobnails ('hobnail burials') occurred in cremations and inhumations from early in the Roman period, and the practice continued throughout the Occupation. It might have been thought to be a Roman innovation, except for the fact it is not found further east than Gaul or Germany. In the absence of evidence to the contrary, one can assume that it followed a native tradition which was archaeologically unde-tectable before the introduction by the Romans of shoes or boots with hobnails. From the excavations at Bar Hill (Robertson *et al.* 1975: 58–92) it is clear that not all shoes even in the Roman period were made with hobnails. Many more burials probably occurred where footwear was worn or placed by the feet of the deceased. The practice of depositing footwear in burials was widespread, but generally more common in rural than in urban cemeteries or at military sites (a notable exception being Lankhills cemetery at Winchester). It has been seen as evidence of pagan belief (Watts 1991: 70–1) and is very rare in putative Christian cemeteries. The persistence of the practice throughout the Roman period in some ways compares with and balances that of coins in mouths, a Graeco-Roman practice (above). As might be expected, a distribution map concentrates burials with hobnails in the central south and west, from Gloucestershire to Dorset, whereas the coin burials are spread further to the east (Philpott 1991: Figures 28 and 34).[40]

The Celtic influence also accounts for the incidence of decapitated burials in Roman Britain and for its increase in the late period. The rite was treated in detail in Chapter 4, where it was shown that it originated in the Iron Age and occurred sporadically through the Roman period until a resurgence in the fourth century. The practice continued into the sub- and post-Roman period. It was found in about 2.5 per cent of all Romano-British cemeteries, which compares with about 3 per cent in the Iron Age (this latter figure is based, it is admitted, on very imprecise and limited data; see above, Chapter 4). The location of most decapitated burials was rural and non-military (Philpott 1991: Figure 23). It is of interest that there are very few known examples from Kent,[41] where cremation was practised from an early date and was perhaps an intrusive rite.

Syncretism in religious art

Clearly, the coming of Rome to Britain had more influence on some aspects of religion than others. It had a considerable impact on the religious art of the native inhabitants. Henig (1995: 91–102) has demonstrated the vitality of Romano-British work during the Occupation, attributable, one would imagine, to the new skills and techniques brought in by the immigrants. Of art that was specifically religious in intent, a fair number of small pieces have survived. Two of the best examples are the Foss Dyke Mars, a bronze statuette commissioned by the Colasuni brothers, Bruccius and Caratius, and executed by one Celatus (*RIB* 274), and the Gosbecks Mercury (Henig 1995: Figure 60). Large sculpture had less chance of survival from the Roman period, but one of the most important finds has been made recently: the oolite limestone figure of Mercury, from Uley. This sculpture, probably of second-century date, was broken up some time after the fourth (see above), but much, fortunately, was preserved. It is almost certainly of native craftsmanship (Henig 1995: 99).

In between these fine examples of the craft of the Romano-British artisan and the crude representations of deities on some of the votive plaques mentioned earlier is a whole range of artefacts with a religious purpose. They are of varying degrees of artistic merit, but all have in common the influence of Rome. In the interests of brevity, only a couple will be used to illustrate further this influence on native religious art.

The first type of object is the sceptre head, usually in bronze and in the Roman period frequently depicting a deity or the head of an emperor, probably the current one.[42] It is almost certain that sceptres were not a Roman introduction. The sceptre binding from Farley Heath (Goodchild 1938) and, more recently, the remains of sceptres from Wanborough (O'Connell and Bird 1994) reflect an earlier tradition: for instance, a sceptre binding was found in the Iron Age Llyn Cerrig hoard at Anglesey (Lewis 1966: 137). The artwork on the Farley Heath binding is primitive and clearly native work, but the later sceptre heads are Roman in inspiration, if not in execution. They are believed to have had a connection with the Imperial Cult, representing the 'incorporation of an imperial element into the rites associated with a Celtic deity' (Fishwick 1988: 400). At the same time they illustrate a Roman rendition of a Celtic form.

This same blending of Celtic and Roman can be seen in the

depictions in stone of the Deae Matres, although the syncretism is a little more complicated. The Matres were Celtic goddesses, but not, apparently, native to Britain. It is likely that they were brought to Britain by the army. They would have been readily accepted by Romans in Britain, since the Romans themselves were already familiar with the concept of triple goddesses such as the Fates (M. Green 1989: 190), and by the native Celtic people, to whom triplism was a common feature of religion. A number of inscriptions are dedicated *DEABUS MATRIBUS OLLOTOTIS* ('to the Mother Goddesses from other folk')[43] or *DEABUS MATRIBUS TRAMARINIS* ('to the Mother Goddesses from over the seas'),[44] as well as more commonly *DEABUS MATRIBUS*. There is also an inscription, probably of the third century, by a government official at Winchester to the Mother Goddesses of Italy, Germany, Gaul and Britain (*RIB* 88). This suggests that by the mid-Roman period the goddesses were established in Britain. This is borne out by almost twenty stone reliefs of them found in a civilian context. The distribution map for the cult shows that, while the inscriptions come mainly from the military areas, including York (i.e. by soldiers from beyond Britain), most of the iconographic evidence is from the west, north of the Severn estuary and in the Cotswolds. The cult was also represented at London (B. Jones and Mattingly 1990: Map 8.19). It has been suggested, on the basis of the lack of refinement in the workmanship of the sculptures, that worship of the Matres was not a focus of the upper classes (M. Green 1989: 198–9). If that were the case, it would be an example of the adoption by the ordinary folk of an imported deity and of a new religious art form. The idea of ordinary folk as patrons of art seems unlikely, however. A more likely interpretation is the lack of accomplished craftsmen in that part of Britain at the time.

Even within the limits of the examples given here, we can see that there was a change in religious art with the coming of Rome. Greater technical skills, a longer tradition of anthropomorphising representations of deities, and new media and subject matter all contributed to a different form of art in the Romano-British period from what had been produced before. While the purpose of art in religion did not change, since it was still to produce objects of worship or votive offerings to the gods, it now reflected the religious traditions of Rome rather than of Iron Age Britain.

We now return to the original question posed in this chapter: an *interpretatio romana* or an *interpretatio celtica*? As was suggested at the outset, the reality is probably somewhere in the middle. There is no doubt that syncretism occurred. In temples, inscriptions and art there is clear evidence for the influence of Rome, but often the evidence is limited to areas where Roman influence was greatest, and to the wealthiest members of the Romano-British community. It does appear, moreover, that this was only a change in the visible aspects of religion and not necessarily the blending of beliefs. The evidence from the cemeteries was more equivocal. In the move to inhumation, coffins, extended burials and tombstones the change was again only cosmetic. In grave goods there seemed to have been a fusion of beliefs in the adoption of some Roman forms. At the same time, however, Celtic grave deposits continued, even in the same graves as the new Roman rites. The answer may be in the growing tendency towards grave goods of a personal nature. Perhaps the introduction of these items and the inclusion of coins in the grave had something in common with hobnailed and decapitated burials, and also, at temples, with the depositing of votive tablets and personal objects by the ordinary Romano-Britons. They all point to a view of religion which had become more 'self'-centred, a view that perhaps the god/s might identify objects with persons, and that one's afterlife might be made more comfortable and agreeable with certain rites performed and certain promises made. All this suggests a higher degree of sophistication in religious belief, for which Romanisation was probably responsible; but it is doubtful that the basic concept of the relationship of religion to self had altered. Roman customs and trappings were introduced which might make the path through life and the hereafter easier: by the late fourth century there may have been a genuine fear for the future. For most Romano-Britons, however, beliefs had not undergone any real change. This came only with Christianity. For those who did not convert to Christianity, although their religion became culturally Roman it seems to have remained ethnically Celtic.

7

CHANGE AND
CONTINUITY

The fourth century was, for Roman Britain, a period of dramatic change. For religion, the changes were equally dramatic. In the first decade of the century the scene presented would have been of bustling towns focusing on Roman-style fora, and temples to Roman, Celtic and more exotic deities reflecting the cosmopolitan composition of the towns and the Romanisation of the local inhabitants. In the countryside, where the bulk of the population lived, the ordinary Romano-Briton worked the land, tended his few stock, paid his taxes to the local *decuriones* and, apart from these financial demands, was probably little affected by events even in his *civitas* capital, let alone by what was happening in Rome. He would have had some awe for the Romano-Celtic temple built by the local grandee, but undoubtedly still more fear of the spirits which lived at the place, and in the groves and streams which formed part of his own limited landscape. He would expect, at his death, to be buried in the local burial ground if there was one, or in the rear of his plot of land or other convenient place. His relatives would bury him in the way his father and grandfather had been buried, with, perhaps, some of the rites brought in by the Romans for good measure.

Let us now move on a hundred years, where the picture is one of towns with population depleted, fora overgrown with weeds, and commercial life all but extinct. The temples are gone and Christian churches have appeared, but these are not as numerous or as opulent as the temples had been. Some of the old superstitions remain. In the country the poor man still works his land or that of his rich neighbour and pays his taxes, still in kind, perhaps even now to a local overlord rather than to Rome. The temple once held in awe is a grass-covered ruin, but the spirits still dwell there and need to be propitiated. No building is necessary for this. The Christian God might be the religious focus for some of the locals, but that religion has waned in popularity over the last few years. This native Briton follows the traditions of his ancestors. Death is always around the corner, and he intends to direct his relatives to bury him as his fore-fathers were buried. But he would not mind if they were to include some of the burial practices brought in by the Romans; and some of the old Celtic rites might be included, even though their origins have been lost in the mists of time. They still seem important, and will be good insurance: even more so now, perhaps, when his familiar world seems to be disappearing and he does not know why.

These two composite scenes illustrate the changes and the conti-nuity in religion in Britain at the end of Roman occupation.[1] The situation had progressed from one where the pagan cults prolifer-ated and Christianity was a proscribed religion to one where Christianity was the religion of the state and the pagan cults were proscribed. Yet, despite imperial patronage and laws, when the Romans left Britain the Christian religion was not in the position it was elsewhere in the empire and paganism had not been eliminated.

An attempt has been made in this study to determine what caused the changes in religion in this important period of Romano-British history. The most radical change to the status quo was in the position of Christianity. Its introduction into Britain is unlikely to have been seen as particularly radical, however. It is more likely that it was regarded as merely another religion brought into Britain by the Romans and, after 313, favourably treated by the imperial court. Nevertheless, in view of such patronage, it was adopted by leaders in the towns and countryside and by ambitious army generals. Given the circumstances in other parts of the empire, especially Gaul, Christianity might have become the dominant reli-gion of Britain by the end of the century. It did not, and it is clear that there were a number of factors which contributed to this.

The most important was the revival of paganism in and following the reign of Julian. Julian's reign was too brief for his policies to have had immediate effect on Christianity, but his Christian successors did not legislate against the enemies of Christianity as the sons of Constantine had done. As a result, in the period from 360 to 391 Roman Britain experienced a resurgence of paganism which had the effect of slowing the growth of Christianity and, in some places, of causing it to be abandoned. In Christian cemeteries pagan practices crept back in, covert and inconspicuous, but nonetheless a threat to the unity of the Church. In the pagan cults the revival was evident in the restoration of existing temples and the building of others, in new cults and in a resuscitation of old Celtic rites. Apart from the legislation of Theodosius, there was little to hinder the movement back to paganism. There was not, as in northern Gaul, a Martin of Tours, who spent fifteen years of his life attacking pagan cults, destroying temples, burning groves and, significantly, setting up an elementary parish system for the Church.

There were inherent weaknesses in Christianity in Britain in the fourth century. One of the most serious was the absence of a well-developed parochial system. It cannot be doubted that Christianity initially had considerable appeal to the masses, as it had elsewhere in the empire; but the demands of the religion on its adherents were great, and its popularity waned without the reinforcement of a well-organised Church structure. Nor would the disrupting events of the second half of the century and the declining economy have given rise to confidence in the new God of the emperors: salvation of the soul in an afterlife was perhaps not as important as survival in this life. The old religions had served the needs of the people well enough in the past. For many they continued to do so.

Other reasons suggested for the failure of Christianity in Roman Britain include a certain 'paganisation' of the religion as a result of church authorities ignoring or conniving at pagan practices which crept into Christianity. This may, perhaps, have made it more acceptable to the masses but in turn weakened its hold. The withdrawal of the Roman army and then the Roman administration would have had a marked effect. The absence of such patronage when Christianity was not yet fully established meant that the Church there was bound to crumble. The barbarian invasions also contributed to the problems of maintaining order and disrupted life (and religion) in both town and country. Without the backing of the imperial house and the imperial army, Christianity in the end was unable to defeat the old Celtic traditions.

During the last decades of the Occupation, the fate of Romano-British religion was to a large extent determined by external political events. The pagan Arbogast had had considerable influence over the young Valentinian II, and ultimately held sway in the western court of Eugenius in the years 392–4. It is easy to see how paganism in Britain initially escaped the force of the legislation of 391. After Theodosius' death the laws closing the temples and banning pagan cults were reinforced by his sons, yet Christianity did not recover its momentum. Stilicho, *de facto* ruler of the West from 395, was preoccupied with the barbarian invasions in Italy and with a struggle with Arcadius, Emperor of the East. Enforcement of the laws regarding religion in distant Britain would not have been high on his priorities. After the inept Honorius became sole ruler in 408, Stilicho was arrested and executed. Any hope of reinforcing Christianity in Britain would by now have gone. The pagan cults, although proscribed, continued in the countryside, where some temples yet stood. Elsewhere, and even in the towns, covert pagan observances continued at sacred places.

Political events outside Britain were also responsible for the piecemeal removal of the army and the subsequent impact on the Romano-British economy. The economy had already been in decline early in the second half of the fourth century. The effect on Christianity became apparent in the lower standard of church building and decoration, and poorer burials in cemeteries, in a number of cases uncoffined. Because the towns were early victims of the economic decline it is certain that the numbers of Christians were reduced as the population dispersed into the country, since Christianity had always been strongest in the towns. Its fate seems to have been shared by other imported religions. While Mithraism was probably all but extinct in military areas from the time of the conversion of Constantine, the cult may have had a longer, poorer life in London until some time in the second half of the fourth century; and at Verulamium, although members of a guild of Cybele carried out their fraternal obligations in the cemetery at Dunstable until around 400, there was no longer any temple honouring the goddess. Undoubtedly poverty as well as the pressures from Christianity had had their effects. For the native cults, a similar decline of temples and shrines is observed, but a building was not necessary for the spirits of the place, and the impact on paganism would have been less.

It is clear that Christianity, despite its privileged position by the end of the century, had not made the advances that it had elsewhere in the empire. There were, it is concluded, several contributing factors, not the least being the strength of paganism in Britain. The continuity of the native pagan cults is indeed an outstanding feature in any survey of the religions of Roman Britain. Many of the Romano-Celtic temples which were constructed during the Occupation have been found to have Iron Age origins. At some, perhaps many, sites this 'tradition of sanctity' (Lewis 1966: 50) extended into the sub- and post-Roman period, long after the buildings themselves were derelict and supposedly deserted.

This continuity is also demonstrated in pagan burial customs, where the practice of decapitated burial, originating in the Iron Age and relatively rare in the early Roman period, was revived in the second half of the fourth century and went on well into the Anglo-Saxon period. The reverence for the head as the source of the soul and perhaps the belief in the transmigration of souls after death had a long history in the Celtic world. Archaeological evidence shows that the importance of the head had been transmitted through the ages.

Such transmission raises the question of 'by whom?'. We can glean from the classical sources that the Druids were the custodians of Celtic religion, traditions, history and philosophy;[2] and, while the Emperor Tiberius had taken steps to abolish the Druids as a class in Gaul and Claudius supposedly destroyed their cults, there is a sizeable corpus of material from the first century up to Diocletian to confirm that Druids and 'Druidesses' (or women prophets) continued to exist and to have a role in religion.

Pliny tells us that in his time (he died in AD 79) Druids were still very numerous in Britain (*N.H.* 30.13). When Suetonius Paulinus invaded the sanctuary on Anglesey in AD 60, he slaughtered the Druids and their women prophets. But neither of the accounts of this event (Tacitus *Ann.* 14.30; Dio *Epit.* 52.7) implies that Druids elsewhere – and as a class – were abolished. It is reasonable to assume that, while their more savage practices would not have been tolerated under a Roman administration, they might have continued in their priestly role. Mention has already been made (Chapter 6) of links between the ritual objects of the Iron Age and the Roman. In rural areas where objects such as crowns and sceptres have been found at temple sites (such as Cavenham Heath, Hockwold and Wanborough) the involvement of Romans in Romano-Celtic cults is unlikely. What is likely is that the priests were also Druids, custodians of the old traditions and secrets. These may have been taught by father to son, as in Ausonius' *Commemoratio Professorum Burgidalensium* 4.7–10 and 10.22–30, and still earning for the priest the respect of the community, as the Druids before them.[3] The forces of change were not as strong as those of tradition, and many aspects of the Celtic religion were retained long after the conquerors had departed.

A study such as this should be the vehicle for pointing the way to areas of future research. Perhaps the most fertile field will be in studies of Romano-British cemeteries. With access to the reports on Poundbury and Butt Road, Colchester, the imminent release of the Cannington report and, it is hoped, publication of the cemeteries at

Ashton and Ancaster, there is opportunity to look at the continuity of Christian burial practices into the Dark Ages. With the addition of these alongside the Lankhills volume and other earlier works, comparative studies in Romano-British burial practice, orientation, ritual or grave goods might be carried out (beyond that already done by Robert Philpott). At the same time, physical aspects of Romano-British society can be examined: studies of cemetery populations in areas such as male/female/child distribution, health and disease, and urban and rural comparisons are possible. The application of DNA analysis to cemetery remains, although in its infancy, promises exciting additions to existing knowledge. All such studies have the potential to add to the total picture of the people of Roman Britain.

Research might be also be carried through to the Anglo-Saxon period, or comparisons made with cemeteries in Gaul, particularly in the northern parts. It is only by drawing together as many data as possible from as many sites as can be analysed that valid conclusions can be drawn about the development of religion in the Roman period and about the depth of native traditions.

Studies on Christianity in Roman Britain have not been exhausted, and from time to time there is a boost with the discovery of a spectacular treasure. The Hoxne hoard is one such discovery and, while interest will probably be concentrated on its numismatic aspects, the Christian elements will provide further links with continental Europe in the Roman period. It is hoped that a study of the new hoard will stimulate interest in reappraising earlier treasures, such as those from Mildenhall and Traprain Law.

Further Christian churches of the fourth century still await discovery and recognition. Recent finds in London seem promising, but archaeological evidence for Christianity in this city from the Roman period is, understandably, particularly elusive and inconclusive.

A number of Romano-British temples have been briefly reported in recent times, and these have been noted in various parts of the discussion. With the careful excavation and reporting which have now become the norm in British archaeology, to the eternal gratitude of those who analyse such reports, there is likely to be a further contribution to knowledge of the pagan cults in an aspect which has received scant attention since the important work of Lewis (1966) and W. J. Rodwell (1980).

This present study has dealt mainly with the fourth century, when the greatest changes to religion occurred in Roman Britain. A chronology for the development of Christianity was charted, and reasons suggested for its failure to achieve a dominant position in Romano-British religion. The forces of change were identified and the results assessed. It was found that both Christian and pagan religions were affected by outside influences, but that the religions of the native Britons were the more resistant and resilient. Perhaps the eminent pagan Roman senator Quintus Aurelius Symmachus should have the final word: *consuetudinis amor magnus est* – 'the love of established practice is a powerful thing' (*Rel.* 3).

APPENDIX 1

Religion and the Fasti 360–95[1]

An examination has been made of the religious affiliations of the men who, from Julian to Theodosius, occupied senior posts (Figure 8). Civilian appointments included the consuls,[2] the praetorian prefects of Italy and Africa, of Illyricum (these three often held as one prefecture), of Gaul and the East, and the prefects of Rome[3] and Egypt.[4] Then there were the *magistri militum*, either *equitum, peditum* or *in praesenti* (i.e. the general who accompanied the emperor). It is evident that from this period on preference came to be given to Christians or pagans according to the religion of the emperor. The notable exception to this later policy was the appointment by Theodosius of military commanders, whether Christian or pagan, who were best suited to lead his largely pagan armies and, in 391, of a group of pagan prefects in what may have been reaction to moral pressure by Ambrose, bishop of Milan. After 394 and the defeat of the usurper Eugenius and his aristocratic supporters, Christian appointments became the norm for civilian posts, although pagan generals continued to lead the armies on occasion.

In order to establish the policies of the emperors with regard to senior appointments and the religion of the appointees, however, it has been thought useful to begin with a brief survey of the period of Constantius' sole rule, 353–61, since many of Julian's actions were reactions to his predecessor's policies.

Initially, Constantius seems to have had a fairly tolerant view in regard to the religion of his senior magistrates and generals. He had, according to Ammianus (21.16.2–3), followed a policy of appointing only men who had served a thorough apprenticeship, either in military or civilian affairs. While he believed that military men should be subordinate to the praetorian prefects, he still appointed former *magistri militum* to the office of consul along with prefects. This elevation does not appear to have been an automatic

Year	Emperor²	Ambrose Bishop of Milan	Consuls	P/Pref Italy/ Africa³	P/Pref Gaul	Prefect Rome	Prefect Egypt	P/Pref Orient	Mag/ Milit. West	Mag/ Milit. East	Mag/ Offic- iorum⁴
360	Julian		C P	X	X	·	C	C?	C	X	P
361			X X	X	P	P?	X	P	C C?	X	P
362			X X	X	P	P	X	P	C	X	P
363	Jul/Jov		P P	X	P X	P	X	P	C C	C C	P
364	JVl/Vlns		C C	C	X	P	P X	P	C X	C C	P X
365	Val/Vlns		C C	P	X	P	X	X	C X	C C	P X
366			C X	P	C	C	X	P	C X	C C	X
367			C C	P	X	P	P	X	C X X	C C	X
368			C C	C	C	P	P	X	C X X	C C	X
369			C C	C	C	C	P	C	C C X X	C C	C P
370			C C	C	C	C	X	C	C X X	C C	C X
371			C C	C	X	P	X	C	C X X	C C	C X
372			C C	C	X	X	X	C	C X	C C	C X
373			C C	C	X	X	X	C	C X	C C	C X
374		+	C C	C	X	P X	X	C	X	C C	C X
375	Grat/Vlns	+	C C	C	X	P P	·	C	X	C C	P? X
376		+	C C	C?	C?	C	X	C	X	C C	X
377		+	C X	C	C C	X	·	C	X	C C	·
378		+	C C	C C	C C	C	·	X	X	C C	X
379	Grat/Thd	+	C C	C	C P?	C X	X X	C	X	C X X	X
380		+	C C	C X	·	C? C?	X	X	C X	C	C?
381		+	X X	P	·	X X	X	C?	C X	C	C?
382		+	X X	C X	C	C C	C?	C	C X	C C	C?
383	V2/Thd/ MagMax	+	C P	C C	X	X	X	C	C X X	C P X	C? X
384		+	P P	C P	C?	P	P	C	C P X	X	C? X
385		+	C C?	X X	C?	C	X	C	P X X	X	X
386		+	C C?	X X	C?	C	X	C	C P X X	X X X	C
387		+	C P	·	·	X	X	C	C P X X	X X X	C
388		+	C C C	·	·	X	X	P	C P X X	P X X X	C
389	Val2/Thd	+	C? X	·	X	P X	X	P	C P	P X X	C
390		+	C X	P X	X	P	X	P	P	P X X X	C
391		+	P P	P	X	P C C	C	P	P	P X X	C
392		+	C C	P	X	P	X X	C	P	C P X X	C
393	Eug/Thd	+	C C P X	P	·	P	·	C	P	C P X	C X
394		+	C C P	P	·	P	·	C	P	C X X	X
395	Theod.	+	C C	C	·	·	·	C	·	C X X	X

Figure 8. Senior Roman magistrates and their religion AD 360–95
1 C = Christian; P = Pagan; X = religion uncertain or unknown; - = incumbent unknown.
2 Emperors: Julian, Jovian, Valentinian I, Valens, Gratian, Valentinian II, Theodosius, and usurpers *Magnus Maximus* and *Eugenius*.
3 Includes Illyria at various times.
4 Combines appointments from Eastern and Western Empires.

promotion, but a reward for services. As a result, there is little evidence of religious bias in his senior appointments from the time he became sole emperor in 353 until about 356.

In 356, however, he banned sacrifice and the worshipping of images (*C.Th.* 16.10.6), and temples were closed in all cities and all places (*C.Th.* 16.10.4). While the picture is not entirely clear, this clampdown on paganism is possibly reflected in

Constantius' senior appointments. If we look at the period 353–6, the position of consul seems reserved mainly for the (Christian) imperial family,[5] although a pagan was elevated in 355, the same year he was prefect in the East. But after 356 through to the death of the emperor in 361, there is no known pagan consul. The religion of the non-imperial consuls from 358 to 361 is not known, but it is likely to have been Christian.[6]

Constantius' appointments to the prefectures for the same period were more ambivalent. Of the eight praetorian prefect appointments from 353–6, in the five cases where religious affiliations are known, four were pagan and only one was Christian. After 356, of seven office holders, there was one known pagan (Anatolius in Illyricum, 357); the others of unknown religion included two who may have been Christian (see note 6 above) and four others. Of the four prefects at Rome, there were two pagans and one Christian, while the four prefects of Egypt included one pagan and one Christian (a heretic) in the period.

This situation was to change with his successors. Where their religion is known, Julian's appointees for 361–3 were pagans, with the exception of Jovinus as *magister militum* in Illyricum and then in Gaul (Ammianus 22.3.1, 25.8.11). In 361 Fl. Sallustius and Salutius Secundus were made prefects of Gaul and the East, respectively (Ammianus 21.8.1, 22.3.1), and by 363 pagans held the consulships and the prefecture of Rome as well. In defiance of Constantius, in 360 Julian had already chosen the pagan Anatolius for the influential position of *magister officiorum* (Ammianus 22.9.8).

The pendulum was to swing in the opposite direction with Julian's successors. While the period of the Christians Valentinian I (364–75) and Valens (364–78) was supposedly one of religious toleration, it is marked by a near monopoly of the consulship by Christians. This is not as significant as it might seem since, of twenty-two consulships (excluding suffects) available in the eleven years to Valentinian's death, thirteen were taken up by the Augusti or members of their families. Nevertheless, of the remaining nine consulships, two were occupied by serving Christian praetorian prefects, six by Christian *magistri militum*, and one by a *magister militum* of unknown religious persuasion.

Most of the praetorian prefects and military leaders of this period were also Christians. Noteworthy was the indefatigable and rapacious senator Sextus Claudius Petronius Probus (cos. 371), who was in charge of Illyricum for a year, of Gaul for another year and of Italy, Africa and Illyricum for a further eight years. Other Christians in praetorian prefectures were Modestus (cos. 372),[7] in the East for four years, and Viventius, who spent four years in Gaul. The pagan Vulcacius Rufinus was in charge of Italy for the period 365–8, and another pagan, Saturninus Secundus, the eastern prefecture for two years (366–7). He had previously held that same post from 361 to 365. There are gaps in detail as regards the religion of other office-holders including Maximus, prefect of Gaul 371–6, the notorious former *vicarius* of Rome, who had been responsible for the prosecution of many senators for sorcery and adultery during the reign of Valentinian I (Ammianus 28.1).[8] In Egypt there were two pagan prefects, but the religion of the others is not known. The office of Prefect of Rome continued to be dominated by aristocratic families, both pagan and Christian. Five of the eleven prefects (the length of term varied) were pagan, including Vettius Agorius Praxtextatus and the elder Symmachus. At least two were Christians, including Quintus Clodius Hermogenianus Olybrius, one of the few urban prefects to progress to praetorian prefect and consul. There were four or five whose religion is unknown. Most of the *magistri militum* at this time seem to have been Christian; at least, no known pagan held a command in the years from 364 to 378.

The reign of Gratian (375–83) might have been expected to have revealed more tolerance of pagan officials than had that of Valentinian, given the certain influence of Decimius Magnus Ausonius[9] and his friendship with Quintus Aurelius Symmachus. Yet this does not show up in the Fasti. Perhaps the later influence of Ambrose was even stronger. Of the sixteen consulships, eleven were held by known Christians, including one by Ausonius and six by the Augusti. One of the consuls for 379, the Christian Olybrius, was at the same time prefect of the East. Another, Fl. Claudius Antoninus, had been prefect of Italy, Africa and Gaul in 376–7 prior to his elevation. His religion is not known, but he may also have been Christian, since he was connected by marriage to Theodosius. The two consuls for 383 were also *magistri militum*: one, Fl. Saturninus, was a Christian, the other, a consul in both 377 and 383, was Fl. Merobaudes, a Frankish general whose religion is not known. In the same unknown category were two prefects of Rome, Fl. Syagrius (cos. 381) and Fl. Afranius Syagrius (cos. 382), the latter holding the offices of consul and prefect concurrently. The other consul of unknown religion was an uncle of Theodosius, Fl. Eucheris (cos. 381).

In the provinces the regional prefectures seem to have been dominated by Christians, but a pagan was known to have held office in Illyricum in 381, and probably another in Gaul in 379. There are four or five years in the two western prefectures where the religion of the incumbents is not known. Those prefects were the two Syagrii and Antoninus (see above) and Proclus Gregorius, appointed by Gratian prefect for Gaul for 383.[10] In the East there are gaps for four years. Back at Rome, the urban prefecture had been held by thirteen or fourteen men during Gratian's reign: four were Christian, one pagan, the others of unknown religious affiliation. All the military commanders whose religion is known were Christian, with one exception, the competent and influential barbarian Flavius Richomeres, *magister militum* in the East in 383.

The death of Gratian in 383 precipitated a crisis. The usurper, Magnus Maximus, had been proclaimed Augustus by his army when in Britain, and proceeded to invade Gaul and cause the defeat and death of Gratian. His success had been aided by the defection of Gratian's general, Fl. Merobaudes. The remarkable appointments of the year 384 must be seen as reflecting the political tensions at the time, rather than, as would seem, a resurgence of paganism. The consuls were Theodosius' *magister militum* from the previous year, Richomeres, and the urban prefect of Constantinople for 383, Clearchus. Both were pagans. Maximus, having set up his court at Trier, appointed to the western prefecture a man whose identity and religion are not now known.[11] In the East the *magister militum* was Ellebichus, whose religion was also unknown, but the praetorian prefect was Maternus Cynegius (cos. 388), a Christian. Valentinian's appointments in the West have been seen by J. F. Matthews (1975: 179, 180) as making his stand against Gaul and Maximus, and reinforcing the legitimate imperial government. There is merit in the suggestion. While the civilian officeholders were a mixture of Christian and pagan, all were from the Roman aristocracy: Nonius Atticus Maximus, a Christian and friend of Symmachus, as praetorian prefect of Italy, succeeded in the same year by the pagan Praetextatus, and, as urban prefect, Symmachus himself. His *magister militum* of the West was Rumoridus, a pagan who would later be recalled to be consul with Theodosius II in 403.[12] Perhaps we see here evidence of the influence of Theodosius I, and of his pragmatic approach to the appointment of pagans and Christians, finding the best man for the job. It is interesting to record that the prefect of Egypt for the year was also a pagan, Optatus.[13] Egypt came under the control of the emperor of the East, who was, of course, Theodosius.

Theodosius was occupied with barbarian threats in the years

following the seizure of the West by Maximus, but it seems that, from 385 to 390, pagans as well as Christians were rewarded for their support and loyalty[14] by the most prestigious appointments. The Frankish general Flavius Bauto who, on the evidence of Ambrose *Ep.* 57, may have been a Christian, was made consul-elect for 385 along with the leading senator and pagan Praetextatus, who died before holding office. Maximus may have been given tacit recognition by Theodosius of his claim to the throne by the awarding of the consulship for 386 to his prefect of Gaul in 385, Euodius. The pagan historian and former prefect of Illyricum, Eutropius, held office in 387, and two *magistri militum* from the East, Fl. Timasius and Fl. Promotus, were consuls in 389, holding military and consular positions concurrently. Theodosius' man in Gaul in 390, the experienced Fl. Neoterius,[15] was consul with Valentinian II in the same year. The religious affiliations of these last three are unknown.[16]

There are the same gaps in knowledge for other major offices during these years. A likely Christian prefect of Rome in 385–7 was the senator Pinianus, whose son and brother were known to be Christian. The pagan aristocrat Caeionius (Rufius) Albinius held the position from 389 to early in 391, and in the intervening years the post was occupied by three different men, at least two of whom were of humble origin, and one of these an appointee of Magnus Maximus. Their religious affiliations are not known. The eastern praetorian prefects from 383 to 388 were Christians, and in 389 Fl. Eutolmius Tatianus, a pagan, replaced a Christian who had died in office. From the list of military leaders there was one known Christian general, Gildo, and two pagans, Richomeres and Arbogast. The other posts were held by Timasius, Promotus and the appointees of Magnus Maximus.

An ominous appointment in the West at this time was that of Arbogast as *magister militum* to Valentinian II. This man, like his uncle, Richomeres, was a Frank and a pagan. Richomeres was acquainted with Symmachus and Flavianus, and it was he who had recommended Eugenius, philosopher and nominal Christian, to Arbogast as tutor to Valentinian. Following the death of Valentinian's mother, Justina, around 389, the court removed to Trier and Arbogast came to dominate the young emperor. It was the *magister militum* who was responsible for the death of Valentinian, and for acclaiming Eugenius as Augustus in 392.

The year 391, like 384, produced another set of extraordinary appointments with pagan consuls, prefects (of Italy, Rome and

Constantinople) and *magistri militum*. The consuls were Tatianus, who was also still eastern prefect, and Symmachus.[17] Rome was under the control of Albinus, although he was succeeded at least as early as February by the Christian Faltonius Probus Alypius. Arbogast and Richomeres were *magistri militum* for the West and East, respectively.

It is difficult to pinpoint any single reason for these appointments for 391. Bloch (1945: 222; 1963: 197) suggests they were made under the influence of the pagan prefect of Italy, Nichomachus Flavianus, who had held his position from at least as early as August 390 and prior to that had been a member of the emperor's court as *quaestor sacri palatii*. This by itself would appear out of character for a war-hardened soldier like Theodosius. Pagan courtiers were not a novelty. Williams and Friell (1994: 66) believe that Theodosius was cultivating the senatorial aristocracy because he would need their support to ensure dynastic succession. This is, of course, true, but the focus particularly on one year for pagan appointments does not sit squarely with that proposal. J. F. Matthews (1975: 227–31) suggests that it was in response to the favourable reception Theodosius received from the senate when he visited Rome in 389 following the defeat of the usurper, Magnus Maximus. That seems hardly sufficient reason for the elevation of three of the leading pagans at Rome, one of whom, Symmachus, had only recently spoken out in favour of the usurper, Magnus Maximus. He had, moreover, never held a praetorian prefecture or been a *magister militum*: of all the consuls (apart from Augusti or their sons) in the period from 360 to 391, Symmachus is one of only three men who advanced to this position without having been a general or having been in charge of a major praetorian prefecture, the others being Eucherius (cos. 381), uncle of Theodosius, and Clearchus, the energetic pagan prefect of Constantinople.[18] This mark of distinction for Symmachus requires more study.

It must be borne in mind that Theodosius had twice been forced into a humiliating backdown by Ambrose: in June 388 over the destruction by Christians of the synagogue at Callinicum, and in the last half of 390 over the massacre of the citizens of Thessalonica. It may be that the elevation of the pagan senator (whose requests to have the altar of Victory restored had been turned down as a result of the influence of the bishop) was, for the emperor, a means of settling the score to some extent. The year 391 was the only one, apart from 384, following the invasion of Gaul by Maximus[19] in which there had been two pagan consuls since the time of Julian. A very well-known pagan as consul – in a prestigious although not powerful position – would no doubt cause discomfort to Ambrose and a certain vindictive satisfaction to Theodosius. It cannot be argued that the appointments for 391 were an indication that Theodosius had softened his attitude to paganism: the prefect in Egypt at the time was Evagrius, who had helped Bishop Theophilus destroy the pagan temples (Socrates *H.E.* 5.16.1). Certainly the anti-pagan legislation of 391 had the stamp of Ambrose's influence. Theodosius was restored to communion with the Church at Christmas 390. Perhaps the appointment of the Christian Alypius as prefect of Rome early in 391, replacing the pagan Albinus, represented a change in attitude towards (and a genuine submission to) Ambrose in matters of religion.

The remaining years of this study cover the the last-ditch effort by senatorial pagans to turn back the clock. The year 392 saw Christian consuls once more: Arcadius Augustus, son of Theodosius, and the prefect of the East, Fl. Rufinus, a native of Gaul. The latter was presumably being rewarded for his years of service as *magister officiorum* by elevation to the consulship as well as being promoted to the position of eastern prefect. But Flavianus senior continued to control the prefecture of Italy, and his son held the post at Rome, after the Christians Alypius and Philippus in 391. Richomeres was still *magister militum* in the East, and Arbogast in the West. The death of Valentinian II led Arbogast to acclaim the *magister scriniorum*, Eugenius, as Augustus, an elevation which Theodosius refused to recognise. When Eugenius declared himself and Theodosius consuls in 393, Theodosius ignored Eugenius and nominated instead his general in Illyricum, Fl. Abundantius (religion unknown). In 393 Eugenius invaded Italy with his *magister militum*, Arbogast. Meanwhile Flavianus, having been reappointed prefect for Italy, was vigorously promoting paganism. The issue was settled when the army of Eugenius was defeated by a Theodosian force in 394.

The following year saw Christians in all positions where the incumbents are known: two aristocrats as consuls, a Spaniard as prefect of Italy, an ex-*magister officiorum* in the East, and barbarians as generals. The reaction of Theodosius had been predictable: pagan senators were removed from the arena, and Christianity had triumphed.

APPENDIX 2

A lead tank fragment from Brough, Notts (Roman *Crococalana*)

Some time in the late 1970s, a metal-detector user discovered a large object in a field east of the A46, opposite the scheduled site of Roman *Crococalana* (SK837584). The object, a sheet of decorated lead (Figure 9), was subsequently acquired by the Newark Museum, and remains on display there. It was assumed that the find was part of a lead coffin, since there are other coffins from the district in the museum (A. Smith 1941; C. M. Wilson 1972). Until now no study of the piece has been undertaken.

On examination, it appears that the sheet of lead was part of a container usually categorised as a circular tank (Guy 1981). While the actual find spot is not recorded, it is likely to have been located within or near the eastern sector of the small fortified town. The close proximity of the field to a known Roman site and the similarity of the object to a number of lead tanks found in Britain make it fairly certain that it too was of Roman date, and probably of the fourth century. The decoration on the fragment can readily be interpreted as Christian. If this is accepted, then the piece is important not only in expanding knowledge of the extent of Christianity in the fourth century, but also as the first known Christian object from this part of Roman Britain.

The height of the fragment varies from 370 mm to 390 mm, with a slight tapering from right to left. The width ranges from 730 mm to 820 mm, and the thickness of the lead is 3–4 mm. A portion of the sheet which formed the base of the tank remains, and this is attached to the sides, sealed between two strips of lead. The construction seems similar to, but not exactly like, that of the tanks from Burwell and Kenilworth (Guy 1978, 1987–8).

Around the top of the fragment is a moulded band of lead 15–17 mm wide, finished with an indented lower edge. The main decoration comprises two registers. The upper is a continuous frieze of Xs

147

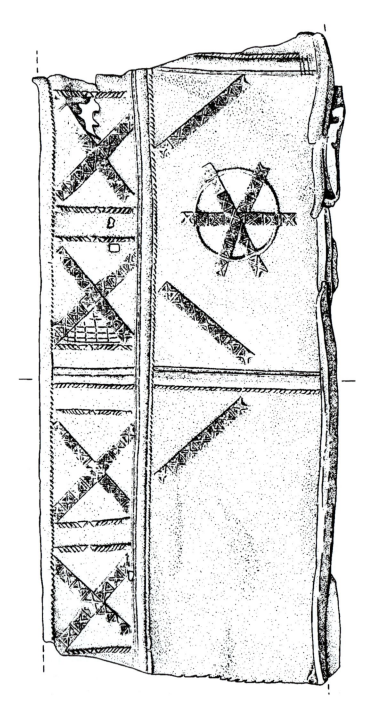

Figure 9. Lead tank fragment from Brough, Notts

in applied straps or bands, 16 mm wide, separated by pairs of narrower verticals which appear to have been part of the original moulding. The main feature of the lower register is a device consisting of a circle overlaid by an intersecting X-and-vertical. This is flanked by a pair of Y-shaped motifs with arms at an angle of about 45 degrees and the vertical extending to the same height as the arms. The intersecting X-and-vertical and the arms of the Ys are applied bands; the circle and uprights are moulded.

The decoration appears to have been carried out with care. All applied bands are themselves decorated with a scored X-and-vertical design and the narrow verticals with a rope-like pattern. Some of this decoration, particularly on the uprights of the Ys, may have been part of the original moulding, but definition of the motifs on the other verticals is sharp, suggesting that much of the decoration was done after casting. The lower edges of all the applied straps are finished with a V-shaped indentation.

There is no evidence that any violence had been used in breaking up the original vessel. The edges appear to have been cut with a sharp object, although there is some tearing and bending at the top right corner, where the reinforced edge may have made it more difficult to cut.

Eighteen or so whole or partial circular lead tanks are known from Roman Britain.[1] The height of the piece (370–90 mm) compares with the tanks from Bourton-on-the-Water (405 mm and 355 mm), Icklingham (370 mm and 330 mm), Ashton (380 mm) and Huntingdon (400 mm).[2] If these are any guide, the diameter of the Brough tank was probably in the range of 810–965 mm.

The decoration is also comparable with that found on other tanks. It does, however, have some features which are unique on such vessels, though found elsewhere in Roman Britain and in a Christian context. The X motif with separate verticals is found on seven tanks or fragments: Pulborough, Willingham, Caversham, Bourton-on-the-Water (two), Huntingdon and Ashton.[3] The last two of these have circles in the four triangles formed by the X. The Pulborough and Caversham tanks also have a chi-rho as decoration. In an earlier study (Watts 1988),[4] it was shown that the X was a form of the Christian cross, the *crux decussata* or St Andrew's cross, and that its presence on these tanks, with or without an accompanying chi-rho, was an indication that the symbol had an association with Christianity.[5]

The Y-type devices reinforce this interpretation. To date, no similar symbol has been found on a lead tank in Roman Britain, but there has been a non-functional metal object in the shape of a Y found in a grave in the cemetery at Poundbury (Farwell and Molleson 1993: Figure 83.40). This object was noted by Sparey Green (in Keen 1981: 133). In a more detailed study by the present author it was concluded that the object gave further weight to a Christian identity for the Poundbury cemetery.[6] The symbol, as it appears on the Brough tank, resembles that still found today on chasubles, with the vertical of the Y extended upwards about the same height as the diagonals. This then resembles the *orans* attitude, found in early Christian art and – most significantly for our purpose here – on the walls of the house church at Lullingstone. It was equated with the cross.[7] The Y symbol was also seen as representing moral choice, an idea borrowed from the Greeks.[8] Such a symbol, with the implication of making a choice for good or evil, would be a singularly appropriate decoration on a vessel used in Christian baptism, a religious ritual in which the candidate was asked to renounce the devil and all his works.

Although the X and Y symbols point to Christianity and may both be seen, among other interpretations, as representing the cross, it is the intersecting X-and-vertical superimposed on a circle which is clearly the central motif on the fragment. It was presumably also the focal point of the complete vessel. In Christian symbolism the device represents the initial letters of *ΙΗΣΟΥΣ ΧΡΙΣΤΟΣ* (Jesus Christ). This iota-chi (⚹) combination was probably the earliest Christian monogram, preceding the chi-rho (☧),[9] which became widely used after the conversion of Constantine in 312.

At least two inscriptions using the iota-chi monogram in place of the words 'Jesus Christ' are known from as early as the third century. The first, of about AD 270, is from Phrygia, and concludes with the words *ΕΣΤΑΙ ΑΥΤΩ ΠΡΟΣ ΤΟΝ* ⚹ – 'he will have to account to Jesus Christ'.[10] The second, from Rome, can be positively dated to 269, and includes the phrase [IN] ⚹ DN (= [IN] IESU CHRISTO DOMINO NOSTRO – 'in Jesus Christ our Lord').[11] A third example, also from Rome,[12] evidently predates the Council of Nicaea of 325 (and affirmation of the nature of the Trinity), since it reads AVGVRINE IN DOM ET ⚹ – 'Augurinus, (may you rest) in (our) Lord and Jesus Christ'.

By the early part of the fourth century the monogram had come to be used as a symbol rather than as an abbreviation (Sulzberger 1925: 397). Nevertheless it continued to be found in various parts of the empire. Later examples from Egypt[13] and Rome[14] date from the sixth and seventh centuries.[15]

The iota-chi may, therefore, be set securely within the context of Christian monograms and symbols of the third to seventh centuries. Its presence in Roman Britain on various artefacts cannot be seen as unusual. While the Brough fragment is the only known example of the use of the device as decoration on a lead tank, there are other artefacts from Britain which bear the monogram.[16] Two of these have known Christian symbols besides the iota-chi. One is an important piece in the British Museum, a pewter plate from Stamford: it has a central motif of iota-chi, encircled by crosses of the *decussata* type, palm leaves and two simplified chi-rho symbols (*RIB* II.2417.41). The other is a pottery platter from Lankhills cemetery, with an iota-chi on one side and what may be a stylised fish on the reverse (G. Clarke 1979: 430, Figure 82.256). The platter was found with burials in Feature 6, an enclosure which is believed to have contained the graves of Christians (Watts 1991: *passim*).

On the Brough fragment the prominence of the iota-chi is enhanced by the circle, over which the straps of lead forming the monogram were laid. Circles are found on a number of lead tanks from Britain, including those from Huntingdon, Oxborough, Burwell, Ireby, Wilbraham and perhaps Cambridge. The device has been variously interpreted as representing eternity, the world, the cosmos, and an everlasting God, as well as a wreath of triumph. It is found in Christian contexts, standing alone and in conjunction with another symbol. In the latter case, this may be seen as intensifying the religious significance of both symbols (Watts 1991: 163–6; Child and Colles 1971: 27).

It will thus be seen that we have considerable evidence for a Christian identity for the lead fragment and parallels from Roman Britain for the complete vessel. The purpose of these tanks has been frequently discussed,[17] and the writer has proposed that they were used at Christian baptism for performing a foot-washing ritual. For this book, however, the importance of the object lies not in its purpose but in its identification as part of a vessel decorated with Christian symbols. It adds to our corpus of similar objects in Roman Britain and to finds with a Christian identity. It also extends knowledge of the distribution of Romano-British Christianity.

Little is known about Roman *Crococalana*. It was established towards the end of the first century. Coins and pottery to the end of the fourth century have been found on both sides of the Fosse Way (Walters 1970). The town appears to have been fortified in the third

century, perhaps because of its position between Leicester and
Lincoln, and is one of only five such fortified small towns on this
section of the Roman road (Burnham and Wacher 1990: 35, 315).
The earliest known excavations were those in 1906 (Woolley 1910),
in the north-east sector of the enclosure. It is the area east of the
A46 which also yielded the lead fragment.[18] However, in view of
the threat to the scheduled site by proposed road widening, the
watching brief in 1980 and subsequent geophysical surveys in 1990
and 1991 were concentrated on the area west of the Fosse Way.

Archaeological evidence, such as painted wall plaster, imported
pottery, glass and bronzework, suggests some wealth in the town;
but in the absence of large-scale excavation at the site little can be
deduced of the activities of Roman Brough, and even less of the religious beliefs of the inhabitants.

Evidence for Christianity in the area generally is sparse. The
nearest large centre, and one with a Christian presence, was Lincoln,
about 16 km north of Brough. Ancaster, some 20 km to the south
east, had a cemetery which appears to have been Christian (Watts
1991: Chapter 3 *et passim*), and recently a fragment of a comma-
terminal implement decorated with a chi-rho was found there.[19]
The lead fragment is thus of great importance in establishing a
Christian presence in the Brough area during the Roman period. It
is the first such evidence from Nottinghamshire.

It raises considerable interest in the scheduled site just across the
A46 from the field where the object was found, and even greater
interest in the field itself. It is known that the lead coffin discovered
during the Second World War was found east of the area explored
by Woolley early this century. A geophysical survey of the field
might, therefore, profitably be undertaken.

The state of the lead fragment is also of great interest. A number
of tanks have been found in a fragmentary state only: some appear
to have been deliberately damaged or to have been abandoned in
unusual places such as wells or streams. Guy (1981: 275) has
suggested that such treatment is evidence of the revival of paganism
in the late fourth century. While the actual provenance of the
Brough find is not known, the sheet of lead appears to have been
carefully cut. It does not seem to have been subjected to violent
treatment or to the kind of damage that would be caused if the
whole vessel had been broken up for reuse of the lead. Nevertheless,
its condition could also fit the theory of pagan revival. If, as has
been proposed in the early chapters of this work, Christianity in
certain areas was under pressure as a result of the efforts of the

pagan emperor, Julian, and the policy of religious toleration of his (Christian) successors, the Brough lead fragment might be evidence of such pressure. Christians, anxious to preserve the sacred monogram on a lead tank which was no longer in use for baptisms, may themselves have cut the piece and hidden it away from pagan zealots.

Such opinion is, at this stage, only speculation. Further research and excavation may help to solve some of the problems. In the meantime, we may be fairly confident in adding the lead fragment from Brough to the list of artefacts with Christian symbols, and thus to our knowledge of Christianity in Roman Britain.[20]

NOTES

1 HISTORICAL BACKGROUND AD 294–360

1 The location of the fifth province, established 369, is a matter of dispute. See Frere (1987: 200).
2 For the view that Druidism was not completely wiped out in AD 60, see below, Chapter 7.
3 The need for Paulinus to achieve a notable victory here may have had as much to do with the success of his rival, Corbulo, in Armenia, however (Tacitus *Ann.* 14.29).
4 For a discussion on syncretism in Romano-British religion, see below, Chapter 6.
5 For thorough accounts of the period, see A. H. M. Jones (1964) and Frend (1984).
6 Maximian had been raised to the rank of Augustus in 286. The tetrarchy dated from 293.
7 E.g. Eusebius *H.E.* 8.11.1; Lactantius *Instit.* 5.11.
8 Persecution of Christians by Jews and Romans began in the first century (e.g. 1 *Peter* 7; *Acts* 7.54–8.3), the first Roman attack by Nero, in 64. Other persecutions of varying intensity were carried out in the reigns of Domitian in 96, Trajan in *c.*112, Marcus Aurelius in 177, Septimius Severus in 203 and 206–10, Maximin of Thrace in 235, Decius in 250, Valerian in 257–60, Maximin Daia in 306–9, and Licinius in 322–3.
9 Four, if one counts the *vicarius* of Africa, Domitius Alexander, acclaimed Augustus by his troops in 308–11. This revolt was put down by Magnentius, and his success may have prompted Constantine to attack Magnentius (A. H. M. Jones 1964: 79).
10 Maximin, nephew and adopted son of Galerius, had also refused the title *filius Augusti* and assumed the title of Augustus.
11 Licinius seized the European part of Galerius' territory. Maximin, as well as supporting Galerius' thrust against Christians, had also made a contribution to the advancement of the Imperial Cult. Perhaps taking the lead from the hierarchy of the Christian Church, he introduced a high priest for each city to supervise cults and sacrifice, and a provincial high priest to oversee the cities. Temples were built and sacred groves revived (Eusebius *H.E.* 8.14.9).

12 The eldest son, Crispus, had been put to death for adultery in 326.
13 E.g. state subsidies for clergy, widows and virgins (Sozomen 5.5), status in law (*C. Th.* 1.27.1), exemptions (*C. Th.* 16.2.1, 2, 21), etc.
14 See, for example, S. Clarke (1996).
15 The Brigantes had once more been subdued; however, the Romans were still engaged in pacifying the Caledonians and Maeatae north of the Wall. See Frere (1987: 155–62).
16 The date of the temple is disputed. See Fishwick (1995).
17 See Frere (1987: 70 and n. 37).
18 Known and postulated examples are limited to towns and military centres; see Lewis (1966: 57–72). Note that, with the exception of the Springhead temples, numerical identification of Romano-Celtic temples in this present work is in accordance with that used by Lewis.
19 But see now Hind (1996), who interprets the figure as Typhoeus, son of Ge (Earth), and sees him as 'a personification of geothermal activity'.
20 E.g. Cunliffe (1984: 41, 43); M. Green (1989: 155); Henig (1995: 39–40). Indeed, Lewis's caveat that 'classical architecture does not necessarily imply the worship of a classical deity' (1966: 56) is most apposite here.
21 The site of a possible classical temple at Buxton (*Aquae Arnemetiae*) was not where the Roman baths were located, but *c.*75 metres from the spring (Lewis 1966: 71).
22 So, too, King (1990), who sees the influence as Graeco-Roman. See below, Chapter 6.
23 Temple 4 at Sheepen, Colchester (Crummy 1980: 256). The sanctuary at Sheepen may well have had Iron Age origins, given its location in relation to the Roman *Colonia Victricensis* (see Crummy 1980: Figure 11.1). Moreover, the earliest phase of Temple 4 seems to have had an open-air cella (cf. Lewis 1966: 18), which may indicate some native nature deity.
24 A notable exception being Caerwent I, now shown to have been built *c.*330 (Brewer 1993).
25 This is in contrast to the situation on the continent, where Romano-Celtic temples were in decline in rural areas from, at latest, the end of the third century (Horne 1981: Figure 3.3). The survival of Romano-Celtic temples in rural areas in Britain will be discussed in detail below, Chapter 3.
26 Wait includes the temple at Bath. Examples of Romano-Celtic temples generally accepted as being built over earlier Iron Age cult structures include those at Gosbecks Farm, Colchester (Crummy 1980: 264), Frilford (Bradford and Goodchild 1939: 11–15), Hayling Island (Downey *et al.* 1980; King 1990; King and Soffe 1994), Harlow (France and Gobel 1985), Lancing Down (see Watts 1991: 114 for references and discussion), Maiden Castle (R. E. M. Wheeler 1943; Drury 1980), Muntham Court (summarised in Lewis 1966: 83–4), Nettleton (Wedlake 1982), Thistleton 1 (Lewis 1966: 84; D. R. Wilson 1965: 207), Uley (Woodward and Leach 1993), Woodeaton (Goodchild and Kirk 1954) and Worth (Stebbing 1937).

27 E.g. Colchester 2 at Sheepen (Hull 1958: 230) and Chelmsford (Wickenden 1992) with possible sacred trees, and Wanborough. The excavators of Wanborough suggest there was originally either a sacred grove or an undetected Iron Age shrine (O'Connell and Bird 1994: 134, 165). A standing stone, post or tree has been suggested as the focus for the Iron Age structure at Uley. This may have been replaced by another feature such as a water tank in the Roman-Celtic successor to the Iron Age shrine (Woodward and Leach 1993: 308, 310). Another possible shrine, built after 337, and connected with a nearby spring and a small theatre, has been proposed at West Heslerton, north-east of York (Denison 1995).

28 Formerly Springhead 1 (Lewis 1966). The revised numerical identification is given by Detsicas (1983: 60–76) in his reappraisal of the material reported by Penn in accounts from 1957 to 1962.

29 Such 'syncretism' will be discussed later in this work (see below, Chapter 6).

30 For a comprehensive study of Romano-British burial customs see Philpott (1991).

31 For a good coverage of the topic, see Harris and Harris (1965).

32 E.g. *RIB* 1545–6 (Carrawburgh); *RIB* 1599–1600 (Housesteads), etc.

33 E.g. Lewis (1966: 106); Thomas (1981: 133–6); Henig (1984: 109, 215); Richmond (1963: 210) considers that the Carrawburgh Mithraeum, at least, was destroyed by Christians.

34 E.g. *RIB* 1022, 1131, 1725.

35 E.g. *RIB* 658.

36 Ll. 1120–5, trans. M. Murray (1921: 21). The rites were performed by women crowned with leaves; they were said to dance and shout even louder than the Thracians.

37 E.g. Thomas (1981: 43); but even he accepts a Christian presence in Britain by the last quarter of the second century.

38 So Toynbee (1953).

39 See Watts (1991: 9–10) for discussion.

40 See Toynbee (1953) and Thomas (1981: 197) for discussion and references.

41 E.g. Toynbee (1953); Frere (1987: 322).

42 See Thomas (1981: 114).

43 This date is particularly imprecise, based as it is on unstratified coin evidence of Constantine and Constans (with no comment in the report on their condition), and of stratified colour-coated ware datable only to the fourth century.

44 There is only the very vague *tpq* of 'a coin of the House of Constantine I' given in the report. See below, Chapter 5.

45 Again, the dating is imprecise. D. J. Smith suggests 'not earlier than c.A.D. 315/15 and not later than c.340/350' (1963: 100–1). These dates fit into the period of the reign of Constantine and his sons.

46 Identification of this site as Christian is based on the cemetery remains, which, from the limited evidence as yet published and that generously supplied by the archaeologist (P. Leach, personal communication), generally fit the criteria for Christian cemeteries as determined by the present author (Watts 1991). The possible identification of the monogrammatic cross as a Christian artefact of Roman date is not

taken into account, nor is it necessarily endorsed. See Gibbs (1997) for details of the controversy.

47 The sites of Richborough, Lincoln, Bradley Hill, Brean Down, Lamyatt Beacon and Uley will be discussed in Chapters 2 and 3.

48 This order was lifted in the following year in respect of rural temples, the emperor recognising the traditional role such places had in the life of rural communities (*C. Th.* 16.10.3).

49 Ammianus 14.5.8 (*iustissimus rector, ausus miserabiles casus levare multorum*).

50 See below, Appendix I.

51 For an assessment of Julian's commitment to Mithraism, see Athanassiadi (1992: xiv, 52–88).

52 In 358, Julian was under the surveillance of Constantius' henchman and *notarius*, Paulus 'Catena' (Julian *Letter to the Athenians* 282C). No doubt this watch on his activities continued.

53 See Matthews (1989: 89–90).

54 To suit his dramatic purpose in justifying Julian's religious policies.

55 E.g. Firmicus Maternus *Err. prof. rel.* 28.6.

56 While such rural sites would have been spared by the revised edict of 342 (*C. Th.* 16.10.3), they would have been targets for the all-embracing edict of Constantius of 356.

57 However, coins up to Arcadius (*c.*405) were found in the latest levels (Niblett 1990). This point will be discussed further below.

58 E.g. see *C. Th.* 16.10.3.

59 Yet coins were found dating 350–402 (Ottaway 1989 and personal communication). This enigmatic evidence will be discussed further below.

60 Or as late as the last decade, when Theodosius banned pagan cults. The location would seem to support an earlier date. A further possible example is the destruction by fire of a Romano-British temple outside the city wall at the west of Roman London early in the fourth century. There is no evidence that it was deliberately destroyed, however. See S. Milne (1988) and Watts (1991: 241, n. 41).

61 Christianity at Roman Wroxeter has now had a boost with the discovery of an apsidal building, probably a church, in the town (*British Archaeology* 7, 1995). Further detail is awaited.

62 Data from a total of forty-two temple sites were examined. Seven of the temples were out of use prior to 360; the other thirty-five are analysed in detail below. See also Figures 3–7.

63 Detsicas has identified three Romano-British temples and a shrine at the site. This compares with the seven temples suggested by Penn in a series of reports from 1952–68. Temple 1 was not known to Penn. Temples 2, 3 and 10 had formerly been given the numerical identification of nos. 1, 2 and 4, respectively, by Penn and by Lewis (1966).

64 When it was in a 'ruinous condition' and given over to industrial pursuits (Detsicas 1983: 70).

65 At Chedworth, the chi-rhos and other Christian symbols on stones and altars (Goodburn 1983: plates 11 and 12; Watts 1991: 173–8); at

Harlow, a strap tag with peacock and tree of life (France and Gobel 1985: 90, Figure 119; Bartlett 1987).

66 The previous Iron Age shrine, and perhaps even the Romano-Celtic one, may have been dedicated to a thunder god. A collection of palaeolithic and neolithic axes was found, and the archaeologist sees these as archaic attributes of a thunder god, similar to Jupiter (Turner and Wymer 1987).

67 As described in Libanius Or. 18.129. See above.

68 One of the problems in studying this aspect of fourth-century religion has been the dearth of cemetery reports which identify the sequence of burial. To date, the only well-published material is from Lankhills, Poundbury Camp and Butt Road, and while a sequence for the formal cemetery at Ashton has been proposed (B. Dix, personal communication), there is very limited evidence for dating for this site.

69 See Watts (1991) for criteria for the identification of Christian cemeteries, and Watts (1993) for a detailed discussion of the west–east cemetery at Butt Road.

70 This, of course, is arguing from negative evidence. There is no archaeological evidence as yet for contemporaneous Christian cemeteries at these locations.

71 The influence of Christianity on the orientation of non-Christian burials and on the relative absence of grave goods in the fourth century is much discussed and disputed. See, especially, Macdonald (1979: 434–8) and Rahtz (1977).

2 THE PAGAN REVIVAL OF THE LATE FOURTH CENTURY AD 360–90

1 For a pertinent discussion of this term, see J. F. Matthews (1989: 425–6).

2 Paganism among the upper classes did not disappear immediately. See Cameron (1993: 75) for examples.

3 There is a considerable corpus of material on the subject. See, especially, Bowersock (1978: 79–93) and Athanassiadi (1992: 121–91) for contrasting views.

4 The deities Julian especially favoured included Mithras, the Magna Mater (Cybele) and her consort Attis, Serapis, Isis, Dionysus and Heracles, all of which had an element of rebirth or renewal in their associated myths.

5 E.g. as he saw himself in his Oratio 7 (233C–34C) when the gods told him they wanted him to cleanse the house of (the Christian) Constantine.

6 He steadfastly refused to use the term 'Christians'.

7 Although examples of torture and martyrdom are given by Socrates (e.g. 3.25) and Sozomen (e.g. 5.5), Gregory of Nazianzus, an earlier source, does not say it was a policy of Julian; and it seems that Julian took deliberate steps to avoid provoking Christians to martyrdom (e.g. Julian To Artarbius 376C–D; Sozomen 5.4), at least in the early part of his reign.

8 For a contrary view see Lieu (1989: 41).

9 A project never finished; an earthquake caused the project, headed by Alypius, to be abandoned (Sozomen 5.22).

10 As at Emesa, where all the churches but one were burnt, and the remaining building converted into a temple for Dionysus (Julian *Misop.* 357C and n. 2 (Loeb edn)).

11 Libanius saw the restoration of the temples and the old religions as symbolic of the restoration of the state (*Or.* 18.22–3).

12 E.g. at Edessa (Julian *To Hecebolius* 424C–425A).

13 So Lieu (1989: 46–50); cf. Bowersock (1978: 93), who refers to the Castalian spring at Delphi.

14 See also *To an Official* (450A–451D), in which Julian deals with a complaint of an attack on a priest, presumably by Christians. The claim was made by the high priest.

15 The same concern regarding households is expressed in a letter *To the Priestess Theodora* (Papadopoulos 2), who may have been reluctant to sell a Christian slave.

16 Pythagoras, Plato, Aristotle, Chrysippus and Zeno were acceptable reading for priests, however.

17 So, too, Gregory of Nazianzus (*First Invective* 113), where he seems to be quoting from one of Julian's regulations on public worship: a purple robe, a fillet around the head and a garland of flowers are mentioned.

18 The same found in the letter *To Arsacius*, where he points to Christians' 'benevolence to strangers, their care for the graves of the dead, and the pretended holiness of their lives' (429D) as attracting converts. He also notes that 'no Jew ever has to beg' and that Christians give charity not only to their own members, but to pagans as well (430D).

19 E.g. Julian *Misopogon* 360C.

20 See, for example, Ephrem Syrus *Hymns against Julian* 3.10 for the view that the army of Constantius was mainly pagan.

21 And following the murder Julian took rapid steps to acquire the bishop's celebrated library (*To Ecdicius* 377D–378).

22 E.g. Gaza (Sozomen 5.3; 9), which came to dominate its neighbour, the Christian city of Constantia (Majuma), in a dispute resolved by Julian.

23 E.g. Nisibis (Sozomen 5.3), which was later surrendered by Jovian to the Persians.

24 Not of the superficial nature of the people's religion!

25 E.g. see *C.Th.* 9.16.9. The laws permitting religious freedom are not extant.

26 Ammianus 30.9.5. Ammianus also relates (29.6.19) that during the reign of Valentinian the prefect at Rome restored many buildings in the city and erected a colonnade called the Colonnade of Good Success (*Bonus Eventus*), because there was a temple of that deity close by. There seems not to have been any restriction on the existence of pagan cults.

27 Valens, on the other hand, was a fierce Arian, but his persecution of Catholics was in the east.

28 For a convenient collection of the documents pertaining to the debate over the Altar of Victory, see Croke and Harries (1982: 28–51).

29 In 389 Theodosius may, however, have vented his spleen against Ambrose for the humiliation by nominating the pagan Flavianus as urban prefect at Rome for 390, and Symmachus and Tatianus, also pagans, as consuls for 391. See below, Appendix 1 for a more detailed discussion.

30 A further attempt by the Roman pagan senators in 391 to have the Altar of Victory restored had previously been rejected by Valentinian II, emperor in the west (Ambrose *Ep.* 57; Paulinus *De Obit. Val.* 52).

31 The status of patrician was, since Constantine, an honour conferred by the emperor. See A. H. M. Jones (1964: 106, 1225, n. 28).

32 However Julian, on becoming sole emperor, had begun measures to improve the standing of eastern senators. See Bowersock (1978: 72-3).

33 These included former *vicarii* and *praesides*, whose service had earned them promotion: *magistri* (both civil and military), *consulares* or *correctores*, whose appointments automatically put them into the senatorial order, and praetorian prefects, traditionally from the equestrian order. (See Ammianus 21.16.2: *nec sub eo dux quisquam cum clarissimatu provectus est. erant enim . . . perfectissimi*).

   Diocletian frequently made his prefects consuls, enrolling them in the Senate with the highest status (A. H. M. Jones 1964: 106). Although Constantine eliminated the old (Augustan) office of praetorian prefect, the new officials he created, eventually controlling four prefectures each made up of a number of provinces, were likewise elevated to the Senate while in office, and some to the consulship. The practice was to some extent continued by his sons, but with the growing threat of the barbarians, and the intense military activity of the last half of the century, many serving *magistri militum* (including a number of barbarian origin) also came to be promoted to the Senate via the consulship. This was particularly so after the death of Julian; and there seems no doubt that the Pannonian Valentinian I had no great regard for the traditions of the Senate. The office of Prefect of Rome, on the other hand, had always been the prerogative of the senatorial order. Overall, in the fourth century the lines between equestrian and senatorial orders and their traditional roles within the state became increasingly blurred.

34 So Frend (1984: 704). Croke and Harries (1982: 63) date the events to 394.

35 See Williams and Friell (1994: 136).

36 There were also old aristocratic families which were Christian, e.g. the Anicii and the Petronii.

37 Yet even he had a Christian wife.

38 In fact it has been seen (Bloch 1945: 225) as a tacit acceptance of Christianity. Symmachus says: *uno itinere non potest perveniri ad tam grande secretum* – 'not by one avenue only is it possible to arrive at so great a secret' (*Rel.* 3.10).

39 *PLRE* I (Jones *et al.* 1971). See Appendix 1 for a more detailed discussion.

40 Such as Publius Caeionus Caecina Albinus, *consularis* in Numidia about 364, and his son Caecina Decius Albinus Iunior, who held the same post some time between 388 and 392.

41 E.g. Ammianus 21.16.2. A notable exception was, of course, the struggle between Julian as Caesar in Gaul and Flavius Florentius, the praetorian prefect (Ammianus 17.3.2–6; Julian *To the Athenians* 280A–B, 282C–D). See also J. F. Matthews (1989: 88–90).

42 There are, it is true, gaps in the Fasti: names and particularly religious affiliations are unknown at various points. Nevertheless, sufficient information is available for these conclusions to be drawn.

43 But temples were not banned at this time, so Praetextatus and Symmachus were not operating beyond the law.

44 This included the temple at Lydney, but the authors note that, at the time of publishing (1979), the dating for Lydney was being revised. See below.

45 As, for example, the actions of the prefect of the east 384–8, Cynegius, at Apamaea and later Alexandria (Theodoret *H.E.* 5.21.1; Zosimus 4.37.3). The involvement of prefects or provincial governors may be implied when Libanius (*Or.* 30.13) complains, ' . . . those allies they [i.e. the pagans] might normally have had in times of trouble are responsible for their experiencing . . . outrages in times of peace' (Loeb trans.).

46 For the original publication, see Wheeler and Wheeler (1932), and for the revised date, Casey (1981). But see also S. Smith (1994) for a view supporting the Wheelers' dating.

47 E.g. Painter (1971), Thomas (1981: Figure 48), and Frend (1992).

48 Most of these have been included in Figure 4. A couple have been omitted in the light of more recent research. Additions to the list not mentioned by the scholars noted above include Brigstock 1 and 2 (Greenfield 1963: 229–40), Coventina's Well at Carrawburgh (Allason-Jones and McKay 1985), Chelmsford (Wickenden 1992), Henley Wood (Watts and Leach 1996), Lamyatt Beacon (Leech 1986), London Mithraeum (Grimes 1968), Maiden Castle circular (Drury 1980), Richborough 1 and 2 (Bushe-Fox 1932), Silchester 1, 2 and 3 (Hope 1908), Thetford (Gregory 1991: 120, 199), Wanborough (O'Connell and Bird 1994), Worth (Klein 1928) and York (Ottaway 1989).

49 The dating is extremely imprecise, as there are few coins. See Grimes (1968: 104).

50 Fortuna was a favourite deity with the army, who also related it to the Imperial Fortune (Henig 1984: 77–9).

51 About 380, although the excavator believes votive offerings may have continued beyond this date.

52 There are many difficulties in making this type of analysis. See above, Chapter 1, n. 67.

53 Burials nos. 658, 755, 756, 1071 and nos. 730 and 734.

54 See Watts (1991: 197) and references.

55 For example, Curbridge (Chambers 1976, 1978), Radley I (Atkinson 1952–3) and probably Radley II (Frere 1984: 302). See also Philpott (1991: 78–9).

56 Burials DD and II. The sequencing of burials at Dunstable is a hazardous undertaking, however.

57 There was one prone east–west burial in the main Late Roman (Christian) cemetery at Poundbury, Dorchester, but this burial (no. 1170A) was very late in the sequence (postdating two earlier burials), and was possibly from the sub-Roman period.

58 For example, at Trentholme Drive, York (Wenham 1968), Radley I (Atkinson 1952–3) and Curbridge (Chambers 1978).

59 For an analysis of Roman burials with animal remains, see Philpott (1991: 195–207).

60 See Ross (1992: 404–17) on Epona and on the importance of the horse in iconography and myth in the Celtic world, and M. Green (1989: 146–9), who gives continental examples of burial of horses.

61 A similar burial has been found at Raffin Fort in Ireland, but the animal bones have not been identified in the report (Newman 1993b: 22).

62 Stanwick has also produced an Iron Age horse mask (Ross 1967: 324, plate 81a).

63 See, especially, Ross (1992: 423–6) on dogs in Celtic mythology and iconography.

64 E.g. at Ilchester, the Late Roman cemetery at Little Spittle comprised forty-two burials, one of which was accompanied by the articulated remains of a dog, and another by the jaws of a sheep and the forelimb of a horse (Leach 1982: 88; plate 15). At Barton Court Farm, Abingdon (Miles 1984: 15–16), in a cemetery of infant burials, two were accompanied by dogs' skulls, and a third by the skull of a sheep. The excavator notes that these infants, aged from a few weeks to nine months old, were the only ones so buried: all other infants seem to have been neonates, and were unaccompanied. A further example from Oxfordshire comes from Yarnton, where, in a small Late Roman cemetery of fifteen burials, two were decapitated and a third was buried with a dog (Frere 1991: 258); and from West Ham in London (Esmonde Cleary 1994: 285) comes a brief report of a site of Roman date of three human burials together with two horses and a dog.

65 See Watts (1991) for criteria. A notable absence is that of neonate burials, but that is not surprising, given the small population of the cemetery (fifteen inhumations). The report does mention an 'infant' burial, however (Wedlake 1982: 91). An investigation of the cemetery was not a primary objective of the excavation.

66 A further example of the deterioration of control in a Christian cemetery is that of Ancaster, full details for which have not been published. See Watts (1991: 254, n. 14 et passim) for material on this site.

67 See Watts (1991: 158–73, 224).

68 Eighteen whole or partial tanks were recognised when my revised article from Antiq. J. 68 (1988) was published in Christians and Pagans in Roman Britain. Since that time another fragment has been published (Watts 1995). See now Appendix 2.

69 See Watts (1991: 172).

3 CLOSURE OF THE TEMPLES AND BEYOND

1 The official was one Chrysanthus. As noted in Appendix 1, the names of the prefects of Gaul who followed Neoterius (390) are not known, nor is his religion or that of the prefect for 389, Constantianus.

2 E.g. *C.Th.* 16.10.22 (423), 16.10.23 (423), 16.10.25 (435).

3 Pagans Hill may have been for a time converted to Christian use. The temple building continued in some role and was still standing into the medieval period. See above and references.

4 No remains *in situ* of a Romano-Celtic temple have been found by aerial survey or by excavation; however, L. Alcock (1972: 173–4) gives persuasive evidence for its existence from the late third century until the end of the fourth. Foundations and walls of a stone building were known to have survived until at least the sixteenth century.

5 A separate deposit of coins and pots was made around a pillar about 1.5 m high at the back of the *cella*. This column may have been the base for a former cult statue (Ottaway 1989), and the temple of classical plan dedicated to a Roman deity.

6 Temple 1 at Caerwent has been suggested by Lewis (1966: 51) as continuing into the second half of the fourth century and perhaps up to 400. A late-fourth-century date for the end of the temple has been confirmed by recent work (Brewer 1993), but it seems very unlikely that the temple continued after 391. The broken pieces of a bronze snake and a bone bird (Ashby *et al.* 1910: 4–7) suggest deliberate destruction of the contents of the temple, as has been proposed for Silchester 3 (Hope 1908: 208–9). There is no doubt that there was a Christian presence in Caerwent: a hoard including a pewter bowl inscribed with a *chi-rho* was found in House VII N (Boon 1962). The continuation of overt pagan practices in a temple so close to the administrative centre of a town after the legislation of Theodosius is unlikely.

7 So, too, Frend (1992: 127), in research independent of this present work, discussing the reasons for the popularity of the pagan cults.

8 In view of the early date of the first votive deposit at the temple site (*c.*AD 60–80), a native deity seems more likely; brooches of the same kind were still being deposited half a century later.

9 It has also been suggested that the temple may have been associated with a local river god (I. A. Richmond, cited in C. W. Green 1966: 360). In either case, a native deity is supposed.

10 Although there may have been some conflation with other deities in the minds of the supplicants. See Tomlin (1993: 115) and below, Chapter 6.

11 I have, for example, suggested (below) that the York temple may have been for the Imperial Cult.

12 This number includes individual structures at a particular location (e.g. three temples at Silchester, two at Brigstock, Maiden Castle and Richborough) but does not include Lowbury Hill and Cosgrove temples, details of which are at present very limited.

13 I.e. Bourton Grounds, Great Dunmow, Jordon Hill, South Cadbury and York; but two of these lasted only a few years after 391.

14 Although in later Irish myths this seems to have become more developed.

15 See Watts (1991: 3) for discussion and references.

16 For example, in the comprehensive study of finds relating to the cult of Bacchus in Britain made by Hutchinson (1986: 38–95), the only artefacts listed from the fourth century as found in rural areas are from Chedworth (listed under 'villas'), Lydney and Thetford. Chedworth 'villa', with its satyr-and-maenad mosaic, also had a temple, possibly to Silvanus or a similar god, in the vicinity; the complex was clearly more than a native-type religious centre, such as that at Springhead. The temple at Lydney yielded a satyr plaque and a mosaic with a central motif of a cantharus, suggesting some connection with Bacchus. But there were many syncretic elements at Lydney, and it, too, is hardly typical of a Celtic shrine. Moreover, it was, on the evidence of the finds, primarily a healing centre. Thetford has yielded the only 'rural' example of a salvation cult in Britain in the fourth century to date.

17 And its classification as a true 'urban' site is open to question. See Cunliffe (1984: 149, 178–81).

18 No evidence for pre-Roman votive activity was found at the well site itself, but I think it not unlikely that the spring had some religious significance for the native people before it was contained in a cistern and the marshy surroundings drained by the Roman army. On the other hand, Allason-Jones and McKay suggest that, while the well was designed to be purely functional, it acquired a religious significance shortly after its construction c.128–30, given the presence of 'soldiers with Celtic superstitions and beliefs regarding springs' (1985: 12).

19 The early archaeological record for the site is not available. In their most recent publication on Pagans Hill, Rahtz and Watts note 'The Iron Age and earlier aspects of the site . . . remain to be elucidated' (1989: 366).

20 Wheeler and Wheeler (1932) did not address this problem; however Woodward and Leach (1993: 305) suggest that the archaeological evidence uncovered by the Wheelers (1932: Figure 2) was that of an Iron Age shrine beneath the Romano-Celtic temple.

21 That is, cults which 'ministered to the needs of a society which continued in ways independent of the survival of Romanised institutions' (Rahtz and Watts 1979: 183).

22 If this were so, then a date for the abandonment of the temple in the reign of Constantius is highly probable. We know that the Imperial Cult continued, if in an 'emasculated form' (A. H. M. Jones 1964: 93), on the evidence of *ILS* 705 of Constantinian date; and Libanius (*Or.* 19.48–9) tells us that Constantius received with good humour news of the overthrowing of a statue of himself by a mob at Edessa.

23 E.g. *C.Th.* 16.10.11 (391): 'no person shall go around the temples; no person shall revere the shrines'.

24 Those events also show that a nominal or half-hearted Christian could readily weigh in on the side of pagans in a challenge to the existing order. See above (Chapter 2) for details of the activities of Eugenius, and Watts (1991: 147) for the suggestion that at least some members of the cult of Faunus had previously been Christian.

25 The increase in the incidence of coins in graves of the fourth century, rather than being seen as a resurgence of a Roman ritual, is attributed to the celticising of the practice. See Philpott (1991: 215-16) and Macdonald (1979: 408-9).

26 Although one might not go so far as Higham, who claims that 'British paganism was in excellent health at the end of the fourth century' (1992: 65).

27 On a suggested baptistery, as well as the font identified previously (P. D. C. Brown 1971), see P. R. Wilson (1988).

28 By the evidence of the 'squatter' phase, it could have been derelict by the late 360s, but Frere (1975: 297) considers the limited coins and pottery evidence likely to be 'irrelevant' for this phase, and suggests the church was unlikely to have been abandoned so early.

29 A number of other urban sites have been suggested as having Roman origins. See Watts (1991: 111-13).

30 See Watts (1991: Figure 28) for a map of the distribution of Christianity.

31 Thomas (1981) takes up Frend's challenge only obliquely, and looks at the period beyond 450. He questions whether it is, in fact, wholly true that Christianity did not become the predominant religion in Britain in the first half of the fifth century; he suggests that by 500, and in certain centres, there may have been more Christians than 'any one other, distinct, form of religion' (1981: 353-4). Thomas's research leads him to propose a continuation of Roman influence, and thus of Christianity, in those areas away from the Saxon invaders: Wales, the north west and south west in particular. He sees Romano-British Christianity as a casualty of the invasions and civil wars after c.450, surviving mostly in distant areas to emerge into fully fledged monasticism by the end of the century.

32 E.g. 1 Cor. 11.4-16; Tim. 2.9; 3.1-12; etc.

33 E.g. Paedagogus, especially Books 1 and 2, on eating, drinking, use of wealth, dress and appearance, behaviour, etc.

34 See below, Chapter 5, for a more detailed discussion on the economy and its effects on religion.

35 In a letter quoted by Hilary of Poitiers. See Frend (1984: 529 and references).

36 See Frere (1987: 358-9) for a convincing account of the events 408-9.

37 On the reluctance of the native Britons to embrace Roman ways, see now S. Clarke (1996).

38 It is difficult now to accept the statement by Henig that 'a large proportion of British society' was Christian by 429 (1984: 224), at the time of the visit of Germanus in connection with the Pelagian controversy.

   For comments on the likely size of the urban population of Roman Britain, see Todd (1993: 6); and for estimates, Millett (1990: 181-6), who calculates the urban population at only about 6.5 per cent of the whole.

39 On the survival of Druids, see below, Chapter 7.

40 Orosius: *Adv. Pag.* 7.34.9–10; Zosimus 4.35.2–6, 37.1–3. Theodosius did not recognise Maximus as Augustus until 386, possibly as a delaying tactic; Theodosius supported the cause of Valentinian II.

41 See Frere (1987: 354–5 and references) for the British campaign, and Williams and Friell (1994: Chapters 3 and 5) for details of Maximus in Europe.

42 Esmonde Cleary (1989: 137–8) questions the sources and details of events in Britain from 409 to 411: the revolt of the Britons in 409, the letter from Honorius in 410, and the devastation by the Saxons 410/11. He says, 'There are reasonable grounds for regarding all these references to Britain in the years around 410 as suspect' (1989: 137–8), and proposes a date of 411 for the end of Roman Britain. After this date, he maintains, there was no evidence of replacement of government officials or of the army, and no coins were shipped to Britain.

43 See Kirby (1976).

44 Bushe-Fox (1932: 7) confirms the increase in coin activity at Richborough fort between 383 and 395; the coin series ends in the time of Constantine III, who withdrew the remainder of the army to Gaul (407).

45 The names of only two are known: ?Constantianus (389) and Neoterius (390, and cos. 390); their religious affiliation is not recorded.

46 Although his mobilising an army against Eugenius and the pagan senators at Rome is testament to his continuing commitment to Christianity.

47 Not all writers believe that Magnus Maximus withdrew soldiers from Britain (e.g. Millett 1990: 215), but it does seem the logical move if he was to have any hope of becoming an effective 'emperor'.

48 E.g. re-enactments of the decrees of 391–2, *C.Th.* 16.10.13 (395), and of earlier decrees, 16.10.20.1 (415 by Honorius and Theodosius II); other decrees 16.10.14–19 (396–9).

49 The withdrawal of troops by Stilicho in 401 probably meant effectively the end of the defence of the Saxon shore (Frere 1987: 356).

50 Cf. Dark (1994: 18–21, 28–39), who maintains, without specific examples and presumably only on the coin evidence produced in 1966 by Lewis, that in the late fourth century 'urban temples survived' (p. 10) and there was a 'continued functioning of temples' (p. 21); thus although, he claims, paganism was supported by the wealthy in the towns and villas (and he gives little evidence for their decline), yet somehow 'as soon as the Roman withdrawal from Britain had occurred, Christianity seems to have become dominant' (p. 32).

51 See Thomas (1981: 240–94).

52 Cf Dark who maintains that 'to Gildas, living in the sixth century paganism was a matter of antiquity' (1994: 32). There is a tension between this and the statement by Bede (*H.E.* 1.30) that Augustine was instructed to destroy idols but to leave the temples and convert them to churches. This implies that, some decades after Gildas was supposedly writing, paganism was, in fact, alive and well in Britain.

4 FURTHER EVIDENCE FOR THE REVIVAL OF PAGANISM

1 On this aspect, see Philpott (1991: 80).
2 I.e. burial 120 at Lankhills (G. Clarke 1979) and burial AR at Dunstable (C. L. Matthews 1981).
3 In view of the difficulty of detecting decapitation in these circumstances, however, it is likely that in earlier excavations other decapitated burials of this type may have been overlooked.

  Philpott (1991: 77) gives examples from Guilden Morden and Bath Gate, Cirencester, and suggests that these were executions. This would seem to be a reasonable proposition. See below.
4 There seems to be a very thin line between burial and votive offering, and one is inclined to agree with Wait that, in some cases in the Iron Age at least, the 'final deposition is probably less a mortuary ritual than a votive or apotropaic treatment of the symbolically potent skulls' (1986: 120). See discussion below.
5 My thanks to Professor Etienne Rynne for drawing my attention to the work on Cahercommaun, Ballinlough and Raffin Fort, and to Mr Conor Newman for additional information on the Raffin Fort skull.
6 Rynne (1974-5). Raftery (1981) gives other examples of extended inhumation which may date from the first century BC; however, see O'Brien (1992), who sees the rite of extended inhumation as introduced into Ireland in the second century AD.
7 E.g. Wait (1986: 51-82) and Ross (1992: 141-3); but Branigan (1990) has now shown that the Wookey Hole material is from regular Romano-British burials.
8 See above, note 4.
9 Iron Age sites with skull burials recorded by Wait (1986: 357-84) include Fengate (Late Iron Age); Fifield Bavant: two, one without mandible (eighth/fifth century); Maiden Castle: two, one with a femur (late first century BC/first century AD); Salmonsbury (second/first century BC).
10 This deposition may have been accompanied by other bones, and therefore may not necessarily be considered in the same category as the other seven (Walker 1984: 452-3). There is no doubt, however, that the mandible was missing here.
11 This percentage is based on the figures given by Wait. It is important to note, however, that he believes that only about 5 per cent of all Iron Age burials survive (Wait 1986: Figure 4.19, p. 90).
12 I thank Mr R. A. Chambers for his generosity in supplying this detail, and particularly for the unpublished information on the skulls from Abingdon, Millstream, Horley and Stadhampton.
13 See R. F. J. Jones (1981) on burial practices in the third century.
14 And also in other parts of the Celtic world. See, for example, Wait (1995: 505) and Whimster (1981: 188).
15 E.g. Ross (1992: 98), Whimster (1981: 185-6), Ritchie and Ritchie (1995), Wait (1986: 191-209; 1995), Brunaux (1988: 109-11), Macdonald (1979: 414-19), etc.

16 Polybius 3.67; Strabo 4.4.5 and Diodorus Siculus 5.29, drawing on the lost account by Posidonius; Livy 23.24; and possibly Herodotus 4.66, if we allow that the Scythians were a Celtic-related people (but see Rankin 1987: 26–30).

17 For the importance of early Irish literature in the understanding of pre-Christian Ireland, see Raftery (1994: 13–16).

18 There are two versions of this (probably the same) story. See Koch and Carey (1995: 191–2).

19 Its final deposition in London ensured protection for the island as long as it was interred there. There is no suggestion that it was reunited with the body. See Ford (1977).

20 Koch and Carey (1995: 344).

21 As related in Ross (1992: 157).

22 On this aspect see C. Murray (1992).

23 There were also single fragmentary pelvic girdles found at Danebury, and Walker suggests these may have been deposited as 'symbol(s) of fertility and regeneration' (1984: 453–4).

24 See Harman et al. (1981: 167) for a summary of interpretations up to that date.

25 So too, Esmonde Cleary (1989: 134), who appears to see decapitated burial as linked with social stress and decline in standards in the late fourth century.

26 On burial in the classical world see R. F. J. Jones (1987), Kurtz and Boardman (1971), Morris (1992), Rowell (1977), Rutherford (1980), Toynbee (1971), etc.

27 One of the decapitated burials at Derby Racecourse cemetery had the head placed at the feet, but set between two stones (H. Wheeler 1985).

28 A likely explanation for the decapitated burials at Bath Gate, Cirencester, is that they were criminals executed by beheading. No one would welcome the transmigration of their souls.

29 I am deeply indebted to Mr Don Benson, Dyfed Archaeological Trust, for his generosity in making available to me his records on this site, for answering endless questions regarding the burials, and for organising the dating at Oxford University. My thanks also to the University of Queensland for providing the funding for the dating; to Dr Simon Mays of English Heritage for assistance in arranging the transport of the skeletal remains to Oxford; and to Mr Brian Dix for first drawing my attention to this excavation and for lively and productive discussions on the interpretation of this cemetery.

30 The pottery has, as yet, not been studied in detail.

31 Details from Oxford OXCAL: Sample 1 (burial S6), Ref. Oxa6718, 985 ±45 bp = AD 970–1170 (95 per cent); Sample 2 (burial S16), Ref. Oxa6719, 1040 ±45 bp = AD 880–1120 (95 per cent) or 880–1050 (99 per cent).

32 There are, indeed, literary references to decapitated burials in a medieval Christian context, and specifically to Church approval for the removal of the head to prevent a spirit from haunting the living. These are isolated incidents and do not relate to whole cemeteries.

(Information from Dr Elizabeth O'Brien, from her unpublished Oxford D.Phil. thesis.)

33 For criteria for the identification of Christian cemeteries, see Watts (1991).

34 My thanks to Ms Sonia Puttock, Department of Classics and Ancient History, University of Queensland, for stimulating discussions on personal ornaments in graves and for drawing my attention to the Clement of Alexandria reference to combs.

35 Philpott (1991: 268) records a wooden comb from a cremation burial in Kent, perhaps dating to the second century. All combs with inhumations that he lists are, with one exception, fourth/fifth century.

36 E.g. Whimster (1981) and Raftery (1981).

37 See G. Clarke (1979: 362) for examples.

5 THE ECONOMY AND RELIGION IN THE LATE PERIOD

1 I do not intend in this study to enter into the debate as to what constitutes a 'town' and a 'small town', but shall limit myself to generalities as far as possible, taking as my guide classifications by Wacher (1995) and Burnham and Wacher (1990). For recent discussion on small towns, see individual authors in A. E. Brown (1995).

2 This suggestion might be compared with the view that being a provincial capital actually gave a town a considerable economic boost. See details below on Lincoln, York and Cirencester, all believed to have been provincial capitals in the fourth century.

3 E.g. B. Jones and Mattingly (1990: 310), Wacher (1995: 238).

4 E.g. Colchester and Silchester (Millett 1990: 135; Crummy 1993).

5 This de-urbanisation seems to have been reflected in the pattern of food consumption. King (1991) has shown that in the late period urban bone assemblages were rather more like those at rural sites than had earlier been the case. This suggests the decline of a more organised and specialised trade, corresponding to a decline in commerce in the towns.

6 E.g. Potter and Johns (1992: 200), Dark (1994: 20), M. J. Jones (1993), Ottaway (1993: 107), Esmonde Cleary (1993), etc.

7 So Burnham (1995); cf. Millett (1990: 143–51), who believes that these centres became 'more prominent' and that 'the peak of their prosperity lay in the later Empire'. Millet does not give specific examples, however.

8 For a connection between small towns and the villas, see Todd (? 1990: 17).

9 E.g. Ilchester (Leach 1982: 12), but even here there may have been some 'continuing function' as late as mid-sixth century.

10 E.g. Kelvedon (K. A. Rodwell 1988: 136); Burnham and Wacher (1990: 317–18) give other examples.

11 One of the outstanding examples of continuity from the Iron Age through to the present day is Rivenhall, which, from the second to the fourth century AD was the site of a substantial Roman villa. See Rodwell and Rodwell (1985).

12 E.g. at Woodchester, Bignor, Chedworth and Rockbourne.

13 Black (1987: 83) has suggested that they may have been inhibited by the presence of the military at the Saxon shore forts, but this seems unlikely. A military presence would very likely have provided a ready market for produce. The Saxon threat itself may have caused instability and decline.

This decline did not necessarily extend to the East Anglian area, however. A recent brief report of a farmhouse and farm at Boreham, near Chelmsford, gives evidence of a quite wealthy lifestyle in the third/fourth centuries, even if it was not in the same class as the villas of the west (Denison 1996).

14 See de la Bédoyère (1993: 123–4) for examples.

15 For a penetrating study on this aspect of the economy of Roman Britain, see Esmonde Cleary (1989: 138–44); also Higham (1992: 51–2), de la Bédoyère (1993: 123–4), etc.

16 See Hopkins (1980) for an important study of the growth of tax in kind and its repercussions.

17 See A. H. M. Jones (1964: 460–1) for details of late-fourth-century tax arrangements. The progressive commuting of tax in kind to tax in gold does not seem to have been complete in the West until the second quarter of the fifth century, and it is likely that Britain was never fully subjected to this reform. It began in Valentinian's reign with nine months' tax in kind and three in gold.

18 For the view that the army was not a big spender, see Creighton (1996).

19 For a discussion on the effects of taxation on landholders in the fourth century, see Percival (1975: 153).

20 I have a certain sympathy with Reece's description of Romano-British towns as 'trading settlement[s] with a classical facade' (1988: 140).

21 Esmonde Cleary (1989: 130) says that there is now 'some evidence' for a similar decline in Gaul and the Rhineland.

22 E.g. Esmonde Cleary (1989: 135), Millett (1990: 196), Potter and Johns (1992: 204), de la Bédoyère (1993: 126), etc.

23 Details of this site are still to be published, and the interpretation above is in contrast to an earlier one given by the present writer (Watts 1991: 182). The size alone of the Witham church suggests a small congregation.

It may have been built by a local leader who, with his family, converted to Christianity, at least for a time.

24 Cf. Crummy et al. (1993: 188), who propose that the first extension (Phase 2) took place in the late fourth century. This would seem to be far too late because the method of construction is virtually identical to that of the original building (Crummy et al. 1993: 166), and because it is unlikely that it took almost eighty years for the building to subside and subsequent repairs and extension (Phase 3) to be undertaken. Furthermore, it would surely be hard to justify this second enlargement of the building so late in the period, when the town was under threat and its population declining.

25 Of the uncoffined burials (including a double burial), two were on the periphery, and are thus difficult to date. The three skeletons, however, were either prone, or placed with head to the east, or both. This suggests a breakdown in Christian burial rites, i.e. occurring after *c*.410–20. Of the other three, two were isolated and thus undatable, but the third was dated to the final phase of the cemetery.

The tree-trunk burials comprised one which was the last in a sequence of five; a second, fourth in a sequence of five, the second of which dated to 360/70 or later; and a third, which occurred before a burial also dated to 360/70 or later. (There is some confusion in the report over this last burial: see Crummy *et al.* (1993: 122; cf. Table 2.67)).

26 See above, Chapter 3, note 28.

6 THE QUESTION OF SYNCRETISM

1 The gods of Roman Britain have been discussed by many writers and it is not intended in this work to replicate their work. For an excellent analysis and distribution maps of the various deities worshipped, the reader is directed to B. Jones and Mattingly (1990: 264–300).

2 So Henig (1984: 66).

3 E.g. Horne (1986), M. Green (1976), Webster (1986).

4 E.g. the *numen* of the emperor (*RIB* 1041), the spirits of the Otherworld (*RIB* 251), Jupiter (*RIB* 797), Neptune and Minerva (*RIB* 91), etc.

5 E.g. Apollo-Maponus (*RIB* 1120), Mars-Lenus (*RIB* 309), Silvanus-Callirius (*RIB* 194), etc.

6 E.g. Sulis-Minerva (*RIB* 146), Vinotonus-Silvanus (*RIB* 732).

7 E.g. Mithras (*RIB* 1545), Astarte (*RIB* 1124), the Syrian goddess (*RIB* 1792), etc.

8 E.g. *RIB* 887 to Belatucadrus.

9 E.g. *RIB* 1534 to Coventina, *RIB* 143 to Sulis.

10 E.g. *RIB* 161, 250, 674, Councillors from Bath, Lincoln and York, respectively; also *RIB* 147, the leaders of the villagers at Old Carlisle.

11 The best known is that of King Cogidubnus (*RIB* 91); other examples: *RIB* 67, 674.

12 E.g. the guilds: *RIB* 270, 271.

13 Towns or *vici* near army bases, e.g. *RIB* 742 found at Greta Bridge or Birdoswald, dedicated by Eunemogenus, who may even have been a British soldier, serving some time after the Severan reforms; *RIB* 1700 from Chesterholm, by the villagers of Vindolanda; and from health resorts such as Bath, e.g. *RIB* 151 etc.

14 E.g. *RIB* 742. See note above.

15 Two examples are *RIB* 192 (to the Mother Goddesses Suleviae, by Similis, son of Attus, a tribesman of the Cantiaci) and *RIB* 194 (to Silvanus Callirius, by Cintusmus the coppersmith). The Matres may not have been native goddesses in Britain, but imported from 'overseas'. (See discussion below.) Cintusmus is a Celtic name. It is

significant that both these inscriptions came from one of the most highly Romanised centres in Britain, Colchester.

16 E.g. *RIB* 19, 293. One of the latest inscriptions (*RIB* 933) comes from Old Penrith and dates to the fourth or fifth century. It was on a tombstone to the spirits of the departed (*dis manibus*) set up by the daughter of a local councillor in the *civitas* of the Carvetti, centred on Carlisle.

17 Most of the data in this discussion have been extracted from Tomlin (1988).

18 The reference is presumably to Bath, although not stated. Solinus writes of 'warm springs adorned with sumptuous splendour for the use of mortals' and of 'Minerva . . . patron goddess of these' (*Collectanea Rerum Memorabilium* 22.10). He seemed to have borrowed extensively from Pliny the Elder and Pomponius Mela.

19 But it is pointed out that, of the inscriptions on stone at Bath, there are also none solely to Minerva.

20 E.g. Henig (1984: 43).

21 Indeed, it may be that the seeming 'obsession of the . . . tablets with "blood"' (Tomlin 1988: 70) reflects a long-held memory of the blood sacrifices of the pre-Roman period.

22 There are three dedications on the Bath *defixiones* to Roman gods: two to Mars and one to Mercury. This may be compared with a similar equivocation at Uley. See below.

23 The material for this section has been extrapolated from the Uley report (Woodward and Leach 1993).

24 Twelve miniature spears made of iron and one of silver with a twisted shaft (Woodward and Leach 1993: Figures 110 and 111) were found. As far as is known, the silver example is unparalleled and indicates some degree of wealth.

25 The earliest *defixio* is by one Cenacus, to Mercury, but confusion as to the god's identity may have continued for some time.

26 See above, Chapter 4.

27 A date of third century BC for this site has rightly been rejected by King (1990: note 2), who proposes a late-first-century BC/early-first-century AD date.

28 Notable exceptions being Hayling Island and Uley, but these have been dealt with elsewhere in this study. For Hayling Island, see Chapter 1; for Uley, see above, this chapter.

29 For references and a discussion of this site, see Watts (1991: 114 and note 15).

30 See Philpott (1991: 53 and note 1) for references.

31 See Whimster (1981: 147–9) for details of the debate.

32 E.g. Lankhills, Winchester (G. Clarke 1979).

33 Even poorly furnished cemeteries such as Bath Gate, Cirencester, had wooden coffins and a few made of stone or lead (McWhirr *et al.* 1982: 86–92).

34 For the Dobunni, see Dio 60.20; for the Cornovii, see *RIB* 288, a dedication of Trajanic date by the *civitas* of the Cornovii, and Frere (1987: 55).

35 This compares with the situation in continental Europe, where glass was a common grave deposit in the fourth century (Harden 1979: 209). The relative rarity of glass in Romano-British graves in the fourth reflects the economic situation. See above, Chapter 5.

36 Classical references to the practice of sprinkling or anointing bodies/cremated bones include Vergil, *Aeneid* 6.219 and [Tibullus] 3.2.19, and there is also the example of the anointing of the body of Christ after his crucifixion (John 19.39–40).

37 See Philpott (1991: 161) for details.

38 There were also four cases where the coin may have originally been placed in the mouth and had fallen on to the chest or by the neck when the body was decomposing. The graves with coins at Poundbury included two small groups of burials, who may have been members of families in which it had been the custom to employ such a rite. See above, Chapter 2.

39 A partial pseudo-Venus was also found in a votive pit at Hammill, in Kent (Black 1986).

40 Philpott lists roughly the same number of inhumation sites with hobnails as coins, but the number of actual Romano-British graves with hobnails (including Poundbury cemetery, figures for which were not in Philpott's analysis) is about 50 per cent higher. The evidence is skewed by the figures for Lankhills, which has 144 burials with hobnails (G. Clarke 1979: 322). It is pointed out, however, that the total numbers for coin (*c.*280) and hobnail (*c.*440) burials would each be but a small proportion of all known burials from Roman Britain, possibly around 5 and 7.5 per cent (based on a very approximate calculation of figures from G. Clarke (1979: Tables 38 and 39) and Watts (1991: Figure 2), with some additions).

41 I have disregarded the example which Philpott (1991: 309) gives from Springhead, Kent, because the two decapitated bodies were clearly foundation burials and, moreover, the heads, the most important part of the body to the Celts, were missing. See above, Chapter 4.

42 E.g. representations of Mars and Minerva, and of the emperors ?Hadrian, Antoninus Pius (Henig 1984: Figures 25 and 61; 1995: Figures 20 and 47) and Hercules/Commodus (Rostovtseff 1923).

43 E.g. *RIB* 574, 1030–2. For this translation of the word *ollototis*, see the commentary on *RIB* 574.

44 E.g. *RIB* 919, 920.

7 CHANGE AND CONTINUITY

1 It has not been my intention in this book to concentrate on the ending of Roman Britain. That important topic has been dealt with by a number of writers in recent times. The most recent work, by Dr Michael Jones, has only just been released and was not available to me prior to completion of the typescript. I have, however, had access to Jones's summary of his book (M. Jones 1996), in which he argues that the end of Roman Britain was due in no small measure to the intransigence and rebelliousness of the Britons themselves and that

'Romanisation had failed in several vital respects', a view with which I am in considerable agreement with regard to religion.

2 E.g. Ammianus 15.9.4; Diogenes Laertius in the Introduction to *Vitae* 1); Dio Chrysostom *Or.* 49; Cicero *De Div.* 1.41.90.

3 In a recent publication, Ross (1995) suggests that under the Romans the term 'Druid' may have been avoided in reference to the function of priests because of its barbaric connotations. Instead, the word 'magus' was preferred. That Druids in this guise continued in Britain beyond the Occupation is shown by the Vortigern story, in which 'magi' feature. Although druidism was effectively destroyed as a formal system, Ross says, there is no doubt that it continued in some form into the later period.

APPENDIX 1: RELIGION AND THE FASTI
360-95

1 Based on Jones, Martindale and Morris (1971) *The Prosopography of the Later Roman Empire*, vol. 1. Individual references will not be given in this analysis.

2 This does not include suffects. I begin with the consuls because although they held no real power they nevertheless occupied a position of great prestige and give an indication of whom the emperor was favouring or rewarding at the time. There is no doubt that the consulship was still a highly coveted honour. It became common for the emperor to nominate himself or members of the imperial family to the senior position and have as *consul posterior* a commoner who was concurrently or had been a prefect or a military commander. These ordinary consuls, in their other roles as prefects or generals, would also have been members of the consistory when the imperial court was in their areas of jurisdiction. See A. H. M. Jones (1964: 333-7) on the consistory.

3 As this study is part of one on religion in Roman Britain for the period it was not thought relevant to include the urban prefects for Constantinople. Of the officeholders from 360 to 394, only two, Modestus (362-3) and Clearchus (372-3 and 382-4), rose to greater heights. The former became prefect of the East in 369-77 and consul in 372, the latter consul in 384. Modestus had declared himself pagan during Julian's reign but was a Christian under Valens. Clearchus was a pagan.

4 This last has very few instances where the religion of the incumbent is known; it is at times a useful addition.

5 Ammianus (16.10.12) tells us that Constantius never allowed any private citizen to share the consulship with him.

6 The aristocratic Naeratius Cerialis (cos. 358) had close connections with the imperial family (his sister was the mother of Gallus Caesar), while Fl. Eusebius and Hypatius (coss. 359) were brothers-in-law of the emperor. Of the last two, Fl. Taurus and Fl. Florentius (coss. 361), the former is known to have had two sons who were Christian, and the latter had a son who was probably a Christian (an assumption based on Libanius *Or.* 56.15-16).

7 See above, note 3.

8 Maximinus was likely to have been pagan, since he was said to have been influenced in his actions by the predictions of augurs, one his own father (Ammianus 28.1.7).

9 What is shown clearly is the self-interest of Ausonius and the ascendency of his family. This is covered well by J. F. Matthews (1975: 56–87).

10 Gregorius had previously been *praefectus annonae* at Rome, and probably *quaestor sacri palatii*. He was apparently being groomed for the consulship. This was upset by the death of Gratian (J. F. Matthews 1975: 71–2). There is no reason to believe that his support of the orthodox line in the Priscillianist controversy was an indication of his own 'personal tastes' (*pace* J. F. Matthews 1975: 164, 196) and/or that he was a Christian. After all, in 391 we have the instance of pagan prefects of Rome and Italy having to carry out the Christian emperor Theodosius' orders to close the temples. It is, I believe, unrealistic to think that prefects would openly act against the orders or desires of the emperor.

11 But probably Christian, since Magnus Maximus was a 'fierce, unbending Nicene Christian' (Frend 1984: 621), and possibly Fl. Euodius, who held the consulship (as Magnus Maximus' nominee) in 386.

12 As *magister militum* he succeeded Bauto (Baudo), who had previously held the position under Gratian. Baudo was a Frankish general who had opted to support the legitimate Augustus, Valentinian, rather than throw in his lot with Maximus. He had also opposed Ambrose in his stance over the altar of Victory (Ambrose *Ep.* 57).

13 Optatus, whose anti-Christian sentiments were sufficient for him to persecute the supporters of John Chrysostom, was nevertheless a man whom Theodosius trusted. He was appointed urban prefect at Constantinople in 404–5 (Socrates *H.E.* 6.18.19).

14 Particularly in the suppression of Maximus in 388.

15 He had begun his career as a *notarius* (Ammianus 26.5.15), and was prefect in the East (380) and of Italy (385) before holding the western prefecture and the consulship. J. F. Matthews (1975: 179) suggests, quite reasonably, that Theodosius had, in 385, established a kind of 'protectorate' over Italy (and thus, presumably, over the youthful Valentinian II). The elevation of Neoterius to the consulship with Valentinian is, therefore, not surprising.

16 When Promotus died in 391 his sons were brought up in the royal household with the children of Theodosius. It is likely, therefore, that Promotus had been Christian.

17 The praetorian prefects in Gaul for the period June 390 to March 396 are unknown.

18 Clearchus had a long career in public service, including as vicar and pro-consul of Asia. He had two stints as urban prefect of Constantinople, one 372–3 and the other 382–4, along with his consulship in 384.

19 There are, it is true, gaps for the years 381 and 382, but Eucherius (cos. 381) was an uncle of Theodosius, and Antoninus (cos. 382) a relative by

marriage to the emperor. They were thus likely to be Christian. The religion of the Syagrii is unknown.

APPENDIX 2: A LEAD TANK FRAGMENT FROM BROUGH, NOTTS (ROMAN CROCOCALANA)

1 See Watts (1991: 158–75). A further (undecorated) tank has since been found at Riby, Lincs, but its date is uncertain. (Information kindly supplied by Dr Ben Whitwell, Archaeology Unit, Humberside County Council.)
2 See Guy (1987–8: Table 1) for a summary of sizes of tanks discovered up to 1988.
3 See Watts (1991: Figures 23(d), 23(f), 24(a–e).
4 This paper was subsequently updated in the 1991 publication.
5 Isidore Orig. 1.3 and possibly Justin Martyr 1 Apol. 60 and Julian Misop. 357A.
6 See Watts (1991: 173–8). This has been challenged, but no satisfactory function for the object has since been proposed. The grave belonged to a male – not a female, as reported in that publication.
7 E.g. Minucius Felix Oct. 29.6; and possibly Barnabas Ep. 12.2.
8 E.g. Isidore Orig. 1.3.7. See Watts (1991: 177 and notes).
9 E.g. Ramsay (1897: 526–7), Marucchi (1910: 59) and Sulzberger (1925: 393–7).
10 CIG 3902o. This seems to be a variant on the formula ἔσται αὐτῷ πρὸς τὸν Θεόν ('he will have to account to God'), which was common in Christian inscriptions in Asia Minor (Ramsay 1897: 514–16).
11 DeRossi (1861: vol. I, 16, no. 10).
12 DeRossi (1867: vol. II, plate xxxix, no. 30).
13 E.g. Oxy. P. I.126 (AD 572), 136 (583), 137 (584), 138 (610–11). This last document, although secular in nature, begins with a Christian invocation.
14 E.g. Diehl (1925: no. 841) (AD 584).
15 The monogram is used only as a symbol in these examples.
16 See Watts (1991: 151, 245, note 9).
17 See Watts (1991: 169) for the main theories and for further details of the argument presented in this present discussion.
18 Information kindly supplied by Mr V. Radcliffe.
19 This item is now in the British Museum.
20 My thanks to Mr Michael Jones and the City of Lincoln Archaeology Unit for organising and supplying the drawing and photograph, and to Newark Museum for permission to publish the object.

REFERENCES
Archaeological and secondary sources

Abbreviations for the titles of journals are in accordance with the system adopted by the Council for British Archaeology. In addition, BAR = British Archaeological Reports, CBA = Council for British Archaeology and OUCA = Oxford University Committee for Archaeology.

Alcock, J. P. (1980) 'Classical religious belief and burial practice in Roman Britain', *Archaeol. J.* 137: 50–85.

Alcock, L. (1972) '*By South Cadbury is that Camelot . . .*': *The Excavation of Cadbury Castle 1966–1970*, London: Thames & Hudson.

Allason-Jones, L. and McKay, B. (1985) *Coventina's Well: A Shrine on Hadrian's Wall*, Hexham: Trustees, Clayton Collection (Gloucester: Alan Sutton).

Anthony, I. E. (1968) 'Excavations in Verulam Hills Field, St Albans, 1963–4', *Hertfordshire Archaeol.* 1: 9–50.

ApSimon, A. M. (1965) 'The Roman temple on Brean Down, Somerset', *Proc. Univ. Bristol Spelaeolog. Soc.* 10.3: 195–258.

Ashby, T., Hudd, A. E. and King, F. (1910) 'Excavations at Caerwent, Monmouthshire, on the site of the Romano-British city of Venta Silurum in the year 1908', *Archaeologia* 62: 1–20.

Athanassiadi, P. (1992) *Julian: An Intellectual Biography*, London: Routledge.

Atkinson, R. J. C. (1952–3) 'Excavations in Barrow Hills Fields, Radley, Berks, 1944–45: the Romano-British inhumation cemetery', *Oxoniensia* 17–18: 1–35.

Baddeley, J. St C. (1930) 'The Roman-British temple, Chedworth', *Trans. Bristol Gloucestershire Archaeol. Soc.* 52: 255–64.

Bartlett, R. (1987) 'A late Roman buckle from Harlow Temple Essex', *Essex Archaeol. Hist.* 18: 115–20.

Birley, R. E. (1961) 'Housesteads civil settlement, 1960', *Archaeol. Aeliana* (4 ser.) 39: 301–19.

Black, E. W. (1983) 'Ritual dog burials from Roman sites', *Kent Archaeol. Rev.* 71: 20–22.

REFERENCES

—— (1986) 'Romano-British burial customs and religious beliefs in South-East England', *Archaeol. J.* 143: 201–39.

—— (1987) *Roman Villas of South-East England*, Oxford: BAR.

Blagg, T. F. C. (1979) 'The date of the temple of Sulis-Minerva at Bath', *Britannia* 10: 101–7.

Bland, R. and Johns, C. (1993) *The Hoxne Treasure: An Illustrated Introduction*, London: British Museum.

Bloch, H. (1945) 'A new document of the last pagan revival in the west, 383–394 A.D.', *Harvard Th. Rev.* 38: 199–244.

—— (1963) 'The pagan revival in the West at the end of the fourth century', in A. Momigliano (ed.) *The Conflict Between Paganism and Christianity in the Fourth Century*, Oxford: Clarendon, 193–218.

Boon, G. C. (1961) 'A temple of Mithras at Caernarvon-Segontium', *Archaeol. Cambrensis* 109: 153–6.

—— (1962) 'A Christian monogram at Caerwent', *Bull. Bd. Celtic Stud.* 19: 338–45.

Bowersock, G. W. (1978) *Julian the Apostate*, London: Duckworth.

Bradford, J. S. P. and Goodchild, R. G. (1939) 'Excavations at Frilford, Berks, 1937–8', *Oxoniensia* 4: 1–70.

Branigan, K. (1977) *Gatcombe: The Excavation and Study of a Romano-British Villa Estate 1967–1976*, Oxford: BAR.

—— (1990) 'The Romano-British finds from Wookey Hole: a reappraisal', *Somerset Archaeol. Nat. Hist.* 134 (1991): 57–80.

—— (1993) '*Venta Silurum*: a civitas-capital', in S. J. Greep (ed.), pp. 56–65.

Brewster, T. C. M. (1971) 'The Garton Slack chariot burial, East Yorkshire', *Antiquity* 45: 289–92.

Brown, A. E. (ed.) (1995) *Roman Small Towns in Eastern England and Beyond*, Oxford: Oxbow.

Brown, P. D. C. (1971) 'The church at Richborough', *Britannia* 2: 225–31.

Brunaux, J. L. (1988) *The Celtic Gauls: Gods, Rites and Sanctuaries* (trans. D. Nash), London: Seaby.

Burnham, B. C. (1995) 'Small towns: the British perspective', in A. E. Brown (ed.), pp. 7–18.

Burnham, B. C. and Wacher, J. (1990) *The 'Small Towns' of Roman Britain*, London: Batsford.

Bushe-Fox, J. P. (1914) *Second Report on the Excavations on the Site of the Roman Town at Wroxeter*, Oxford: Soc. Antiq.

—— (1932) *Third Report on the Excavations of the Roman Fort at Richborough, Kent*, Oxford: Soc. Antiq.

Buxton, L. H. D. (1921) 'Excavations at Frilford', *Antiq. J.* 1: 87–97.

Cameron, A. (1993) *The Later Roman Empire*, London: Fontana.

Casey, P. J. (1981) 'Lydney Park Roman temple SO6102', *Trans. Bristol Gloucestershire Archaeol. Soc.* 99: 178.

REFERENCES

Challis, A. J. and Harding, D. W. (1975) *Later Prehistory from the Trent to the Tyne* (2 vols), Oxford: BAR.

Chambers, R. A. (1976) 'A Romano-British settlement at Curbridge', *Oxoniensia* 41: 38–55.

—— (1978) 'Two radio-carbon dates from the Romano-British cemetery at Curbridge, Oxon', *Oxoniensia* 43: 252–3.

—— (1987) 'The late- and sub-Roman cemetery at Queensford Farm, Dorchester-on-Thames, Oxon', *Oxoniensia* 52: 35–69.

Child, H. and Colles, D. (1971) *Christian Symbols*, New York: Scribner.

Clarke, G. (1979) *Pre-Roman and Roman Winchester Part II: The Roman Cemetery at Lankhills*, Oxford: Clarendon.

Clarke, S. (1996) 'When Romans and natives didn't mix', *Brit. Archaeol.* 14: 7.

Creighton, J. (1996) 'Tight-fisted soldiers of Roman Britain', *Brit. Archaeol.* 18: 7.

Croke, B. and Harries, J. (1982) *Religious Conflict in Fourth-century Rome*, Sydney: Sydney University Press.

Crummy, N., Crummy, P. and Crossan, C. (1993) *Colchester Archaeological Report 9: Excavations of Roman and Later Cemeteries, Churches and Monastic Sites in Colchester, 1971–88*, Colchester: Colchester Archaeol. Trust.

Crummy, P. (1980) 'The temples of Roman Colchester', in W. J. Rodwell (ed.), pp. 243–83.

—— (1993) 'The development of Roman Colchester', in S. J. Greep (ed.), pp. 34–45.

Cunliffe, B. (1984) *Roman Bath Discovered*, rev. edn, London: Routledge & Kegan Paul.

—— (ed.) (1988) *The Temple of Sulis Minerva at Bath, Vol. 2: The Finds from the Sacred Spring*, Oxford: OUCA.

Cunliffe, B. and Davenport, P. (1985) *The Temple of Sulis Minerva at Bath, Vol. 1: The Site*, Oxford: OUCA.

Dark, K. R. (1994) *Civitas to Kingdom: British Political Continuity 300–800*, Leicester: Leicester University Press.

de la Bédoyère, G. (1993) *Roman Villas and the Countryside*, London: Batsford/English Heritage.

Denison, S. (1995) 'Roman theatres', *Brit. Archaeol.* 9: 4.

—— (1996) 'Late Roman farm yields image of the good life', *Brit. Archaeol.* 11: 4.

DeRossi, G. B. (1857–61) *Inscriptiones Christianae Urbis Romae*, vol. 1, Rome, with Supplement 1, ed. I Gatti, Rome (1915).

—— (1867) *La Roma Sotterranea Cristiana* (3 vols), Rome (reprinted 1966, Frankfurt: Minerva).

Detsicas, A. (1983) *The Cantiaci*, Gloucester: Alan Sutton.

Diehl, E. (1925) *Inscriptiones Latinae Christianae Veteres*, Berlin: Weidmann.

Dix, B. (1984) 'Ashton Roman town: archaeological rescue excavation', *Durobrivae* 9: 26–7.

—— (forthcoming) *Excavations at Harrold Pit, Odell, Bedfordshire (1974–78)*.

Dorcey, P. F. (1992) *The Cult of Silvanus*, Leiden: Brill.

Downey, R., King, A. and Soffe, G. (1980) 'The Hayling Island temple and religious connections across the Channel', in W. J. Rodwell (ed.), pp. 289–31.

Drury, P. J. (1980) 'Non-classical religious buildings in Iron Age and Roman Britain: a review', in W. J. Rodwell (ed.), pp. 45–78.

Ellison, A. (1980) 'Natives, Romans and Christians on West Hill, Uley: an interim report on the excavation of the ritual complex of the first millennium A.D.', in W. J. Rodwell (ed.), pp. 305–28.

Esmonde Cleary, A. S. (1989) *The Ending of Roman Britain*, London: Batsford.

—— (1993) 'The Late Roman towns in Britain and their fate', in A. Vince (ed.), pp. 6–13.

—— (1994) 'Roman Britain in 1993: sites explored (England)', *Britannia* 25: 261–91.

Farwell, D. E. and Molleson, T. L. (1993) *Excavations at Poundbury 1966–80, Volume II: The Cemeteries*, Dorchester: Dorset Nat. Hist. Archaeol. Soc.

Fishwick, D. (1988) 'Imperial sceptre heads in Roman Britain', *Britannia* 19: 399–400.

—— (1995) 'The temple of Divus Claudius at *Camulodunum*', *Britannia* 26: 11–27.

Fletcher, E. and Meates, G. W. (1969) 'The ruined church of Stone-by-Faversham', *Antiq. J.* 49: 273–94.

—— (1977) 'The ruined church of Stone-by-Faversham: second report', *Antiq. J.* 57: 67–72.

Ford, P. K. (ed. and trans.) (1977) *The Maginogi and other Medieval Welsh Tales*, Berkeley: University of California Press.

France, N. E. and Gobel, B. M. (1985) *The Romano-British Temple at Harlow* (ed. F. R. Clark and I. K. Jones), West Essex Archaeol. Group: Gloucester.

Frend, W. H. C. (1979) '*Ecclesia Britannica*: prelude or dead end?', *J. Eccles. Hist.* 30: 129–144.

—— (1982) 'Romano-British Christianity and the West: comparison and contrast', in S. M. Pearce (ed.), pp. 5–16.

—— (1984) *The Rise of Christianity*, London: Darton Longman & Todd.

—— (1992) 'Pagans, Christians, and the "barbarian conspiracy" of A.D. 367 in Roman Britain', *Britannia* 23: 121–31.

Frere, S. S. (1975) 'The Silchester church: the excavations by Sir Ian Richmond in 1961', *Archaeologia* 105: 277–302.

—— (1983) 'Roman Britain in 1982: sites explored', *Britannia* 14: 279–356.

—— (1984) 'Roman Britain in 1983: sites explored', *Britannia* 15: 266–332.

REFERENCES

—— (1987) *Britannia A History of Roman Britain*, 3rd rev. edn, London: Pimlico.

—— (1991) 'Roman Britain in 1990: sites explored', *Britannia* 22: 222–92.

Fulford, M. (1991) 'Britain and the Roman Empire: the evidence for regional and long distance trade', in R. F. J. Jones (ed.), pp. 53–66.

Gibbs, G. (1997) 'Cross found in Roman grave may be a fake', *Guardian*, 28 May, p. 12.

Gillam, J. P. and MacIvor, I. (1954) 'The temple of Mithras at Rudchester', *Archaeol. Aeliana* (4 ser.) 32: 176–219.

Goodburn, R. (1983) *The Roman Villa at Chedworth*, London: National Trust.

Goodchild, R. G. (1938) 'A priest's sceptre from the Romano-Celtic temple at Farley Heath, Surrey', *Antiq. J.* 18: 391–6.

Goodchild, R. G. and Kirk, J. R. (1954) 'The Romano-Celtic temple at Woodeaton', *Oxoniensia* 19: 15–37.

Green, C. J. S. (1982) 'The cemetery of a Romano-British community at Poundbury, Dorchester, Dorset', in S. M. Pearce (ed.), pp. 61–76.

Green, C. J. S., Paterson, M. and Biek, L. (1982) 'A Roman coffin-burial from the Crown Building site, Dorchester: with particular reference to the head of well-preserved hair', *Proc. Dorset Natur. Hist. Archaeol. Soc.* 103: 67–100.

Green, C. W. (1966) 'A Romano-Celtic temple at Bourton Grounds, Buckingham', *Rec. Bucks.* 17. 5: 356–66.

Green, M. (1976) *A Corpus of Religious Material from the Civilian Areas of Roman Britain*, Oxford: BAR.

—— (1989) *Symbol and Image in Celtic Religious Art*, London: Routledge.

—— (1992) *Dictionary of Celtic Myth and Legend*, London: Thames & Hudson.

—— (ed.) (1995) *The Celtic World*, London: Routledge.

Greenfield, E. (1963) 'The Romano-British shrines at Brigstock, Northants', *Antiq. J.* 43: 228–68.

Greep, S. J. (ed.) (1993) *Roman Towns: The Wheeler Inheritance*, York: CBA.

Gregory, T. (1991) *Excavations in Thetford, 1980–1982, Fison Way, Volume One*, East Anglian Archaeol. Rpt 53.

Grimes, W. F. (1968) *The Excavation of Roman and Mediaeval London*, London: Routledge & Kegan Paul.

Guy, C. (1978) 'A Roman lead tank from Burwell, Cambridgeshire', *Proc. Cambridge Antiq. Soc.* 68: 2–4.

—— (1981) 'Roman circular lead tanks in Britain', *Britannia* 12: 271–6.

—— (1987–8) 'A lead "bucket" from Kenilworth, Warwickshire', *Trans. Birmingham Warwicks Arch. Soc.* 95 (1990): 107–9.

Harden, D. B. (1979) 'Glass vessels', in G. Clarke, pp. 209–40.

REFERENCES

Harman, M., Molleson, T. I. and Price, J. L. (1981) 'Burials, bodies and beheadings in Romano-British and Anglo-Saxon cemeteries', *Bull. Brit. Mus. Nat. Hist.* 35: 145–88.

Harris, E. and Harris, J. R. (1965) *The Oriental Cults in Roman Britain*, Leiden: Brill.

Haselgrove, C. (1990) 'Stanwick', *Curr. Archaeol.* 10.12: 380–4.

Henig, M. (1984) *Religion in Roman Britain*, London: Batsford.

—— (1995) *The Art of Roman Britain*, London: Batsford.

Henig, M. and King, A. (eds) (1986) *Pagan Gods and Shrines of the Roman Empire*, Oxford: OUCA 8.

Higham, N. (1992) *Rome, Britain and the Anglo-Saxons*, London: Seaby.

Hind, J. (1996) 'Whose head on the Bath temple-pediment?', *Britannia* 27: 358–60.

Holder, P. A. (1982) *The Roman Army in Britain*, London: Batsford.

Hope, W. St J. (1908) 'Excavations on the site of the Roman city at Silchester, Hants, in 1907', *Archaeologia* 61: 199–218.

Hopkins, K. (1980) 'Taxes and trade in the Roman Empire', *J. Rom. Stud.* 70: 101–25.

Horne, P. (1981) 'Romano-Celtic temples in the third century', in A. King and M. Henig (eds), pp. 21–6.

—— (1986) 'Roman or Celtic temples? A case study', in M. Henig and A. King (eds), pp. 15–24.

Hull, M. R. (1958) *Roman Colchester*, Oxford: Soc. Antiq.

Hutchinson, V. J. (1986) *Bacchus in Roman Britain: The Evidence for his Cult* (2 vols), Oxford: BAR.

Hutton, R. (1991) *The Pagan Religions of the Ancient British Isles*, London: BCA/Blackwell.

James, H. (1993) *Roman Carmarthen* in S. J. Greep (ed.), pp. 93–8.

Jenkins, F. (1976) 'Preliminary report on the excavations at the church of St. Pancras at Canterbury', *Canterbury Archaeol.* 1975–6: 4–5.

Johns, C. M. and Potter, T. W. (1983) *The Thetford Treasure: Roman Jewellery and Silver*, London: British Museum.

Jones, A. H. M. (1964) *The Later Roman Empire 284–602*, Oxford: Blackwell.

Jones, A. H. M., Martindale, J. R. and Morris, J. (1971) *The Prosopography of the Late Roman Empire*, vol. 1, London: Cambridge University Press.

Jones, B. and Mattingly, D. (1990) *An Atlas of Roman Britain*, London: Guild/Blackwell.

Jones, M. (1996) 'Rebellion remains the decisive factor', *Brit. Archaeol.*, 20: 8–9.

Jones, M. J. (1991) 'Lincoln', in R. F. J. Jones (ed.), pp. 69–74.

—— (1993) 'The latter days of Roman Lincoln', in A. Vince (ed.), pp. 14–18.

—— (1994) 'St Paul-in-the-Bail, Lincoln: Britain in Europe?', in K. S. Painter (ed.) *'Churches made in Antiquity': Recent Work in Britain and the East Mediterranean*, London: Soc. Antiq., pp. 325–47.

REFERENCES

Jones, M. K. (1982) 'Crop production in Roman Britain', in D. Miles (ed.) *The Romano-British Countryside: Studies in Rural Settlement and Economy*, Oxford: BAR, pp. 95–107.

Jones, R. (1975) 'The Romano-British farmstead and its cemetery at Lynch Farm, near Peterborough', *Northamptonshire Archaeol.* 10: 94–137.

Jones, R. F. J. (1981) 'Cremation and inhumation – change in the third century', in A. King and M. Henig (eds), pp. 15–19.

—— (1987) 'Burial customs of Rome and the provinces', in J. Wacher (ed.), pp. 812–37.

—— (ed.) (1991a) *Roman Britain: Recent Trends*, Sheffield: Collis.

—— (1991b) 'Cultural change in Roman Britain', in R. F. J. Jones (ed.), pp. 115–20.

Keen, L. (ed.) (1981) 'Dorset archaeology 1979', *Proc. Dorset Nat. Hist. Arch. Soc.* 101: 133–43.

King, A. (1990) 'The emergence of Romano-Celtic religion', in T. Blagg and M. Millett (eds) *The Early Roman Empire in the West*, Oxford: Oxbow, pp. 220–41.

—— (1991) 'Food production and consumption – meat', in R. F. J. Jones (ed.), pp. 21–8.

King, A. and Henig, M. (eds) (1981) *The Roman West in the Third Century*, Oxford: BAR.

King, A. and Soffe, G. (1994) 'The Iron Age and Roman temple on Hayling Island', in A. P. Fitzpatrick and E. L. Morris (eds) *The Iron Age in Wessex: Recent Work*, Salisbury: Association Française d'Étude de l'Age du Fer, pp. 114–16.

Kirby, D. P. (1976) 'British dynastic history in the pre-Viking period', *Bull. Bd. Celtic Stud.* 27: 81–115.

Kirk, J. (1949) 'Bronzes from Woodeaton, Oxon', *Oxoniensia* 14: 1–45.

Klein, W. G. (1928) 'Roman temple at Worth, Kent', *Antiq. J.* 8: 76–86.

Koch, J. T. and Carey, J. (eds) (1995) *The Celtic Heroic Age: Literary Sources for Ancient Celtic Europe and Early Ireland and Wales*, 2nd edn, Malden: Celtic Studies Publications.

Kurtz, D. C. and Boardman, J. (1971) *Greek Burial Customs*, London: Thames & Hudson.

Leach, P. (1982) *Ilchester, Volume I: Excavations 1974–1975*, Bristol: Western Archaeol. Trust.

—— (1990) 'The Roman site at Fosse Lane, Shepton Mallet: an interim report of the 1990 archaeological investigations', *Somerset Archaeol. Nat. Hist.* 134: 47–55.

—— (1991) *Shepton Mallet Romano-Britons and Early Christians in Somerset*, Birmingham: University Field Archaeol. Unit & Showerings Ltd.

Leech, R. H. (1980) 'Religion and burials in South Somerset and North Devon' in W. J. Rodwell (ed.), pp. 329–66.

—— (1981) 'The excavation of a Romano-British farmstead and cemetery on Bradley Hill, Somerton, Somerset', *Britannia* 12: 177–252.

—— (1986) 'The excavation of a Romano-Celtic temple and a later cemetery on Lamyatt Beacon, Somerset', *Britannia* 17: 259–328.

Lewis, M. J. T. (1966) *Temples in Roman Britain*, London: Cambridge University Press.

Lieu, S. N. C. (1989) *The Emperor Julian Panegyric and Polemic*, 2nd edn, Liverpool: Liverpool University Press.

Lynn, C. (1993) 'The Navan landscape', *Curr. Archaeol.* 12.2: 53–5.

Macdonald, J. (1979) 'Religion', in G. Clarke, pp. 404–33.

McWhirr, A. (1993) 'Cirencester – *Corinium Dobunnorum*', in S. J. Greep (ed.), pp. 46–9.

McWhirr, A. D., Viner, L. and Wells, C. (1982) *Cirencester Excavations II: Romano-British Cemeteries at Cirencester*, Cirencester Excavation Committee.

Marucchi, O. (1910) *Christian Epigraphy* (trans. J. A. Willis), reprint 1974, Chicago: Ares.

Matthews, C. L. (1981) 'A Romano-British inhumation cemetery at Dunstable', *Bedfordshire Archaeol. J.* 15: 4–137.

Matthews, J. F. (1975) *Western Aristocracies and Imperial Court AD 364–425*, Oxford: Clarendon.

—— (1989) *The Roman Empire of Ammianus*, Baltimore: Johns Hopkins University Press.

Mawer, C. F. (1995) *Evidence for Christianity in Roman Britain: The Small Finds*, Oxford: Tempus Reparatum.

Mays, S. and Steele, J. (1996) 'A mutilated human skull from Roman St Albans, Hertfordshire, England', *Antiquity* 70: 155–61.

Meates, G. W. (1979) *The Roman Villa at Lullingstone, Vol. I: The Site*, Kent Archaeol. Soc. Monograph 1.

Merrifield, R. (1977) 'Art and religion in Roman Britain: an inquest on the sculptures of Londinium', in J. Munby and M. Henig (eds) *Roman Life and Art in Britain*, Oxford: BAR, pp. 375–406.

—— (1986) 'The London hunter god', in M. Henig and A. King (eds), pp. 85–92.

Miles, D. (ed.) (1984) *Archaeology at Barton Court Farm Abingdon, Oxon*, Oxford: Oxford Archaeol. Unit/CBA.

Millett, M. (1990) *The Romanisation of Britain*, London: Cambridge University Press.

Milne, G. (1993) 'The rise and fall of Roman London', in S. J. Greep (ed.), pp. 11–15.

Milne, S. (1988) 'Roman temple find changes view of London', *Guardian*, 3 July.

Morris, I. (1992) *Death-ritual and Social Structure in Classical Antiquity*, London: Cambridge University Press.

Murray, C. (1992) 'Heads will roll: a diachronic look at cranial deposition', *Trowel* 3: 18–22.

Murray, M. A. (1921) *The Witch-cult in Western Europe*, Oxford: Clarendon.

REFERENCES

Neal, D. S. (1974) *The Excavation of the Roman Villa in Gadebridge Park, Hemel Hempstead, 1963–8*, London: Soc. Antiq.

Newman, C. (1993a) 'Raffin Fort, Co. Meath: neolithic and Bronze Age activity', in E. Grogan and C. Mount (eds) *Annus Archaeologiae Archaeological Research 1992: Proceedings of the OIA Winter Conference 1993 held in University College Dublin 30 January 1993*, Dublin: Office of Public Works, pp. 55–65.

—— (1993b) 'Sleeping in Elysium', *Archaeology Ireland* 25(7. 3): 20–3.

Niblett, R. (1990) 'Verulamium', *Curr. Archaeol.* 10. 3: 410–17.

—— (1993) '*Verulamium* since the Wheelers', in S. J. Greep (ed.), pp. 78–92.

O'Brien, E. (1992) 'Pagan and Christian burial in Ireland during the first millennium AD: continuity and change', in N. Edwards and A. Lane (eds) *The Early Church in Wales and the West*, Oxford: Oxbow, pp. 130–7.

O'Connell, M. G. and Bird, J. (1994) 'The Roman temple at Wanborough, excavation 1985–1986', *Surrey Archaeol. Coll.* 82: 1–168.

O'Kelly, M. J. (1993) *Newgrange, Co. Meath, Ireland: The Late Neolithic/Beaker Period Settlement*, Oxford: BAR.

O'Neill, B. H. St J. (1935) 'Coins from Jordon Hill Roman temple' *Proc. Dorset Natur. Hist. Archaeol. Soc.* 57: 140.

Ottaway, P. (1989) 'The Empire strikes back – new discoveries in the Roman town at York', *Rescue News* 49, p. 3.

—— (1993) *Roman York*, London: Batsford/English Heritage.

Painter, K. S. (1971) 'Villas and Christianity in Roman Britain', *Brit. Mus. Q.* 35: 156–75.

—— (1977) *The Water Newton Early Christian Silver*, London: British Museum.

Parfitt, K. (1990) 'Excavations at Mill Hill, Deal 1982–1989: an interim report', *Kent Archaeol. Rev.* 101: 9–18.

Parker, A. J. (1987) 'Trade within the Empire and beyond the frontiers', in J. Wacher (ed.), pp. 635–57.

Pearce, S. M. (ed.) (1982) *The Early Church in Western Britain and Ireland*, Oxford: BAR.

Percival, J. (1975) *The Roman Villa*, London: Batsford.

—— (1987) 'The villa in Italy and the provinces', in J. Wacher (ed.), pp. 527–46.

Philpott, R. (1991) *Burial Practices in Roman Britain*, Oxford: Tempus Reparatum.

Potter, T. W. and Johns, C. (1992) *Roman Britain*, London: British Museum.

Powell, W. R. (ed.) (1963) *A History of the County of Essex*, vol. III, London: Univ. London Inst. Hist. Research.

Raftery, B. (1974) 'Report on the excavations of some passage graves, unprotected inhumation burials and a settlement site at Knowth, Co. Meath', *Proc. Royal Irish Academy* 74: 111–112.

REFERENCES

—— (1981) 'Iron age burials in Ireland', in D. O'Corráin (ed.) *Irish Antiquity: Essays and Studies Presented to Professor M. J. O'Kelly*, Cork: Tower Books, pp. 173–204.
—— (1994) *Pagan Celtic Ireland*, London: Thames & Hudson.
Rahtz, P. (1977) 'Late Roman cemeteries and beyond', in R. Reece (ed.) *Burial in the Roman World*, London: CBA, pp. 53–64.
—— (1991) 'Pagan and Christian by the Severn Sea', in L. Abrams and J. Carley (eds) *The Archaeology and History of Glastonbury Abbey*, Woodbridge: Boydell, pp. 1–37.
Rahtz, P. and Watts, L. (1979) 'The end of Roman temples in the west of Britain', in P. J. Casey (ed.) *The End of Roman Britain*, Oxford: BAR, pp. 183–210.
—— (1989) 'Pagans Hill revisited', *Archaeol. J.* 146: 330–71.
Rahtz, P., Woodward, A., Burrows, I., Everton, A., Watts, L., Leach, P., Hirst, S., Fowler, P. and Gardner, K. (1992) *Cadbury Congresbury 1968–73: A late/post Roman Hilltop Settlement in Somerset*, Oxford: Tempus Reparatum.
Ramsay, W. M. (1897) *Cities and Bishoprics of Phyrgia*, Oxford: OUP.
Rankin, H. D. (1987) *Celts and the Classical World*, London: Croom Helm.
Reece, R. (1984) 'The coins', in S. S. Frere, *Verulamium Excavations*, vol. III, Oxford: OUCA, pp. 3–17.
—— (1988) *My Roman Britain*, Cirencester: Cotswold Studios.
Rees, S. (1987) 'Agriculture and horticulture', in J. Wacher (ed.), pp. 481–503.
Richmond, I. A. (1963) *Roman Britain*, 2nd edn, Penguin: Harmondsworth.
Richmond, I. A. and Gillam, J. P. (1951) 'The temple of Mithras at Carrawburgh', *Archaeol. Aeliana* (4 ser.), 29: 39–43.
Richmond, I. A. and Toynbee, J. M. C. (1955) 'The temple of Sulis-Minerva at Bath', *J. Rom. Stud.* 45: 97–105.
Ritchie, J. N. G. and Ritchie, W. F. (1995) 'The army, weapons and fighting', in M. Green (ed.), pp. 37–58.
Robertson, A. *et al.* (1975) *Bar Hill: A Roman Fort and its Finds*, Oxford: BAR.
Rodwell, K. A. (1988) *The Prehistoric and Roman Settlement at Kelvedon, Essex*, London: CBA.
Rodwell, W. J. (ed.) (1980) *Temples, Churches and Religion in Roman Britain* (2 vols), Oxford: BAR.
Rodwell, W. J. and Rodwell, K. A. (1985) *Rivenhall: Investigations of a Villa, Church, and Village*, London: Chelmsford Archaeol. Trust/CBA.
Rostovtseff, M. (1923) 'Commodus-Hercules in Britain', *J. Rom. Stud.*, 13: 91–109.
Ross, A. (1959) 'The human head in insular pagan Celtic religion', *Proc. Soc. Antiq. Scotland 1957–8* 91: 10–43.

—— (1967) *Pagan Celtic Britain: Studies in Iconography and Tradition*, London: Routledge & Kegan Paul.

—— (1992) *Pagan Celtic Britain: Studies in Iconography and Tradition*, rev. edn, London: Constable.

—— (1995) 'Ritual and the druids', in M. Green (ed.), pp. 423–44.

Ross, A. and Feachem, R. (1976) 'Ritual rubbish? The Newstead pits', in J. V. S. Megaw (ed.) *To Illustrate the Monuments*, London: Thames & Hudson, pp. 229–237.

Rowell, G. (1977) *The Liturgy of Christian Burial*, London: Alcuin Club/SPCK.

Rutherford, R. (1980) *The Death of a Christian: The Rite of Funerals*, New York: Pueblo.

Rynne, E. (1972) 'Celtic stone idols in Ireland', in C. Thomas (ed.) *The Iron Age in the Irish Sea Province*, London: CBA, pp. 79–98.

—— (1974–5) 'Ancient burials as Ballinlough, Co. Laois', *J. Kildare Archaeol. Soc.* 15: 430–3.

—— (1992) 'Dún Aengus and some similar Celtic ceremonial centres', in A. Bernelle (ed.) *Decantations: A Tribute to Maurice Craig*, Dublin: Lilliput Press, pp. 196–207.

Smith, A. (1941) 'Lead coffin found at Crocolana (Brough, Notts)', *Trans. Thoroton Soc.* 45: 106–9.

Smith, D. J. (1963) 'Three fourth-century schools of mosaic in Roman Britain', *La Mosaïque gréco-romaine*, Paris: Colloques Internationaux du Centre National de la Recherche Scientifique, pp. 95–115.

Smith, K. (1977) 'The excavation of Winklebury Camp, Basingstoke, Hampshire', *Proc. Prehist. Soc.* 43: 31–129.

Smith, S. (1994) 'A reassessment of the dating evidence for the Lydney temple site', *Dean Archaeol.* 7: 28–33.

Stead, I. M. (1965) *The La Tène Cultures of Eastern Yorkshire*, York: Yorkshire Philosophical Soc.

Stebbing, W. P. B. (1937) 'Pre-Roman, Roman and post-Roman pottery from burials at Worth, East Kent', *Antiq. J.* 17: 310–13.

Sulzberger, M. (1925) 'La symbole de la croix et les monogrammes de Jésu chez les premiers Chrétiens', *Byzantion* 2: 337–448.

Thomas, C. (1981) *Christianity in Roman Britain to AD 500*, London: Batsford.

Todd, M. (?1990) 'Villa and fundus', in K. Branigan and D. Miles (eds) *The Economies of Romano-British Villas*, Sheffield: Dept. Archaeology & Prehistory, Univ. Sheffield, pp. 14–20.

—— (1993) 'The cities of Roman Britain: after Wheeler', in S. Greep (ed.), pp. 5–10.

Tomlin, R. S. O. (1988) *Tabellae Sulis Roman Inscribed Tablets of Tin and Lead from the Sacred Spring at Bath*, Oxford: OUCA.

—— (1993) 'The inscribed lead tablets: an interim report', in A. Woodward and P. Leach, pp. 113–30.

Toynbee, J. M. C. (1953) 'Christianity in Roman Britain', *J. Brit. Archaeol. Ass.* (3rd ser.), 16: 1–24.

—— (1971) *Death and Burial in the Roman World*, London: Thames & Hudson.

—— (1978) 'A Londinium votive leaf or feather and its fellows', in J. Bird, H. Chapman and J. Clark (eds) *Collectanea Londiniensia: Studies Presented to R. Merrifield*, London: London & Middlesex Arch. Soc.

Turner, B. R. G. (1982) *Ivy Chimneys, Witham: An Interim Report*, Chelmsford: Essex County Council.

Turner, R. and Wymer, J. J. (1987) 'An assemblage of palaeolithic handaxes from the Roman religious complex at Ivy Chimneys, Witham, Essex', *Antiq. J.* 67: 43–60.

Vince, A. (ed.) 1993) *Pre-Viking Lindsey*, Lincoln: City of Lincoln Archaeology Unit.

Wacher, J. (ed.) (1987) *The Roman World* (2 vols), London: Routledge & Kegan Paul.

—— (1995) *The Towns of Roman Britain*, 2nd rev. edn, London: Batsford.

Wait, G. A. (1986) *Ritual and Religion in Iron Age Britain*, Oxford: BAR.

—— (1995) 'Burial and the Otherworld', in M. Green (ed.), pp. 489–511.

Walker, L. (1984) 'The deposition of the human remains', in B. Cunliffe *Danebury: An Iron Age Hillfort in Hampshire, Vol. 2: The Excavations 1969–1978: The Finds*, London: CBA, pp. 442–63.

Walters, H. B. (1970) 'Romano-British Nottinghamshire', in W. Page (ed.) *A History of the County of Nottinghamshire*, vol. II, London: Univ. London Inst. Hist. Research, pp. 1–36.

Watts, D. J. (1988) 'Circular lead tanks and their significance for Romano-British Christianity', *Antiq. J.* 68: 210–22.

—— (1991) *Christians and Pagans in Roman Britain*, London: Routledge.

—— (1993) 'An assessment of the evidence for Christianity at the Butt Road site', in N. Crummy, P. Crummy and C. Crossan, pp. 192–202.

—— (1995) 'A fragment of a lead tank from Brough (Roman *Crococalana*)', *Britannia* 26: 318–22.

Watts, L. and Leach, P. (1996) *Henley Wood, Temples and Cemetery Excavations 1962–69 by the Late Ernest Greenfield and Others*, York: CBA.

Webster, G. (1986) *The British Celts and their Gods under Rome*, London: Batsford.

Wedlake, W. J. (1982) *The Excavation of the Shrine of Apollo at Nettleton, Wiltshire 1956–71*, London: Soc. Antiq.

Wells, C. (1981) 'Report on three series of Romano-British cremations and four inhumations from Skeleton Green', in C. Partridge *Skeleton Green a Late Iron Age and Romano-British Site*, London: Soc. Promotion Rom. Stud., pp. 277–304.

Wenham, L. P. (1968) *The Romano-British Cemetery at Trentholme Drive, York*, London: HMSO.

West, S. (1976) 'The Romano-British site at Icklingham', *East Anglian Archaeol.* 3: 63–126.

Wheeler, H. (1985) 'The Racecourse cemetery', *Derbyshire Archaeol. J.* 105: 222–280.

Wheeler, R. E. M. (1943) *Maiden Castle, Dorset*, London: Soc. Antiq.

Wheeler, R. E. M. and Wheeler, T. V. (1932) *Report on the Excavation of the Prehistoric, Roman and Post-Roman site at Lydney Park, Gloucestershire*, London: Soc. Antiq.

—— (1936) *Verulamium: A Belgic and Two Roman Cities*, London: Soc. Antiq.

Whimster, R. (1981) *Burial Practices in Iron Age Britain*, Oxford: BAR.

Wickenden, N. P. (1988) 'Excavations at Great Dunmow, Essex: a Romano-British small town in the Trinovantian civitas', *E. Anglian Archaeol. Rept. 41*, Chelmsford.

—— (1992) *The Temple and Other Sites in the North-eastern Sector of Caesaromagus*, Chelmsford: Chelmsford Museums Service/CBA.

Williams, S. and Friell, G. (1994) *Theodosius: The Empire at Bay*, London: Batsford.

Wilson, C. E. (1981) 'Burials within settlements in southern Britain during the pre-Roman Iron Age', *Bull. Instit. Archaeol.* 18: 127–69.

Wilson, C. M. (1972) *Lincolnshire Hist. Arch.* 7: 10.

Wilson, D. (1992) *Anglo-Saxon Paganism*, London: Routledge.

Wilson, D. R. (1965) 'Roman Britain in 1964: sites explored', *J. Rom. Stud.* 55: 199–220.

—— (1968) 'An early Christian cemetery at Ancaster', in M. W. Barley and R. P. C. Hanson (eds) *Christianity in Britain, 300–700*, Leicester: Leicester University Press, pp. 197–9.

—— (1970) 'Roman Britain in 1969: sites explored', *Britannia* 1: 269–305.

—— (1975) 'Roman Britain in 1974: sites explored', *Britannia* 6: 220–83.

Wilson, P. R. (1988) 'The Richborough font – some additional structural detail', *Britannia* 19: 411–12.

Woodward, A. (1992) *Shrines and Sacrifice*, London: Batsford/English Heritage.

Woodward, A. and Leach, P. (1993) *The Uley Shrines*, London: English Heritage/British Museum.

Woolley, T. C. S. (1910) 'Crocolana, the Nottinghamshire Brough', *Trans. Thoroton Soc.* 10: 63–72.

Wright, R. P. (1947) 'A Roman shrine to Silvanus on Scargill Moor, near Bowes', *Yorkshire Archaeol. J.* 36: 383–6.

Wright, W. C. (trans.) (1990) *The Works of the Emperor Julian*, vol. 3 (LCL), Cambridge, Massachusetts: Heinemann.

NAMES AND PLACES INDEX

GENERAL INDEX

administration
  Britain: civic 96, 97, 100, 101,
    102, 104, 107, 116;
    provincial 1, 2, 4, 5, 16, 52,
    60, 63, 67, 97, 98, 99, 100,
    101, 102, 105, 106, 107,
    116, 132, 134, 154, 165,
    166, 169; tribal 70, 101
administration (Empire) 3, 4, 5,
    16, 32, 33, 34, 36, 68, 69,
    70, 71, 72, 139, 141, 143,
    145, 146, 160, 174, 175
Afterlife, the 60, 82, 92, 94, 127,
    131, 134
Altar of Victory, the 6, 31, 33, 35,
    145, 159, 160, 175
altars
  Christian 157
  pagan 6, 7, 9, 16, 17, 18, 19,
    35, 38, 53, 54, 62, 108, 115,
    116
Ambrose of Milan
  influence 30, 31, 32, 43, 68,
    139, 142, 145, 146, 175
amulets 66, 81, 85, 87, 125, 126
apostasy 25, 28, 29, 33, 37, 38, 50,
    63, 164
army
  Britain: militia 70, 72, 106, 108
  Roman: 1, 3, 159, 161;
    influence on religion 10, 36,
    116, 130, 133, 139, 143;
    influence on the economy 99,
    100, 102, 105, 107, 170;
    Legion VI Victrix 99; loyalty

  69, 70; paganism 28;
    payment 105; political
    influence 4, 5, 36, 43, 67,
    68, 114, 124, 126, 143;
    withdrawal from Britain 18,
    52, 63, 67, 69, 70, 71, 100,
    105, 107, 134, 135, 166
Arras culture, the 125
art
  Celtic 81
  religious 9, 18, 80, 115, 125,
    127, 129, 130, 131;
    Christian 111, 112, 113;
    motifs 147, 149, 150, 151,
    152; mosaics 21, 109, 111,
    112, 164; Romano-British
    10; sceptre heads 129, 136;
    sculpture 119, 129, 130;
    syncretism 129–31
  wall painting 100, 152
assassination 3, 5, 29, 31, 33, 159
Aylesford Culture, the 122

baptism 32, 49, 71, 150, 151, 153
baptisteries 13, 14, 20, 42, 64, 80,
    165
barbarian conspiracy, the 66, 68,
    103, 104, 106
barbarian invasions
  Britain 18, 32, 60, 64, 67, 71,
    72, 96, 98, 99, 100, 101,
    106, 107, 108, 134, 165,
    166, 170
  Empire 3, 24, 69, 72, 105, 107
    134, 143

classical 2, 6, 7, 19, 42, 55, 102,
    108, 116, 117, 155, 163
closure 2, 6, 15, 25, 52, 61, 72,
    134, 140, 175
construction 26
continuity of use 17
destruction 15, 17, 32, 33, 39,
    52, 134, 146, 157, 161
Mithraea 10, 18, 43, 108, 156
octagonal 15, 20, 21, 41, 42,
    53, 56, 109, 110, 112
rebuilt 17, 26, 159
rectangular 53
refurbishment 38
restoration 26, 38, 159
Roman: architecture 7
Romano-British 63
Romano-Celtic 2, 7, 8, 9, 20,
    39, 42, 43, 53, 54, 78, 108,
    110, 117, 119, 120, 121,
    132, 135, 155, 156, 158,
    163, 164, 172
rural 39, 52, 157
sites: reuse by Christians 20
square 42, 56
triangular 55, 57, 61, 95
urban 15
tetrarchy 5
    first 3, 154
    second 4
theatres 19, 55, 61, 97, 98, 100,
    101, 156
Theodosius
    religious policies 32
tombstones see burial practices:
    tombstones
towns 55, 57, 97, 105, 106, 113,
    120, 170, 171
    Britain: decline 67

continuity 169
decline 97, 99, 100, 101, 102,
    103, 105, 107, 111, 132,
    135, 169, 170
    large 97, 98, 100, 101, 102,
    103, 107, 116, 169
    small 96, 102, 103, 107, 152,
    169
    walled 97, 98, 100, 101, 102,
    107, 108
tradition of sanctity 7, 13, 38, 43,
    67, 80, 86, 111, 135, 164
transmigration of souls, the 60, 84.
    85, 87, 136, 168
treasures see hoards

Ulster Cycle, the 79
unguentaria 125
usurpation 3, 16, 31, 33, 35, 43,
    68, 69, 70, 72, 96, 105, 114
    139, 143, 144, 145, 146,
    154, 166

veterans 99, 100
villas 2, 11, 15, 55, 60, 67, 96, 97.
    100, 101, 102, 103, 104,
    106, 107, 109, 111, 113,
    120, 121, 164, 166, 169,
    170
votive offerings 8, 42, 54, 55, 56,
    57, 62, 75, 76, 78, 81, 89,
    92, 94, 95, 108, 111, 117,
    119, 120, 121, 130, 131,
    161, 163, 164, 167; see also
    coins
    leaves 119
    plaques 9, 119, 129, 164
    weapons 117, 119, 172
Votive Pits 42, 75, 110, 111, 173

Lightning Source UK Ltd.
Milton Keynes UK
UKOW042225300712

196804UK00013B/27/P